The Ethics of Teaching:
A Casebook

(2nd Edition)

The Ethics of Teaching: A Casebook

(2nd Edition)

Patricia Keith-Spiegel
Bernard E. Whitley, Jr.
Deborah Ware Balogh
David V. Perkins
Arno F. Wittig
Ball State University

2002

LAWRENCE ERLBAUM ASSOCIATES, PUBLISHERS
Mahwah, New Jersey   London

Lawrence Erlbaum Associates, Inc.
10 Industrial Avenue
Mahwah, New Jersey 07430

Cover design by Kathryn Houghtaling Lacey

Library of Congress Cataloging-in-Publication Data

The ethics of teaching : a casebook / Patricia Keith-Spiegel ... [et al.].-- 2nd ed.
  p. cm.
  Includes bibliographical references and indexes.
  ISBN 0-8058-4062-1 (cloth : alk. paper) -- ISBN 0-8058-4063-X (pbk. : alk. paper)
    1. College teachers--Professional ethics--Case studies. 2. College teaching--Moral and
ethical aspects--Case studies. I. Keith-Spiegel, Patricia.

LB1779 .E76 2002
174'.9382--dc21

                                                                              2002024254

Printed in the United States of America
10   9   8   7   6   5   4   3   2   1

Contents

4.   Required In-Class Learning Activities   50

PART III: ASSESSMENT OF STUDENTS

5.   Testing and Other Academic Evaluations   61

6.   Grading Methods   77

Preface

- *I want to start my classes on time, so no one is allowed in the door after I start talking.*
- *Students learn much better if I reveal personal experiences about myself.*
- *I never allow make-up exams because I don't have the time to check out all of their stories, and some are going to be lies anyway.*
- *My students are offered plenty of ways to bolster their grades through extra credit opportunities.*
- *I am flattered by a cute student who flirts with me, so I play along even though I would never take it any further.*
- *When a colleague supports a stupid theory, I make sure that my students know how wrongheaded the ideas are.*
- *I can't help it. I just like some students much better than others.*
- *Developing friendships with students has a positive impact on them.*
- *Because students need to learn more than just subject matter, I actively try to influence them in other ways.*

People studying for the medical and human services professions take courses in professional ethics. People preparing for research careers take courses in research ethics. However, for the most part, people preparing for college teaching careers receive no systematic education about ethical issues related to teaching. To be sure, we all know that it is wrong to exploit students or to accept money or gifts in return for grades. But what about situations such as those listed above? Do they raise ethical issues? Although you might not have thought "That's unethical!" as your read through the list, each statement has potential ethical implications.

As we thought about issues such as those listed above and the ethical lacuna they represented in the professional education of college-level teachers, we also realized that such matters are usually not clearly covered in professional ethics codes or institutional policies. Nevertheless, these and other "low profile" behaviors can harm students and coworkers, be it overtly or indirectly. In many instances they can also lead or evolve into more serious predicaments. We therefore prepared this casebook as a way to stimulate discussion and raise consciousness about ethical issues that may lurk unnoticed in the halls of academe.

We have focused our casebook on educators' ethical responsibilities because we believe that members of a profession who undertake an open and constructive examination of their own behaviors are less likely to fail in their obligations to meet the needs and expectations of their students, their institutions, and, ultimately, the profession itself. We believe that a casebook can be of greatest service by identifying the more common types of ethical dilemmas that can arise between educators and their students. We also cover relationships between colleagues in situations in which the quality of the educational experience and attention students receive are affected.

Ethical dilemmas are presented as scenarios, most of which are based on actual situations. We selected this approach because it furnishes more realistic, concrete, and (we hope) interesting stimuli for individual reflection and group discussion than would a presentation of abstract principles. Case material also provides fertile ground for evaluating decision options, and often allows for the additional benefit of forcing people to consider the process by which they arrive at solutions. Case material also allows for consideration of the many subtle complexities inherent in the social and psychological contexts in which educator–student interactions occur and the effects of those complexities on ethical decision making.

About the Second Edition

We began our work on the first edition of this casebook (Keith-Spiegel, Wittig, Perkins, Balogh, & Whitley, 1993) by collecting scenarios reflecting situations and practices that can occur in college and university settings. We obtained our case material from a variety of sources, including experiences relayed by colleagues, public domain media reports, and the ethical dilemmas we personally encountered or observed during our 100 plus combined years of college-level teaching. We then created our responses through consensus after considerable and sometimes lively debate, consultation with outside experts, and, in some instances, compromise. The cases and responses were circulated for comment among volunteer reviewers at colleges and universities throughout the United States. The first edition was sponsored by the Society for the Teaching of Psychology (Division 2 of the American Psychological Association).

Ethical practices continue to evolve in higher education. For this revised edition we have added many new cases to reflect recent trends and events related to academic ethics. We also deleted some cases that are no longer at the forefront of concern, either because the issues have been resolved or because an interest in them has dwindled. We also included, new to this edition, questions designed to stimulate discussion and to further elaborate the issues.

The Many Ways to Use the Casebook

Our cases are almost always "discipline-free" in that the issues they raise would apply regardless of the school or department in which the incident occurred. This means that the name of any field can usually be substituted for those that we selected for illustrative purposes only.

The book was designed to be used in a number of ways, from private reading to a textbook for workshops, continuing education classes, and faculty development programs. The casebook is also well-suited for graduate teaching assistant training and new faculty information packets. All of the authors have tested this material in a variety of venues, using traditional presentations as well as breakout groups, skits and role play, and debates. A leader guide, based on the techniques we have developed for use with groups, has been created for group adoptions. For more information on how to obtain the Leader Guide, please visit www.erlbaum.com.

Although not research-oriented itself, this book may also suggest new problems and directions for empirical research on ethical issues in university teaching. We hope you will find our book as useful as we have.

Patricia Keith-Spiegel
Bernard E. Whitley, Jr.
Deborah Ware Balogh
David V. Perkins
Arno F. Wittig

Introduction

Colleges and universities may seem, at first blush, to be among the places where the highest ethical ideals are held and routinely practiced. However, the potential for ethical conflict in institutions of higher education is ever-present. The organizational culture typically found in college and universities creates a fluid context in which role and authority relationships are asymmetrical and complicated, individual players are ever-changing, needs exceed available resources, and policies and technologies are continuously evolving. In a complex environment such as this, it is important to confront ethical dilemmas as a means of strengthening the relatively stable features that maintain the integrity of the educational enterprise.

Professional Experience and Ethical Risk

Most academic ethical issues concern all members of a college or university faculty. However, younger and less-experienced faculty members may be especially vulnerable to error when faced with an ethically difficult or ambiguous situation.

Beginning Faculty. A wave of retirements in coming years will bring many new faculty members to colleges and universities. Too often, newcomers to teaching are warned only about the more obvious forms of unethical or dishonest workplace behaviors. The more subtle ethical dilemmas that arise frequently in the course of teaching are rarely discussed. When such circumstances present themselves, as they definitely will, those new to teaching may not recognize them as ethical matters, or may feel uncomfortable discussing them with others for fear that they, themselves, will be viewed as incompetent or unprepared for the job. A clear need exists to engage new faculty members in frank discussions of the ethical dilemmas that can arise during interactions with students, and such discussions should be coupled with constructive suggestions both for avoiding ethical predicaments and for dealing with them when they occur. We have observed that new teachers find it reassuring to learn that ethical dilemmas are common and that most of their colleagues have faced similar ones. Many novice teachers also find such discussions extremely enlightening, unaware that some actions that seemed acceptable at the time will likely have unethical features or ethically questionable consequences later.

It is worth remembering that many new instructors are not far removed from being students themselves. They are still learning their new roles. New instructors may have difficulty recognizing their weaknesses or how their personal style affects students (Prieto, 1995, 2001). They comprise a group that is likely to make some ethical mistakes, albeit usually unintended ones. For example, because newer instructors may feel a closer kinship to their students than to their fellow faculty members, they are especially vulnerable to forming potentially hazardous dual role relationships with students.

Graduate Teaching Assistants. Even more vulnerable than new faculty who have completed their degrees are graduate teaching assistants. GTAs may still display behaviors that were acceptable in their student roles but are counterproductive to their roles as educators (Keith-Spiegel, Whitley, Perkins, Balogh, & Wittig, 2001). GTAs may be very excited about their new status, but they may also be more focused on their job performance and the resultant outcomes for themselves than on the needs of their students.

GTAs' views of what constitutes ethical and unethical behavior may differ from those of more experienced faculty members. Based on a survey of 123 GTAs and 124 regular teaching faculty, Keith-Spiegel et al. (2001) found that graduate assistants believed many behaviors to be considerably *less* ethically problematic than did experienced teachers. Examples of these behaviors include hugging a student, accepting a student's expensive gift, teaching a class without being adequately prepared, adopting a textbook because the publisher paid a bonus, and selling personal items to one's students. GTAs may be less able to see the potential negative consequences of certain actions because they have not yet been socialized into the role of professional educator.

Part-Time and Contract Faculty. Although we could not find anything in the literature about the unique ethical problems among those who teach part time or in non-tenure track time-limited positions, we suggest that this increasingly large group may share circumstances that might sometimes limit ethical awareness. These educators are typically paid very little compared to their tenure track colleagues, are assigned high class loads, may not be eligible for certain resources, and are not usually viewed as among the in-group members of the campus community.

Some who may feel exploited and alienated may act on their resentment, and their actions may reveal themselves in conduct toward students and colleagues that is not ethically sound.

Junior Faculty. Newer faculty members who are on the tenure track but who have not yet received tenure face a long period replete with a variety of pressures. They have but a few years to prove themselves when measured against the criteria their institutions have set. Most often, nontenured faculty are expected to produce at least some, and often considerable, independent scholarly or creative work as well as teach classes and participate in the activities of the institution and its local community. Ethical dilemmas can present themselves in a multitude of ways, such as finding ethically questionable shortcuts to getting work done, slighting students while attending to research, and caring more about how to get high student evaluations than about what students learn. Specific acts could include committing scientific misconduct, preparing inadequate teaching materials, and giving overly simple exams and assignments in an effort to attract student support.

Tenured Faculty. One would think that once tenure is achieved, most faculty members are likely to have adapted to the norms and expectations of the good faculty member, and, we believe that most have done so. But regardless of the number of years they have been teaching, educators continue to confront and are expected to manage a broad range of students and learning environments throughout their careers. Education is a context in which challenging new relationships regularly form and may evolve unpredictably. Therefore, factors that affect the interpersonal processes of teaching and learning deserve close attention regardless of one's status or level of experience in the profession.

Achieving tenure may bring out adverse behaviors in some faculty members. Having endured a lengthy probationary period, some newly tenured professors may slack off, reducing the attention they pay to their students and taking less care with their teaching. Others, relying on the safe cloak of tenure, may begin to act in inappropriate ways toward students, staff, and colleagues. Some may become jaded by students who often seem less interested in learning than in just getting a degree, and become sour and less caring. Some may burn out along the way, a condition that often leads to poor ethical decision making unless an investment in their calling is restored.

Senior professors are not exempt from ethical risk vulnerability. Scathing books in the popular press describe veteran academics as a lazy, egocentric, and uncaring lot who barely tolerate their teaching duties, especially when the students are undergraduates (e.g., Anderson, 1992; Sykes, 1989). Although such accusations are most certainly overblown, the danger of stagnation and arrogance is ever-present and, if left uninterrupted, can lead to actions that are inappropriate, out-of-step, and unethical.

Our Approach to Ethical Standards in Academic Settings

We approached our task primarily as advocates of a healthy, comfortable, and active learning environment. We see higher education as a privilege with attendant responsibilities on the part of both faculty and students. However, we also recognize that students are vulnerable to the consequences of the actions and inactions of faculty. We can, without even full awareness, cause students undeserved harm.

We applied a number of well-accepted, general ethical principles as we deliberated our cases. These principles, illustrated with some specific adaptations to the academic community, include the following:

1. *Respect for the autonomy of others:* acknowledging the right of students, faculty, and staff to choose their own ways in life as long as their actions do not interfere with the rights and welfare of others; valuing the free expression of ideas and of appropriate, nonviolent reaction to ideas; fostering student discovery appropriate to their level of academic development, as opposed to indoctrination; maintaining a comfortable environment that is conducive to learning.

2. *Doing no harm (physical or emotional resulting from acts of commission or omission):* engaging in nonexploitive relationships with students and colleagues; a willingness to seek consultation when ethical or personal problems arise that may result in poor judgment; attempting consciously and actively to eliminate any injurious effects of bias in our work; refusing to tolerate passively unethical behavior on the part of colleagues and students.

3. *Benefit to others:* accepting responsibility for student welfare and development; maintaining our own competence; delivering, in a conscientious manner, the services to which students are entitled, such as dependable performance in the execution of teaching and advising; recognizing our roles as models and exemplars.

4. *Fairness and equity:* treating others as we would like to be treated under similar circumstances; maintaining fair practices and objectivity when evaluating students, staff, and peers.

5. *Fidelity and honesty:* exhibiting loyalty, truthfulness, integrity and

promise-keeping in our dealings with students, staff, and peers; labeling our opinions as such; avoiding behavior that would reduce the trust of others in the teaching profession; displaying openness in dealings with students and the use of informed consent procedures whenever applicable.

6. *Dignity*: according dignity to students, staff, and peers; avoiding arrogance and inappropriate displays of emotion; respecting diversity.

7. *Caring*: exercising professional and institutional duties with care; extending compassion to the greatest extent possible toward students, staff, and peers.

8. *Doing one's best*: valuing the pursuit of excellence; taking pride in one's work.

Issues Not Addressed

Broad Policy Issues. We have chosen to focus on ethical decisions over which faculty members have considerable and direct control. Therefore, some of the broad and profound academic issues with ethical implications that have attracted considerable attention in recent years have been excluded. These include concerns about the growing use of graduate students to teach undergraduate courses, the huge class sizes and lack of professor contact in lower division courses, and the misleading recruiting pitches used to attract prospective undergraduate students (e.g., boasting that several Nobel prize winners are on the faculty, but not including the fact that they do no teach undergraduates, or do not teach at all). Because these types of issues are very complicated—involving interactions among administrative leadership and departments, funding priorities, university-wide policies, and other entities including legislatures and the public-at-large—our book does not deal with them.

Issues Only Remotely Related to Teaching Students. Other situations in which ethical issues can arise have been purposely eliminated to allow us to focus on teaching functions, interactions with students, and situations that affect students directly. Generally excluded are ethical issues related to hiring, retention, and promotion; the conduct of research, except for student research in collaboration with their educators; conflicts with administrators and policy; nonteaching staff (e.g., librarians or counseling center professionals); unethical acts perpetrated by students, except as instructors may become involved with such behaviors (e.g., dealing with student cheating).

Egregious Violations of Ethical and Moral Standards. Blatant sexual harassment of students and staff, physical assaults on students or coworkers, forging scientific data, gross incompetence, commission of serious crimes, and the like require immediate action to protect students, colleagues, the institution, and society. We believe that there is little or no room for debate and reflection about such extreme instances. Therefore, clear-cut, egregious breaches of ethical standards and moral codes of conduct that instructors might commit as a result of neglect, willful intent, or serious mental disorder are largely absent from this book. Most colleges and universities have established policies for the disposition of serious problems having ethical and moral ramifications.

Caveats and Disclaimers

We have aspired to cover a great many potentially problematic situations that can arise in the course of teaching , but recognize that we could not exhaust every possibility. If a common behavior or activity with ethical dimensions is excluded in this book, its omission should not be interpreted to mean that it is ethically acceptable or that we considered a scenario but judged it to be unimportant.

We make use of unlikely names in our vignettes, usually echoing the theme of the case. By doing so, we do not intend to trivialize the issues involved. Rather, the names of our characters may assist in recalling information for discussion purposes and reduce the risk of using names of real people. Although most of our cases are based on incidents known to or shared with us, we have heavily disguised them through alteration or truncation, or by combining two or more similar stories. Therefore, any resemblance between our fictitious names and those of actual people and particular events is coincidental.

"Instructor" is the title we use most frequently when referring to college and university-level educators. Because this book will be of interest to those who are teaching while still in training as well as full professors, we decided on this all inclusive title. When referring to particular players in our cases, however, we use the title "Professor X" to differentiate them clearly from students.

We do not offer legal advice. This book does not address or determine what may be the competing rights and obligations of teachers under an institution's rules and policies. For matters that may have implications beyond ethics—such as concerns about institutional roles, contracts, and legal consequences—faculty should seek appropriate professional consultations. We intend for our cases to provide an impetus for academics to think about and formulate positions on ethical issues. These cases can also be used as a starting point for creating departmental and institutional ethical standards.

Finally, it is very important for us to note that any actual event to which one of our case scenarios might be compared has its own peculiar mix of situational and contextual factors, power differentials among the participants, personality variables and differences of intentions and interpretations of acts, and previous history among the parties involved. Therefore, it should be recognized that actual incidents may exhibit features that would make the application of our analysis or advice less relevant or even inappropriate.

I

The Classroom Ambiance

Instructors' Classroom Policies

Discussions of classroom learning environments typically focus on obvious factors such as class size and available resources. Less-often discussed issues that impact on learning and student morale include the role of instructors' methods and practices regarding the maintenance of discipline and order, excuse policies for missed classes, and making changes in the course after the term is under way. The ethical aspects of such methods and practices are the topics of this chapter.

Case 1-1. Discipline in the Classroom

> Professor Stern reminds students that certain behaviors are out of place in the classroom. Students caught sleeping, talking to their neighbors, passing notes, or reading newspapers are penalized by having points subtracted from their grade base.

College-level students, especially recent high school graduates, can act very childishly. Such behavior can be very annoying. Expectations of adult behavior are ethical and proper. They help ensure an appropriate learning environment. Overly severe punishments, however, are likely to have a negative impact on the classroom climate.

Even though this behavior may not bother other students, reading a book for another class is an irritating and demoralizing sight when one is attempting to deliver a lecture Nonetheless, serious students might develop an unfavorable perception of an instructor who does not maintain a classroom atmosphere that is conducive to learning.

Professor Stern deducts already-earned academic credit for behavior he has defined as objectionable. Stern's specific tactic cannot be supported. He could tactfully explain his expectations for proper behavior in his syllabus, and orally, at the first class meeting. Sometimes a general reminder is all that is needed to elicit proper behavior during an actual incident.

Students who behave inappropriately, despite being informed of expectations can be given fair warning. If a warning is ineffective, students can be separated or asked to conduct their conversations elsewhere, perhaps adding that they are welcome to return when they have finished. Such methods can be implemented in ways that minimize the students' embarrassment or humiliation (e.g., the initial discussion of the problem can be conducted privately, outside class). Severely disruptive students and students who do not respond to other tactics should be referred for disciplinary action to the appropriate office.

(For other cases dealing with the management and mismanagement of disruptive and difficult students, see 2-4, 2-5, 2-6, 2-7, and 2-9. For other cases involving academic penalties for reasons related to other than academic performance, see 6-8 and 6-9.)

Discussion Questions

1. Although it is not appropriate to subtract academic credit for behavioral infractions, would it be acceptable to award *extra* points for proper behavior? What are the risks in this course of action?

2. Some disruptive behavior in the classroom can be very aggravating. Is it ever justifiable for an instructor to display that aggravation in the form of expressing anger toward the offending student in front of the whole class? For example, how appropriate are each of the following responses?

     a. "I am very unhappy with you."
     b. "You are an irresponsible and inconsiderate person."
     c. "I can no longer tolerate your rudeness."
     d. "It is students like you who ruin it for everyone else."
     e. "You are a real jerk, you know that?"

3. Are there certain student behaviors that should prompt an instructor to attempt to permanently remove an offending student(s) from the classroom? If so, what are they?

4. Is an instructor ever justified in simply ignoring inappropriate student behavior? If so, what might be an example?

5. Are ingrained habits and quirks (such as repetitive coughing, finger tapping, and knuckle cracking) as offensive as behaviors committed with the intent to disrupt? How should the instructor respond to unintentional interruptions?

Case 1-2. Questions Unwelcome Here

> Professor Mutem seldom provides opportunities for students to ask questions or to offer comments during his lectures. He rarely acknowledges students who raise their hands. Students seeking clarification are often frustrated. Mutem, however, insists that class periods are for the purpose of lecturing, and that he needs all available time to present his lecture material. Mutem informs students that they may come by during his regular office hours to ask questions or to discuss lecture material. But, by that time, students say they have lost the context.

Assuming that Mutem's class presentations are clear and well crafted, his policy is probably not blatantly unethical. But, it is likely too rigid to be pedagogically effective. Whenever course content is complex or confusing, students deserve opportunities for clarification. The welfare of students is often compromised by policies that are too unyielding.

Mutem can ease up and still deliver his lectures efficiently and maintain classroom decorum. He could pause occasionally, especially when he senses that the students are uneasy, and ask for questions. He can consistently reserve a few minutes at the end of the lecture for questions. No matter how much instructors have to say, it is for naught if the students do not understand what it is. (See also Cases 1-3 and 9-6.)

Discussion Questions

1. Would it be acceptable to allow students to ask questions for the purpose of clarification, but disallow any other kind of commentary?

2. Is class size a factor? In a class with 200 or more students, is it possible to field questions and comments in a way that does not disrupt the flow of the planned classroom experience which, usually by necessity, is more structured?

Case 1-3. Reactions to Remarks
Made by Students in Class

> The students in Professor Poke's class rarely speak up. Although Poke praises questions and comments he views as intelligent, he blasts students whose remarks

> he finds obtuse or off-target. Examples include telling a young man that he came to class without having packed his brain and asking a woman if her IQ exceeds room temperature.

Students are in school to learn. And, although we all suffer what seem to be silly questions or questions already answered minutes earlier, it serves no purpose nor is it ethically defensible to humiliate students in front of their peers. A classroom controlled by intimidation is not an effective or acceptable learning environment. Students who seem to have genuine problems with the material or who make off-the-mark contributions and, as a result, waste class time consistently should be called into the instructor's private office for a discussion. (See also 1-2, 3-1, 9-6, and 9-9).

Discussion Questions

1. Is Poke ethically obligated to call in disruptive or poorly performing students for a consultation?

2. Do any ethical concerns apply to praise of an individual student in the classroom? That is, is it OK to single out a student by saying, "That was an outstanding comment, which suggests that you are an extremely insightful young woman"?

3. Can a comment that may cause a student to feel humiliated be ethically defensible if it is offered in private? For example, in the instructor's office with the door closed, can an instructor say, "Your behavior in class is disgraceful, worse than that of my 5-year-old on a bad day"?

Case 1-4. Ready, Set, Go! Strict Class Start-Up Time

> Professor Timelock comes to class early and keeps her eye on the wall clock. If students arrive even a few seconds past the onset of the class period, Timelock does not allow them to enter the room. Students are upset because reasons beyond their control, such as trouble finding a parking place or a long walk from a previous class, may cause them to be a few minutes late. Professor Timelock defends her practice by asserting that late arrivals disrupt the rest of the class and that students need to learn to manage their contingencies in advance.

Late students are disruptive and also model irresponsibility. Interruptions caused by late arrivals, however, can be rather easily minimized. A few seats near the door could be reserved, allowing latecomers to enter quickly and quietly. Alternatively or concurrently, there might be a short grace period to allow students having a long distance between classes or who are unavoidably detained to be seated. We do *not* recommend delaying the start-up time for a few minutes because students rapidly adapt to this ploy, and it cuts into time that should be used for teaching and learning purposes. However, the first few minutes can be reserved for questions or informal commentary and announcements, thus providing a more informal ambience as latecomers settle in.

Professor Timelock's policy can bring harm to students who are late for unavoidable reasons, but who fully intend to attend class. If each class presentation builds on the one before, late students are deprived of needed learning experiences.

Whatever course of action Timelock chooses, she must inform students of her policy and give them periodic reminders. She should be flexible enough to allow conditions that may cause some students delay, such as inclement weather or a physical disability that impairs mobility. If she locks students out on exam day, she should have a make-up policy that allows for legitimate excuses.

Finally, we should note that sometimes late students cause problems extending beyond momentary disruption. Whenever the planned classroom experience is jeopardized by late-arriving students (such as music rehearsals, simulations, or team laboratory exercises) a strict late policy is appropriate. (See also 5-6.)

Discussion Questions

1. A student claims that her daily ride to campus does not enable her to get to your class until the lecture is about half over. Is this pushing the grace period too far?

2. You see your student talking to his girlfriend outside her classroom every time you enter your classroom. He always wanders in about 5 minutes late with a goofy smile on his face. How will you handle this situation?

3. An instructor told a student that because he could not get from his previous class (3 blocks away) to the instructor's class within the 10 minute break time, the student should drop the class or switch to another section. Is such a policy ever justifiable?

4. When points are given for attendance, is it ethically acceptable to count a student who arrives late as absent?

Case 1-5. Double-Standard Absence Policy

> Professor Dockem deducts attendance points if students
> miss more than three class periods. However, Dockem
> allows excused absences for "educational reasons."
> When Steven Sevenfoot brings a travel itinerary to
> Dockem regarding the basketball team's trip, Dockem
> tells him, "Sports aren't educational. I won't accept this."
> But, just yesterday, Dockem excused several members
> of the student symphony for a concert tour.

Dockem is making a value judgment as to what is educational and what is
not. Regardless of individual opinions, given the place of athletics in the
fabric of many colleges and universities, this policy constitutes a double
standard. Indeed, many students have been lured into institutions of
higher learning based on athletic ability and are expected to participate
on the team. Also, there is an intriguing irony here: Dockem apparently
considers classroom attendance to be so critical that missing classes counts
against students. Yet, at the same time, attendance can be superseded by
any other educational pursuit.

Whenever daily participation in classroom activities constitutes a goal
of a course (with obvious examples being classes in drama and counseling
techniques, hands-on laboratories, and small discussion seminars) this fact
should be detailed in the syllabus. A policy would also need to be spelled
out, preferably with some flexibility for dealing with unavoidable absences.
However, if course goals do not require classroom participation, and
students master the material despite their absences, we believe that
occasional nonattendance should not be held against a student. Some
campuses have established policies or guidelines as to what constitutes
"excused absences," and these should be consulted. (See also 1-6, 1-7, and
1-8 for differential policies regarding excuses.)

Discussion Questions

1. What if the absence is for a trip with educational value, but not sponsored
by the university or an affiliated organization? For example, what would you do
if a business major asks to be excused because she has been invited to observe an
important business conference?

2. To what extent should the type of course affect decisions regarding absence
policies? What are the markers of differential policy?

Case 1-6, A & B. Conflicts Between Academic Assignments and Other Campus Activities

Bonny Basketeer checks her syllabus at the beginning of the term and realizes that she will be absent on two occasions when a quiz is scheduled when she will be traveling with the university's basketball team. She approaches her instructor, Dr. Nochange, to explain the situation. Nochange responds with, "Well, you can drop the class right now, or plan to get two zeroes on those quizzes, or give up basketball."

Meanwhile, Andie Arkie checks her syllabus at the beginning of the term and realizes that a major paper is due when she will be on an archeological dig in South America. This paper involves attending a talk on campus (which she will miss) and providing an analysis and critique of the speaker's ideas. Andie approaches her instructor, Dr. Musthear, to ask if she can complete an alternative assignment. Musthear responds, "Well, that's tough. Those archeologists are arrogant to think they can take you away from class for a week without affecting your grade. Sorry."

Nochange and Musthear create no-win dilemmas for their students by being unwilling to adjust assignments when other college-related activities overlap. A college-level experience includes more than classroom activities, and when an institutionally sponsored activity or a field trip for another class creates problematic situations, students should be accommodated if at all possible. We believe that Bonny should be given the opportunity to take the quizzes, perhaps before she leaves on the team trips. Andie ought to be given some reasonable alternative, such as reporting on some of the speaker's work or writing her report from an audiotape of the speech upon her return.

Instructors should attempt to make the quality of college life as fulfilling and rewarding as possible. Sometimes this will mean being tolerant of schedule adjustments and showing some flexibility. (See also 1-7 and 1-8.)

Discussion Questions

1. Should instructors expect conflicts with other campus activities or classes? Should a statement about such conflicts appear in the syllabus and be discussed at the beginning of the term?

2. Instructors are often asked to make adjustments for activities that are not directly related to the college experience, such as family vacations, weddings, and funerals. What accommodations should the instructor announce at the start of the term to handle these situations?

3. Does your campus have a policy related to excused absences? If so, what are its provisions?

Case 1-7. Conflicts Between Academic Assignments and Student Employment

> Professor Noslack creates a detailed syllabus that spells out absolute due dates for term assignments. Late papers are never accepted. Shortly into the term, Manny Mustwork realizes that one paper is due during the period of a major seasonal holiday when the company conducts almost half its annual business. Manny asks Noslack for an extension of a few days after the holiday to complete the assignment, explaining the demands of his work schedule. Noslack denies his request.

With so many students in the work force, conflicts between assignments and employment are common. Many instructors see this as a "Catch 22," with no easy resolution. The timing of Noslack's assignment could mean that Manny either would have to sacrifice a good grade to stay employed or forsake employment to maintain a good academic performance. Neither choice serves Manny's needs.

Assuming the assignment cannot be completed early and turned in prior to the holiday rush because, for example, it depends on knowledge being gathered from classroom materials that have not yet been presented, we recommend that Noslack's policy be reconsidered. Manny's case is just one of many that may deserve an adjustment. Noslack should be willing to make adjustments that allow Manny to complete the assignment in a timely manner, yet not jeopardize his employment. The determination of what constitutes "timely" will have to be negotiated between the instructor and student. (See also 1-6, 1-8, 5-6, 9-4, and 9-5 for policy exceptions regarding students with special circumstances.)

Discussion Questions

1. How much flexibility can an instructor provide if the student undertakes

an inordinate load, such as 18 hours of academic work and 40 hours of work per week? Where is the point at which an instructor can conclude that the student is trying to do too much and refuse any accommodations?

2. Does Noslack's syllabus present a picture of the "real world," where schedules are important and require adherence? Is part of the total college experience learning about such responsibilities?

Case 1-8, A, B, C, & D. Excusing Students for Relationship-Related Matters

> Emily Cruise explains to her instructor that the annual family vacation trip to the Bahamas starts on the day of the second midterm. She adds that school is very important to her, but that this is also a special tradition for her and the 32 family members who participate. This is the only time she ever sees most of these people because they travel to meet from all over the country. She asks to either take the exam early or upon her return.
>
> Dick Papa expresses concern to his instructor that spring break for his young daughter falls two weeks earlier than the institution's spring break. He is the primary caretaker, and an exam is scheduled during the time his daughter will not be in school.
>
> Marla Bridesmaid had no control over the place or timing of her best friend's wedding date, which turned out to be 2,000 miles away on the day before a big exam.
>
> Ned Nephew says he cannot take the exam because his uncle is in the hospital, and he is expected to go home to see him.

Emily's family gathering in an exotic location would, at first blush, appear to be an unacceptable one. Whereas one could respond, "I am not going to make your pleasure my problem" and force Emily to make a choice, the fact remains that Emily is in a painfully difficult dilemma.

Dick is also caught in a bind familiar to many students with small children. This case, however, may be more easily managed because Dick does have sufficient time to locate alternative care for his child on exam days. Marla is also in a bind, but because most weddings are not on a week day, the instructor may believe Marla can manage both. We note that avoiding scheduling exams on Mondays and Fridays precludes many requests for excuses involving special weekend events.

A very sick child, mother, or father usually elicits our sympathy and a willingness to make accommodations. Where to draw the line when it comes to more distant sick relatives poses another frequent dilemma, especially in regions where large, very closely knit extended families are common. Furthermore, exactly how sick does a relative (close or more distant) have to be before excuses are granted? Is it our responsibility or right to attempt to get involved in making such distinctions? For example, would we excuse Ned if his uncle is near death, but not if he broke a few bones in a motorcycle accident? It is also known that many students create bogus excuses (e.g., illness) that would be acceptable only if true. Many instructors become jaded after too many "grandmother death" excuses.

Making decisions on these distinctions is difficult, especially when we have neither the time nor the inclination to investigate every request. It is even unlikely that any absolute policy would serve every student well. Instructors might consider allowing one make-up exam during the semester for any reason whatsoever. Although this policy may raise the number of make-up exams taken, it does level the playing field for all students in the class. (See also 1-6, 1-7, 5-6, and 10-8.)

Discussion Questions

1. When instructors allow excuses for reasons like the ones described in this case, should they also attempt to verify them? That is, should Ned provide a hospital note regarding his uncle's illness? Should Emily present a hotel bill?

2. "When students request absences for the reasons presented in the foregoing scenarios, is that an indication that school is not a priority for them? We should remember such choices when a student requests a letter of recommendation." Do you agree with this opinion? Why or why not?

Case 1-9. Changing the Course in Midstream

> The syllabus that Professor Alter gave students on the first day of class stated that grades would be assigned based on four exam scores. However, after two exams are given on the specified dates, Alter announces that there will be only one more exam.

Because syllabi constitute a contract with students, instructors have an obligation to avoid major changes in course requirements. Circumstances, however, can affect the strength of the obligation. Whereas mere convenience should never justify major changes, unforeseen and uncontrollable circumstances (such as a weather emergency that closed the school for several days) might make schedule changes unavoidable. Under less extreme circumstances, such as discovering new material for the course that would require alterations in requirements, the legitimacy of the change should be balanced against any additional burdens placed on the students.

Alter's decision does not appear to be based on any justifiable stand. Nevertheless, some students may be delighted to learn that they would have to study for one less exam. But other students who have been projecting their schedules or current class status based on two more performance opportunities could be considerably disadvantaged. (See also 5-3.)

Discussion Questions

1. What if, halfway through the course, Alter decides to add a fifth exam? Is this more or less justifiable than deleting an exam?

2. What if Alter changes only the form of the evaluation? For example, an announced multiple choice exam is switched to an essay exam. Or, a planned exam is changed to a term paper. Under what circumstances could these alterations be justified?

3. What if an instructor adds extra credit opportunities toward the end of the semester, indicating that he is giving students an opportunity to pump up sagging grades? Is this a caring and ethical act or a disservice to students who have worked diligently to maintain a good record based on the provisions in the original syllabus?

Student Deportment in the Classroom

Good manners, social skills, and self-control are not competencies that today's educators can assume all students have mastered. Nationwide reports suggest that incivility in the classroom has reached a critical mass (Schneider, 1998; Trout, 1998). Accounts of menacing forms of student misbehavior have become more commonplace in such publications as the *Chronicle for Higher Education.*

Theories abound, often centering on the premise that today's young people are poorly socialized due to such factors as two-income families with too little time for their children, as to why incivility is on the rise. The prevalence of violent images and multiple opportunities to commit "virtual barbarism" through computerized games are also among the usual suspects accounting for rough-edged student behaviors.

Managing disruptive, difficult, disturbed, and scary students requires intervention for the sake of maintaining a healthy classroom environment as well as for the ultimate welfare of students. This task is rarely easy, and ethical issues are ever-lurking whenever intervention is necessary. The cases in this chapter illustrate a range of student behaviors, from the near-benign to the terrifying.

Case 2-1. Love Birds in Class

> Jena Heart and Tom Throb sit next to each other in class, gaze into each others' eyes while holding hands much of the time, and occasionally pass notes. They are not disruptive in any noisy way, but students in the vicinity intently watch them, and the instructor finds their off-task behavior distracting to her own train of thought. The instructor also wonders what these two enamored students are learning in class.

Not all disruptive behavior is loud or blatant, nor is it always meant to be disrespectful of the learning environment. Manifestation of young love is a sturdy phenomenon on any campus. However, in the classroom, learning is the main agenda. To the extent that the couple's behavior compromises other students' ability to concentrate and the instructor's ability to teach, steps should be taken to cool down the situation.

If Heart and Throb are unresponsive to the usual and mild classroom control techniques (e.g., glances in their direction, or walking over close to the action, perhaps pausing momentarily until their amorous activity subsides) they should be called aside outside of class or during office hours. The confrontation need not involve impugning the relationship itself. We suggest simply informing the couple that the active exhibition of their relationship in the classroom distracts both students and instructor, thus diminishing the quality of the classroom environment. The instructor can also express concern about the worth of their own learning experiences.

If the behavior remains unabated, or resumes after a short period of compliance, separating them would be an acceptable solution. If, after warnings, the students continue the behavior from a distance (e.g., passing notes down the line), then more invasive discipline techniques are warranted, including openly admonishing the behavior.

This case illustrates one of many advantages of seating charts that the instructor devises. When lovebirds as well as other close chums are separated, the classroom may be more conducive to teaching and learning. (See also 2-4, 2-5, and 2-9.)

Discussion Questions

1. The situation described in this case may elicit an urge to have some fun at the couple's expense, such as "threatening" to hose them down with cold water. Would teasing them be an ethical means of social control?

2. Sometimes lovebirds stand right outside the classroom doors, embracing as if they will never see each other again. Should such passionate behavior be frowned upon, or does it just make the hallways more interesting?

Case 2-2. The Class Monopolist

Hedda Gabber is an active participant in World Literature 355. She enjoys responding to other students' observations and has something to add to most points made by the instructor. She frequently uses questions to mask a vehicle for lecturing her classmates on her

interpretations of literary works as well as her
perspectives on life in general. Sometimes her
comments are enriching, but most of the time she comes
across as grand-standing. The course instructor has used
various indirect strategies to reduce Hedda's daily
commentary, but Hedda seems unable to take a hint.
Some students in the class have become so fed up with
her that they roll their eyes, carry on conversations
amongst themselves while she is speaking, or loudly
whisper"will you just shut up." Some students
complain to the instructor about the rude behavior of
others while Hedda speaks and others complain that the
instructor is not active enough in controlling Hedda's
monopoly of class time.

Hedda's classroom behavior raises two important classroom management
issues: how to respond to discourteous behavior and how to control a
student who routinely attempts to monopolize class discussions. We have
found that a bit of prevention on the first day of class often goes a long
way to minimize both classroom management problems. If discussion is
encouraged, the ground rules should be stated in the syllabus. These rules
serve a dual purpose: They set a standard for classroom decorum, and
they help to create an atmosphere of openness and trust. Students actually
feel more comfortable participating in class, knowing that expectations of
courtesy and acceptance of different points of view have been put in place.

In this case, however, an unfortunate situation appears to be escalating.
The rude behavior of Hedda's classmates, although inappropriate, is likely
an expression of their increasing frustration with Hedda and with the
instructor who has failed to effectively control her. Some students may
feel that Hedda is wasting time that would be better spent reviewing critical
course material. Or, they may feel that Hedda's monologues are
condescending. Others may feel that her long speeches limit the
opportunities for others to contribute. Such resentment can be avoided if
the instructor intervenes early.

Some monopolizing students respond well to hints to back off. This is
not the case with Hedda. The instructor needs to deal tactfully, but directly
with her in a private conversation. The instructor can acknowledge
Hedda's uncommon enthusiasm for contributing to class discussion, but
point out that spending extra time on her comments has resulted in running
out of valuable time needed to cover the day's lesson and insufficient time
for other students to speak. Hedda should be asked to be more selective
with her commentary or else the instructor will not call on her in the future.

An invitation to discuss course-related issues during office hours or via email might be extended to Hedda as well. (See also 2-3, 2-4, 2-6, 2-10, and 21-2.)

Discussion Questions

1. What ground rules for class participation could be included in course syllabi?

2. How should the instructor deal with the obviously frustrated and openly rude students?

3. How would you deal with Hedda?

Case 2-3. The Student Who Discloses Too Much

> An obviously enthusiastic Maggie Mouth raises her hand often during the daily discussions in Professor Brown's creative writing class. Her comments and questions are usually relevant to the topic at hand, but almost always contain a disclosure of extremely personal information about herself and her family. Her classmates have learned about her brother's multiple felony convictions, her sister's unusual sexual practices, her mother's mental illness, her father's philandering, and her own abortion. Professor Brown notices other students' eye-rolling and hand-over-mouth snickering whenever Maggie releases yet another family skeleton from the closet. He also notices that students increasingly shy away from her in and out of class. Professor Brown worries that Maggie is harming herself by being so open. However, he also believes that it is not his business to gag Maggie's right to free expression.

Professor Brown is in charge of the room and, as such, what occurs in class is not only his business but his responsibility. In some cases it might be possible to modify the content of comments of a student who reveals too much by not responding in a way that encourages more of the same and calling on the student less frequently.

When a student consistently puts herself in social jeopardy, the instructor needs to intervene. The instructor should call Maggie into the office and, while maintaining sensitivity to Maggie's feelings and perhaps complimenting her on her enthusiasm, inform her that others do not need to know her personal business and that some students may even hold what she discloses against her or hold her up to ridicule. To mitigate against totally silencing Maggie, the instructor might also try to teach her to frame her comments in a way that precludes revealing her sources.

We do not know the motivation behind Maggie's self-disclosures, which could range from naivete to an unhealthy form of attention-seeking. If one talk does not solve the problem, the instructor should consider consulting a counselor for additional advice about how to deal with this student. (See also 2-2 and 4-6.)

Discussion Questions

1. What if an inappropriate disclosure by a student occurs only once, but it is a profound one? Should this just be ignored?

2. Should a student ever be removed from a class for highly inappropriate disclosures that do not subside after several attempts to alter the behavior?

3. What if, as part of the personal disclosure, the student reveals a serious problem that requires some sort of intervention (e.g., heavy drug use, involvement in a violent crime, or sexual abuse)? Does the instructor have a responsibility to intervene? If so, what course of action should be taken?

4. Have you had an experience with students such as Maggie? If so, how did you deal with it? Was your effort successful?

Case 2-4, A & B. Disruptive Students

> Barbie Babble whispers to her classmates frequently. The instructor has spoken to her twice and has moved her seat. Barbie keeps on chattering, pausing only briefly when she gets "the look." The instructor is considering putting Barbie's seat off in a corner by itself.
>
> Obby Noxious disrupts the class with loud noises whenever the instructor turns to the blackboard and asks annoying ("What good will knowing this do me in life?") or nonsensical ("Did Napoleon have a pet?") questions. Some students laugh, but many others have expressed negative feelings to both Obby and the instructor. Several private talks with Obby have not altered his behavior appreciably. The instructor decides to see if some policy will allow her to expel Obby from the class.

Students have ethical responsibilities, and disrupting the learning environment is prohibited by most codes of student conduct in institutions of higher education. The instructor may also want to discuss the problem with the department chair. Once satisfied that a reasonable effort has been made to encourage a difficult student to shape up (e.g., speaking to the student, a seating change, asking the student to leave the room, consulting the counseling staff, and possibly referring the student to the dean of students), a final warning could be given, followed by instituting the dismissal process. (See also 2-5, 2-6, 2-7, 2-9, and 21-2.)

Discussion Questions

1. Students often have different ideas from those of their instructors about what constitutes appropriate and inappropriate disciplinary measures. For example, a technique that seems appropriate to an instructor, such as asking a student who is constantly whispering to share his comments with the entire class, is viewed as humiliating by students. How should one deal, on-the-spot, with Barbie and Obby? Is it OK to embarrass them in the process?

2. These cases focus on the behavior of identifiable, individual students. Should the class size influence the instructor's expectations about classroom deportment or methods of dealing with students when they are more difficult to identify? Is it reasonable to expect all members in a class of 200 students to avoid private conversations?

3. What are the dangers of simply ignoring all instances of rude, disruptive behavior?

4. Some instructors take the approach of allowing the class to decide how to handle offending students, reasoning that all members of the class should share responsibility for the quality of the classroom community. What are the benefits and dangers associated with this practice?

5. What techniques have you used to deal with disruptive students? Which ones have been effective? Which ones have failed?

Case 2-5. Just a Pinch

> Dennis Dipsit settles into the first row of Professor Noskoal's class with a wad of tobacco tucked in his mouth and a paper cup in his hand in which to expectorate. Dr. Noskoal tells Dennis that his behavior is inappropriate and that he is not allowed to stay in the classroom if he plans to chew and spit. Dennis protests

and points out that the school rule says that "no smoking
is allowed," and adds, "It doesn't say I can't chew."

It is difficult to think that Dipsit's behavior would not be disturbing to the
class. In general, we believe that an instructor has the right to establish a
reasonable code of classroom behavior for any acts that might be disruptive
to the teaching/learning process. Not only might chewing and spitting be
banned, but other disruptive activities such as eating and drinking, use of
a cell phone or beeper, listening to a headset, or personal grooming actions
such as clipping fingernails can be included on the list of disallowed acts.

Where to draw the line is a personal decision. Some teachers we know
will not allow students to wear caps in class. Some allow beverages and
"quiet snacks," whereas others do not. We recommend that, at the
beginning of a term, instructors let their classes know that certain forms
of disruption will not be tolerated, including concrete examples of
inappropriate behaviors. This should help prevent the kind of
confrontation that occurred between Dipsit and Noskoal. (For other cases
dealing with disruptive students, see 2-1, 2-2, 2-4, 2-6, and 2-9.)

Discussion Questions

1. What other disruptive behaviors should be considered when setting the
level of tolerance? How much can an instructor legislate the personal behaviors
of members of the class?

2. What about behaviors that disrupt only the instructor, such as a sleeping
student or a quiet comic-book reader? Should these behaviors be interrupted on
the spot? If so, how can it be done most effectively?

Case 2-6. Very Difficult Students: The Profane

Lew D. Conduct is a student in Professor Penalty's
French class. Lew and a friend repeatedly disrupt class
by shouting at one another across the room during class,
making obscene remarks while the professor is lecturing,
and attempting "baskets" in the trash can by the door.
Penalty's attempt to control this behavior by speaking
individually with the offenders has only resulted in an
escalation of the problem. Fed up, Penalty told the
misbehaving students they were required to stay after
class and complete an extra assignment as punishment
for their inappropriate behavior. Lew responded by

> grabbing his crotch as he strolled out of class. Penalty, an untenured assistant professor, considered further action, but decided against it for fear that doing so might bring her negative attention.

Unfortunately, Lew's behavior is not all that rare on college campuses (e.g., Schneider, 1998). In some cases faculty members have been threatened, verbally abused, or assaulted by students like Lew. Requiring students to stay after class or do extra work when they already have a record of overt hostility is likely to be ineffective, may only increase the volatility of the situation, and may even place the instructor's safety at risk. Instructors who encounter such students need to take swift and decisive action by involving the dean of students or campus security personnel who may be in a better position to apply university-sanctioned or legal consequences.

Penalty's effectiveness as an instructor and the other students' learning are seriously compromised by Lew's disruptive actions. This case, however, included an added twist. Untenured, contract, and graduate student faculty have much to lose if they are perceived as being unable to control their classrooms, yet these may be the faculty who are most vulnerable to disruptive students. This case suggests that Penalty anticipates a lack of support from others in her department and within the administration. Her perception may be a signal that administrators within her institution need to be more readily and forcefully available to support faculty when a student's classroom behavior reaches such startling proportions as does Lew's. Furthermore, if Penalty does not respond, she may risk retaliation from other students, such as complaints to her department chair and poor teaching evaluations. (See also 2-7.)

Discussion Questions

1. What recourse does Penalty have if she seeks help from her department chair, and is simply told, "If you can't stand the heat, get out of the kitchen"?

2. How should the instructor respond when students use inappropriate language or engage in inappropriate behavior (e.g., profanity, offensive slang, and obscene gestures)?

3. Have you had an experience with a student like Lew? If so, how did you manage the situation, and what was the outcome?

Case 2-7. Very Difficult Students: The Scary

Professor Wary is becoming increasingly nervous about the behavior of one of his students. Mike Menace wears an intimidating, disapproving frown throughout every class session and, most days, loiters around in the halls near Wary's office. He does not, however, attempt to make contact. Last week Mike followed Wary to his car from a distance. This week, Wary noticed Mike across the street from his home, standing against a tree while causally smoking a cigarette. Wary wants to the call police but does not know what to say because Mike has not made any direct threat. Wary is afraid to call Mike in for a private confrontation. He is also reluctant to tell anyone else because he feels like a coward and cannot bear admitting to others that he is terrified of one of his own students. Wary has, however, purchased a gun which he keeps with him at all times.

Unfortunately, actual reports of obsessed students have surfaced. Students who have issues, real or perceived, with one or more of their educators are now less likely to remain passive. Those with rage or emotional problems can be dangerous.

Professor Wary should take some form of action. Although we cannot tell if he (and his family) are in any real danger, Mike's shady behavior, especially if it continues to escalate, is well outside the norm. Instructors should never be embarrassed about seeking help in such situations. Wary's gun toting, while against most campus policies, could also lead to a tragic outcome.

Immediate consultations with trusted colleagues, the department chair, or the institution's counseling center will likely provide advice and support to follow through with appropriate action. In a situation with which we are familiar, the embarrassed colleague was being stalked and threatened for months by a student before confiding in a colleague. The colleague was forbidden to tell anyone, but chose to call one of us without revealing identities. We were able to convince the faculty member, through a second party, that the campus police be called. It was discovered, fortunately in time, that the emotionally disturbed student believed that he had been sent on a mission to "delete" the instructor. We recommend that all campuses provide their faculties with guidance on how to manage a hostile, threatening, or frightening student. (See also 2-6.)

Discussion Questions

1. What would you have done if you were Professor Wary?

2. Does your campus distribute information about managing menacing or threatening students?

3. Do you know of or have you ever faced a situation involving a student like Mike? If so, what happened, and what was the final outcome?

Case 2-8. Handling Students
Who Are Cause for Concern

> In the middle of the semester, a student who has appeared to be extremely depressed comes to Professor Alarm after class to say "goodbye" and to thank Alarm for being a very kind person. The student then abruptly leaves before Alarm can respond. Although suicide was not explicitly threatened, Alarm feels extremely uneasy about what has just happened.

If clues of danger to self or others appear to be probable, as in this case, some form of immediate action using any available resources should be taken. Professional consultation should be available to faculty members and staff for this purpose, such as a psychologist from the counseling center. Most colleges and universities have set plans for such eventualities, and all faculty members should know what they are in advance. Professor Alarm would also be wise to keep notes concerning the actions he takes in response to the student's behavior and comments. These notes would reveal that signs of contemplated suicide were not simply ignored should any unfortunate event ensue that would trigger an investigation. (See also 2-3 and 18-10 for managing students who may have serious emotional problems.)

Discussion Questions

1. Professor Alarm decides to confront the student before the student leaves. The student quickly assures Alarm that his concerns are not warranted. Has Alarm met his obligation to assist a potentially suicidal student?

2. Professor Alarm has a colleague who teaches in another department who is a licensed clinical psychologist but not a staff member at the student counseling center. Is it appropriate for Alarm to ask this colleague to intervene with the

student? What confidentiality or dual-role issues exist? Does a potential suicide override these issues?

3. Suppose the student calls Professor Alarm at home in the evening to say "goodbye." What should Alarm do in this situation, knowing that he cannot contact any appropriate campus personnel until the next morning?

4. Have you had any experiences with a troubled student about whom you were very worried? What did you do? How was the matter resolved?

5. What if the student was a minor? Would you consider calling the parents?

Case 2-9. The Large and Talkative Class: How Far Can We Go?

> When students in his large core curriculum class did not respond to several requests to be quiet, Professor Hadit stopped in the middle of a sentence. "That is it," he yelled. He stomped into the audience, demanding certain students give their names and writing them down. With the list waving in his hand, he went back to the podium and announced that the identified students were "put on notice." Furthermore, if he caught them talking to neighbors or engaging in any other behavior that made it difficult for "good students to hear," he would take steps to have them removed from the classroom. One student in the back yelled out that Hadit was a dictator. Professor Hadit pointed his finger in the direction of the shouter and said, "And this fellow had better watch his backside." With that, a now enraged Professor Hadit stomped out of the room.

Anyone who has taught a very large class probably has empathy for Professor Hadit. Many of today's students, stimulated with fast images and sound bites, find it extremely difficult to sit still in a sea of peers for 50 minutes (or more) as the instructor lectures from afar.

The students cannot be totally faulted, however, because a sense of anonymity reduces their connection to the course, and inappropriate in-class behavior is disinhibited. Furthermore, most large classes are lower division, which means that the least socialized students on campus are in them. Whereas smaller classes would be the best resolution for everyone concerned, the realties of resources and other institutional needs that are fulfilled by offering large classes usually take precedence.

Professor Hadit's tactics reveal desperation that is likely to add to the negative classroom ambience. Hadit's vague threats are irresponsible. Talking during class, although disruptive, does not meet the customary strict criteria for removing a student from the course. Finally, Hadit's more sinister intimidation of the student protester is reckless and possibly actionable.

Although an extended discussion is beyond the scope of this book, techniques and procedures that can help mitigate the problem of talking students can, if feasible, be considered. A teaching assistant can double as a roving reminder ("Shhhh!") when conversations break out. A 2-minute stretch break is sometimes helpful, especially for classes that run more than 50 minutes. The use of short videotapes or other methods that break up a lecture may keep students more focused on what is going on in the front of the room. Brief quizzes at the end of class sessions may foster better attention Finally, strong-voiced, exuberant instructors seem to report fewer problems with chatty students in large classes. (See also 3-13.)

Discussion Questions

1. How might Professor Hadit have handled his class more effectively?

2. Are very large classes ethical?

3. What do you do when students become overly talkative in a large class?

Case 2-10. Handling Prejudicial Statements Made by Students in Class

> During a discussion of contemporary military policies, a student comments to the class that women and men should never be allowed to fight in the same unit because "women would create too much of a distraction for the men." The student continues, "We would lose every war if we let women fight alongside the men."

This remark is sexist, and students might expect the instructor to assail the student immediately. When possible, as it seems to be in this particular case, instructors should turn a biased remark into a positive learning experience. Here we have a comment directly about the topic at hand.

The instructor can ask for reactions to the student's statement and guide the discussion in such a way that the student's attitude can be called into question. If skill is exercised, the student who made the comment can also learn without being humiliated or attacked.

There can be times when a student's offensive class remark is way off-target or has no redeeming qualities that a instructor can build upon to steer the discussion back to a productive track. Although reports of extreme instances are rare, instructors are advised to handle them quickly and decisively by saying something like, "That is not the kind of comment that belongs in an educational setting." (For other cases dealing with students' offensive behavior in class, see 2-2, 2-4, 2-5, 2-6, 2-7, and 2-9. For a case dealing with an student's offensive remark outside of class, see 12-1.)

Discussion Questions

1. The commentary for this case suggests the need for skillful management of this type of student attitude. What are some ways to deal with such remarks that minimize defensiveness or a student feeling humiliated or attacked?

2. Often remarks are a springboard for much (and often spirited) disagreement among students that can be very pedagogically beneficial. However, discussion can reach an uncomfortable impasse. How should the instructor end or resolve an ongoing debate?

3. Have you had a similar incident that required your careful intervention? How did you deal with it?

II

The Classroom
Learning Experience

Instructors'
Presentation Style
and Content

How instructors present themselves to students, including the teaching methods they employ, can have ethical implications. This chapter explores a variety of issues including the use of profanity, the presentation of sensitive materials, self-disclosures, biases that can enter into pedagogical content, emotional outbursts, and other examples of possibly irresponsible or inappropriate behavior displayed in the classroom by the instructor.

Case 3-1. Irritable Instructors

> Students complain that Professor Bark is often petulant in class. They are actually afraid of her if she is having a particularly bad day. The department chairperson assures himself that the quality of her lectures is not being compromised by her less-than-civil demeanor. He advises students who complain to ignore her outbursts and reminds them of how fortunate they are to have an educator who is "tops in her field."

Somewhere along a continuum instructors can create a classroom environment that is hostile and not conducive to learning. Young and inexperienced students may be especially disadvantaged by such a circumstance. Although we would need more detail about the particular incidents involving Professor Bark, the fact that a number of students have approached the chairperson indicates that the departmental leadership should not simply turn them away while suggesting they are ungrateful. That this pattern is apparently consistent differentiates it from the "bad day" experienced by Sad and Adlib. (See 19-4 and 19-5.)

Faculty members are human beings and cannot be expected to have a congenial disposition at all times. However, a consistent pattern of outbursts resulting in abusive behavior that undermines the students' trust and self-confidence requires intervention. In the case of Professor Bark, we would advise that the department chair speak with her and, depending how the consultation goes, appropriately monitor the situation. Academic institutions are increasingly developing impaired-faculty services.

This case raises the intriguing question of whether competence and scholarly accomplishment can compensate for a weakness, in this case extreme and relatively frequent moodiness. Brilliant people with trying quirks have been tolerated in many contexts, from movie sets to research labs, because of their otherwise considerable talents. College-level faculty are traditionally selected on the basis of their command of subject matter and the potential for scholarly contribution to their discipline. However, we believe that interpersonal style and the ability to relate to students can be as important as the other qualifications required of teaching faculty.

Discussion Questions

1. Does your institution have any policies or guidelines for dealing with faculty who are cantankerous or verbally abusive toward students? How would Professor Bark be handled by your institution?

2. Do you agree that competence in one area (e.g., an outstanding, nationally recognized research publication record that brings great honor to your department and the institution) is a sufficient reason to tolerate personal traits that are not admired (e.g., excessive arrogance, angry outbursts, or regular demeaning interactions with students and colleagues)? Why or why not?

Case 3-2. Frequent Use of Profanity in Class

> Professor Colorful uses profanity in his classes on a fairly regular basis. Although he never directs vulgarities toward students, a few have complained they are bothered by his cussing. Professor Colorful defends his lecture style by asserting that most students enjoy it and that it helps sustain students' attention.

Student enjoyment, per se, is different from student comfort. It is certainly possible to provide enjoyable experiences for students while not, at the same time, making others uncomfortable. Professor Colorful seems to be assuming that because some students may be laughing or expressing approval in some form, his classroom technique is, therefore, sound or at least harmless. He also seems to be creating his assessment of the positive impact of his style without benefit of objective evidence. Shock value usually wears off over time whereas the level of offensiveness may actually increase.

We believe that the extent to which profanity in the classroom constitutes unprofessional conduct depends on several factors. One is the context in which it occurs. For example, references to taboo slang terms could be appropriate in lectures on certain subjects (e.g., human sexuality, language, or literature courses), and students taking such courses might expect such references. Profanity could also be used appropriately for illustrative purposes, for example, in direct quotations or to illustrate the emotional effect of taboo vs. nontaboo words. In such cases, however, it might be wise to gently inform students of the possibly offending terminology.

Colorful's constant use of profanity, however, does not appear to have any discernible pedagogical justification. The regular use of taboo words in lectures does not enhance the image of the teaching profession and models a style that parents and others may not appreciate. Freedom of expression, however, is not a value that academics restrict lightly. Acceptability is probably best judged by community standards. In Colorful's case, a 2% complaint rate might suggest that such standards are not being violated. However, because there might be a silent majority of offended noncomplainers, Colorful needs to reexamine his technique. Furthermore, Colorful should keep in mind that it takes only one student to make a major (and public) issue of behavior that many might find unbecoming in the academy. Colorful might, at the very least, be encouraged to include a specific item on the anonymous student course evaluation asking for frank feedback on his teaching style.

Colorful might want to hold discussions with other colleagues, a third party (such as the department chair), or interview students to determine their opinions. If Colorful is offending a substantial number of students, he should desist. In one survey of undergraduate students, it was discovered that most students would not appreciate teachers using profanity for its own sake, and an even higher percentage would find telling "dirty" jokes inappropriate (Keith-Spiegel, Tabachnick, & Allen, 1993). In any case, students should know about Colorful's lecture vocabulary repertoire at the start of the course so that those who do not welcome such exposure can drop out. If Colorful is teaching the only section of a required course, he has a stronger obligation not to give this brand of offense. Finally, college instructors are powerful role models to students even though we may not always be aware of it. We could easily argue that modeling profanity has no apparent redeeming qualities.

Discussion Questions

1. The media are increasingly liberal in the use of taboo words and share a willingness to quote directly others who use them. Should not, then, instructors feel comfortable making liberal use of offensive language? Why or why not?

2. Someone once said that the truly great comedians are those able to amuse without resorting to vulgar language. Might the same apply to the truly great educator?

3. What about the student whose contributions to class discussions are laced with considerable expletives? What should the instructor's response be?

Case 3-3. Oral Plagiarism

> **Professor Copy uses the written work of others to create all of her lectures. However, she never gives the sources credit for her verbatim presentations. Students have never raised the issue because they are unaware of the origins of the lectures.**

Oral plagiarism is a rarely discussed issue in the ethics literature and perhaps raises a pang of dread in most instructors. After all, we did not independently create most of the information we impart to our students. And, at some point, basic knowledge becomes part of the public domain.

When one uses common information and embroiders it in one's own style, to credit all the sources would be cumbersome and unnecessary. Complete attributions would take up class time that could be used for more productive reasons.

However, when one uses materials verbatim beyond a fair use criterion, or presents theories and research findings in a way that would be assumed by the listener to be the original thinking or labor of the speaker, a question of ethics arises. With just a little effort and creativity, instructors can extend proper credit without using up considerable time or confusing students. For example, one might say at the beginning of the period, "Today we will be discussing multivariate statistics, and I will be adapting many of my points from the materials provided to me at a workshop I attended that was conducted by Dr. Tabachnick and Dr. Fidell." For more specific presentations, mentioning the name of those who created the theory or scholarly work or who did the research should not take more than a few seconds. When these names will not be part of an examination, the instructor can also add, "I will not be testing you on the authors' identities, but I do want you to recall the general findings of their work." (See also 3-7.)

Discussion Questions

1. How do you define what is in the public domain in your field?

2. Does the level of the course make a difference? For example, is it more important to cite sources in a graduate or advanced undergraduate seminar than in an introductory survey course?

3. Does the fact that oral plagiarism is not permanent (i.e., it is uttered and then gone) mean that it is also a less severe breach of ethics than is written plagiarism?

Case 3-4. Criticism of Colleagues in Class

> When a student praises the work of an instructor at another institution, Professor Jab replies, "His work is mostly crap and the rumor is that he is facing disciplinary charges for scientific misconduct."

Critical analyses of the work of others is an important component of the socialization of academics. Criticism of a colleague's work is not, therefore, unethical *per se*. However, Jab has behaved unprofessionally in front of students. Describing work of another as "crap" explains nothing, yet teaches disrespect. Furthermore, the accusation that the colleague might be facing disciplinary proceedings appears to be without substantiation. Unless such accusations are part of the public domain, Jab has no business spreading possibly false or unauthorized information in class. Even when formal accusations have been made, the colleague may later be exonerated and Jab may not have an opportunity to modify earlier remarks.

A more legitimate response to scholarship with which one disagrees is to say something like, "Not everyone sees it that way, and personally I think that the work to which you are referring is problematic because. . . ." In other words, rather than letting students' statements evoke displeasure or a lapse in objectivity, instructors can use such incidents as catalysts for a positive and memorable learning experience.

It may be that Jab has other problems, possibly of a personal nature, with his colleague. The classroom is not, however, an arena for personal battles. (See also 14-1 and 14-2.)

Discussion Questions

1. What if the colleague was a faculty member in Jab's institution (or department)? Must commentary about a colleague's work, unless complimentary, be made even more carefully than if the colleague is somewhere else?

2. How should an instructor handle the reverse situation, that is when a student makes an extremely derogatory comment about another instructor or someone else in the instructor's field and the instructor fully agrees with the student's negative comments?

Case 3-5. Little White Lies to Make a Point

> Professor Ceeare uncritically presents results of a study in support of a social policy position to which she adheres to her sociology classes. This work, however, has been found to be invalid by several other researchers. When asked in private about this discrepancy by a colleague, she replies that the original results represent a higher truth, validated by people's personal experiences, that is inaccessible to the traditional logical positivist approach to research. She also replies that consciousness raising is part of a college education, and that the benefits of making students aware of the social problem illustrated by the research outweigh the distortions entailed by presenting possibly flawed research.

Ceeare's arguments for the "experiential validity" of her view are not unethical *per se*. However, if that is the basis of her argument, that is all she should claim to support it. Ceeare should not present a flawed study as if it provides objective support for her view. It is unethical for her to distort another kind of evidence to make it look like something it is not.

We believe that Ceeare's manner of handling this question does a disservice to students because "logical positivist" ideas are probably what most of them learned in research methods classes, and few of them will understand her argument that ideas that fail to achieve this kind of scientific support may nevertheless be considered valid by some people. Confusing students does not make for good teaching, and Ceeare may undermine her credibility in students' eyes concerning other material as well.

Ceeare would be better off acknowledging that there can be different sides to a question and note the nature of evidence for each. It is more appropriate (and less confusing for students) to leave a question unsettled than to answer it on the basis of arguments that seem to undermine other foundations that students are being taught. Handling it this way allows Ceeare to be a better role model for how instructors deal with our sometimes limited understanding of complicated issues. (See also 3-6.)

Discussion Questions

1. Although Ceeare's case is more extreme, it does raise the question of the extent to which it is proper to simplify the results of research or the content of a critique to avoid confusing students with complexities that are beyond their current level of understanding. At what point does simplification become distortion?

2. What are the ethical implications of these alternative scenarios?

a. Rather than presenting flawed research, Ceeare presents valid research, but only those studies that support her stand. She ignores equally valid research that provides contrary evidence.

b. Ceeare presents research that provides evidence in support of both sides of the question, but points out only the strengths of the research supporting her point of view, ignoring its weaknesses, and points out only the weaknesses of the other research, ignoring its strengths.

3. How does a research-based argument, as seen in this case, differ from an artistic, philosophical, religious, or other type of argument? Or does it differ? Are there common standards of validity for all fields?

Case 3-6. Twisting Facts

> **Professor Revision proclaims to his Twentieth Century History class that President John F. Kennedy's assassination was the result of a conspiracy involving the Central Intelligence Agency. He dismisses students who question his certainty on this point with the retort, "You just don't want to see the truth."**

In clear-cut examples, such as whether the Holocaust occurred, it is entirely appropriate to treat an event as historical fact without bringing up extremist claims to the contrary. Students are shortchanged and misguided, however, when one side of an important controversy is dismissed, and the other is enshrined as fact, when respected authorities consider the relevant evidence to be mixed at best.

Professor Revision may be fully convinced that his conclusion is accurate and will eventually be confirmed, but in his excitement to have students credit him with this insight he has stepped away from his role as their mentor for 20th Century History. His intellectual stance on this matter is not sufficiently circumspect and critical. Even if students prefer Revision's self-assured style of instruction, they will not learn as much of value when given only his cut-and dried conclusions.

Students in any field need to understand how trained professionals evaluate evidence, make inferences, and defend their interpretations in the face of relevant criticism. When a course topic is completely value-driven, such that no hard data are available, instructors must still emphasize the process of how a given discipline analyzes ideas rather than the notion that some ideas are necessarily more correct than others.

It is acceptable for Revision to conclude a thorough, objective presentation of the pertinent evidence with his own argument that belief in a conspiracy is defensible. He can add the point that such a disturbing conclusion may be difficult for many people to accept, even if there is some supportive evidence. However, he should not try to undercut students who hold a contrary position especially when they can easily muster other evidence to support a contradictory view. Revision should strive to expand students' mastery of the process and content of his field, not to increase the number of new adherents to his particular hypothesis. This approach also makes it less awkward for instructors when new evidence comes to light that conclusively refutes their position. (See also 3-5.)

Discussion Questions

1. Suppose an instructor's position on a major issue completely changes in light of critical new evidence. Would the instructor have any responsibilities to previous students?

2. What if a dispute is the other way around? What obligation does an instructor have to listen at any length to a student's notion that most scholars consider indefensible or unproven?

Case 3-7. Lecturing From the Textbook

Professor Reader believes that everything her students need to know in her introductory level course is contained in the textbook. Her lectures are merely repetitions of textbook material. She asserts that

> beginning students benefit from repetition and that her
> time is freed to prepare more sophisticated material for
> her advanced classes.

If everything students needed to know were in textbooks, there would be no need for classes. It is our firm belief that textbooks usually do not contain everything students need to know. For example, even the newest textbooks are usually 2 or more years behind current knowledge simply because of the time it takes to write and produce them. The classroom is the place to inform students about what is current in the field. Students, especially introductory students, do not always understand what is in the textbook, so lectures can add explanations and examples. Because of the size of the knowledge base, authors of introductory textbooks often have to pick and choose what to include. Lectures can inform students about topics omitted or treated with insufficient depth. Some textbooks are written from a particular theoretical or philosophical point of view, ignoring or giving little attention opposing theories or viewpoints. Lectures can provide students with different perspectives on a topic. In fact, part of what instructors can accomplish in introductory courses is to teach students the limitations of considering only one viewpoint or approach to a topic.

Finally, all students should be accorded the same degree of the instructor's knowledge, talents, and effort. Professor Reader willfully short-changes her lower division students. If anything, introductory students deserve special attention because of their status as novices. It is also the introductory courses from which advanced students are recruited. If they are uninspired by their introductory course, they may inappropriately label the entire discipline.

Discussion Questions

1. Are there circumstances when going over what is in the book constitutes responsible teaching? What are some examples?

2. To some degree, the question of how much time to allocate to one's courses is one of robbing Peter to pay Paul. What criteria could one use in making a decision to spend more time and effort on one course than on another?

Case 3-8. Risky Class Presentations

> Professor Carnal read an erotic poem, published in a
> legitimate literary journal, to his English Poetry class.
> Two students complained that the poem was "verbal

> pornography" and that they were subjected to it without warning. They further argued that institutions of higher education should function at a level "higher than the gutter."

Today's diverse student population creates a dilemma for instructors who deviate from a relatively narrow, traditional pathway. And yet institutions of higher education remain as one of the few places where any idea or writing can be put forth, critically examined, debated, and accepted or rejected. This process is unfamiliar to many of today's students who are socialized into quick and often unexamined judgments of what is right and what is wrong. (This is not to say that *all* material is automatically suitable for the classroom, as we examine in 3-6 and 3-9.)

When "risk management" figures into ethical decision making, instructors may find themselves needing to become less spontaneous when it comes to controversial or sensitive material. The first step is to be in touch with the campus administration regarding the *actual* amount of support given to the concept of academic freedom. Given any potential dangers, we suggest that instructors protect themselves in the following ways:

1. Be able to support the premise that class lectures, activities, and materials are relevant to the course topic and goals set forth by the department and the syllabus.

2. If any material might offend or disturb some students, describe it briefly on the first day of class, thus allowing students to select themselves out by dropping the class.

3. Invite students to come in during office hours to discuss anything presented in class (and, should any take advantage of an opportunity to criticize it, allow them their say without ridicule or censure while also taking an opportunity to better explain your choices).

4. If upcoming material is likely to be problematic for some students, warn them in advance. Being "tipped off" may be all some students require to alleviate conflict. Others may choose to miss class that day. (See also 3-9, 4-4, and 4-5. See 5-11 for a case dealing with assigning risky course assignments.)

Discussion Questions

1. Should students be responsible for the content of sensitive material on an examination?

2. What if a student refused to learn material with erotic content because it violated his or her moral standards? How would you handle such a confrontation?

Case 3-9. Instructors' Personal Disclosures

Some students are offended by Professor Open's willingness to discuss her private life in her public health services class. She has, on various occasions, described her sexual relations with her spouse, getting a tattoo (and where it is), and her menstrual cycle.

Although students enjoy anecdotes that reveal an instructor's human side, it is a misuse of the instructor's power to relate examples that do not assist student learning or that show disrespect for student sensibilities. We believe that the use of real-life examples to illustrate points should also have some pedagogical value, remain within the limits of propriety, and conform to normative community standards. For example, an instructor's personal experience with jury duty would certainly enhance a presentation of the jury system.

The intimate nature of Open's self-disclosures does not meet any of the three criteria noted earlier. Furthermore, Open's behavior forces her captive audience into a personalized relationship with her. Thus, Open has violated ethical propriety by creating a dual-role situation that has extended beyond some students' comfort zone. Maintaining an appropriate level of professional decorum has the benefits of establishing role boundaries for students, of enhancing respect for faculty, and of providing good role modeling. (See also 3-8.)

Discussion Questions

1. Is telling personal stories *not* relevant to the class topic at hand acceptable? What might be some examples?

2. How can one draw the limits of propriety? How much does the personality style of the instructor influence those limits? Can a witty instructor's stories be more acceptable than the same stories told by a humorless instructor?

3. How much does the class level (say, first-year students as compared to seniors or graduate students) have to do with the degree of appropriate self-revelation?

Case 3-10. Disparities in What Students Are Being Taught

> When Professor Misinfo gives what some students in the class think is factually incorrect information during a lecture, the students go to Professor Expert for an opinion. Expert confirms the students' view. The students then confront Misinfo, who refutes Expert's version and defends his own statements as correct. The students are confused.

Such situations are not uncommon, given the sprawling and fast-emerging nature of many academic disciplines and the inability of any single human being to have total command of his or her own discipline. In this case, the students have, unwittingly, put two instructors in conflict with each other. It would have been better had Expert gone to Misinfo to discuss whether the two of them were approaching the evidence from the same perspective. The students might then be given an account of such a discussion.

When colleagues are genuinely collegial, getting together to sort out the differences in what they are teaching students can be a good learning experience for all concerned. Despite their conflicting theories, methods, or interpretations of fact or fiction, the class could benefit from a debate on the theoretical issues and from the model of scientists and scholars dealing constructively (or at least amicably) with differences.

If the colleagues are not friendly or passionately hold conflicting theories, the disagreement is likely to defy mediation. Moreover, it is not inconceivable that students may knowingly pit instructors against each other, most likely when a grade is in dispute.

Finally, we believe that it is appropriate for instructors to admit when they are in error. In our experience, students handle that well and do not diminish their respect for us. On the contrary, many find the humanity in such an admission refreshing.

Discussion Questions

1. What would you do if these students came to you?

2. What if, based on widely accepted and verifiable information, Misinfo is found to be passing along information of some consequence that is flat-out wrong? Must he be persuaded to change his presentations? If so, how and by whom?

Case 3-11, A & B. Teaching to Which
Student Audience?

> Professor Reach teaches her upper-division, under-
> graduate class in business law at a highly advanced level.
> Her textbook is often used during the second year at law
> schools. Her lectures are well crafted, but complicated
> and fast paced. Students complain they do not
> understand what is going on. During a meeting with
> the department chair, Reach strongly defended her
> teaching approach as the appropriate way to give the
> excellent students the edge they need to compete in
> today's marketplace or for entry into the best law schools.
> Professor Rudimentary believes that every student
> in the room must have a full grasp of the material before
> moving ahead. He goes over the same material several
> times in lecture. He also selects a very basic textbook
> that the better students find unchallenging. By the end
> of the term, only two thirds of the book has been covered.

Most large, comprehensive postsecondary institutions present the
frustrating dilemma of where to aim in terms of difficulty or sophistication
level of the subject matter in heterogenous classes. Reach and Rudimentary
have both shot too far in opposite directions. Both may have the best
interests of students in mind, but their solutions are worse than the problem.

We cannot keep every bright student challenged, and we cannot ensure
that every mediocre student succeeds. We can attempt to offer experiences
that may help those hovering at both poles get more from our classes. The
highly advanced student, for example, can be given some leeway to
upgrade a project if that is what the student wishes to do. A parallel
independent study project may be fitting for a truly gifted student who is
treading water during the regular classroom experience. Special tutoring
or review sessions can be made available for slower students. (See 6-3, 6-
4, 6-6, 6-12, and 6-13 for related grading issues.)

Discussion Questions

1. How do you handle this dilemma?

2. If special provisions or opportunities are made available to the best or
weakest students, are instructors obliged to make the same opportunities available
to all other students in the class?

3. Are there pedagogical techniques that simultaneously could enhance both the work of both mediocre and outstanding students? What might be some examples?

Case 3-12. Course Descriptions
Versus Actual Course Content

> Students complain that Dr. Tune's Music Appreciation 335 is very unlike the catalog description. The catalog described activities and assignments that were never incorporated into the course as it was actually taught, and the general content description was of a substantially different focus from that of the actual course.

Although courses and the instructors who teach them earn reputations that circulate widely among students, many will still select their educational experiences on the basis of the authorized course descriptions. We believe that because instructors do not always control the descriptions that appear in catalogs (or similar announcements) is not an acceptable excuse for such disparities. The students' complaint is legitimate.

Departments and individual instructors should monitor the catalog entries to ensure that the descriptions are congruent with the actual design of the course. If the description and the course design are disparate, and the instructor has a clear rationale and support for *not* conforming to the description, announcements should be made through as many communication channels as possible, ideally before registration, but most certainly on the first day of class.

Discussion Questions

1. Different instructors teach the same courses differently. How should this reality be reconciled with the single authorized descriptions found in the course catalog?

2. Are there special ethical considerations that apply when courses appear in a sequence? That is, when one course prepares the students for the next course, taught by a different instructor, is there an ethical responsibility to teach the first course uniformly (or nearly so)?

3. How would you get the word out to students at your institution if the course description did not match the course as you plan to teach it?

Case 3-13. Why Are You Wasting My Time?

> In a seminar entitled Current Research in the Field, each student must make an in-class presentation on a topic that has been "hot" during the last 5 years. Ned Nadanew cites only work that is more than 10 years old. After several minutes, Professor Getup Sett interrupts Ned and asks for the current materials. When Ned can produce none, Sett becomes irate and storms out of the room, yelling "Why should I waste my time?" The students wait for almost 20 minutes, but finally leave when they realize that Sett is not going to return that day.

Sett's reaction was inappropriate, no matter how bad Nadanew's work has been. We believe that regardless of the acceptability of a student's work, a basic obligation to remain civil is required in every classroom.

Nadanew's poor performance could be used to great advantage by Sett. Discussion of responsibility, expectations in employment settings, or techniques for gathering appropriate materials are all possible topics that Sett could use to gain something positive out of Nadanew's poor showing. Having a temper tantrum serves no good purpose. However, Sett must try not to use the circumstance to publicly derogate Nadanew. Sett can call students who perform poorly into her office for a private discussion that includes an expression of disappointment. (See also 1-3 and 2-9.)

Discussion Questions

1. Does it make a difference if Ned is the first student to present? The last? That is, is Sett's angry reaction more justifiable if many acceptable presentations were completed before Nadanew is scheduled?

2. What techniques might Sett employ to avoid such a situation from arising in the first place? That is, might Sett be largely to blame for not offering students clear guidelines? When a class requires students to use class time for presentations, does an instructor have an ethical obligation to exert extra efforts (e.g., reviewing the students' presentations beforehand) to ensure that the class learns something of value?

3. What resolution can be employed for Nadanew's very poor performance? For instance, should Professor Sett tell Nadanew to turn the presentation into a paper, giving Nadanew a second chance? Or must Nadanew accept his earned failure?

Case 3-14, A & B. When Instructors Cut Classes

> Professor Tardy is almost always between 5 and 15 minutes late to his classes. Students have adjusted to his pattern and also wander in late, often after Tardy has arrived. Colleagues have noticed his pattern and have asked Tardy about it. He replies that he sometimes gets phone calls just before class, or that he misplaced his lecture notes, or that a student appointment ran late. Some students complain because by the time Tardy arrives and straggling students enter, the session can be almost a third over.
>
> Professor Shortchange, who teaches a late evening section, regularly dismisses classes 20 minutes before the scheduled quit time. Most students either do not mind or welcome the early departures. A colleague, however, has taken notice and is concerned that Shortchange is not fulfilling her academic obligations.

Tardy is derelict in his duties. He is not providing adequate services to students. He is a poor role model. Tardy gives the message that teaching is less valuable than just about anything else that comes along, and he also suggests that the subject matter being taught is not worth full consideration. Tardy needs to understand, even if it takes a formal complaint to issue a wake-up call, that he must reorganize his priorities.

All instructors will be late to class on occasion; sometimes for good reason and sometimes not. We suggest that teaching faculty who enter the room late acknowledge their tardiness and even apologize for it, thus giving students correct messages about the expectations of professionals.

Like Professor Tardy, Shortchange is shirking her duties, depriving students of potentially important instructional material and giving the message that both she and her students have much better things to do with their evenings. Sometimes—and this may happen more often in evening classes when hours are usually blocked together—all of the material can be covered a little ahead of the allocated time. If so, the instructor could dismiss the class and stay around for the remainder of the session to confer with students. (See also 3-15. See 11-1 and 11-2 for related issues involving office hours.)

Discussion Questions

1. Are Tardy and Shortchange any more at fault than an instructor who rambles during class, telling lengthy, irrelevant stories?

2. Is "I finished the day's lecture early" ever an acceptable answer for early dismissal? If so, how often can this reason be used?

3. Is a presentation transition that occurs a few minutes before the end of the session (i.e., there is a major shift from one topic to a new one) an acceptable reason to release the students early that day?

Case 3-15. No-Show Instructors

> **After the third time it happened, a student told another instructor that Professor Absent had never arrived and left the class sitting. This student was upset because, as he put it, "I have better things to do than wait for an instructor who never appears." The other instructor was distressed by the student's revelation and told colleagues about the incidents, including his hypothesis that Absent may be using illicit drugs.**

Although instructors may not always respect the criteria that students use to define "good use of time," no one should have to wait more than 10 minutes for an instructor who is not coming. Except in unavoidable circumstances, instructors should get information about an absence to the students in the classroom. Assuming that Absent could have called the department office each of the three times, he is showing disrespect to his students and his department. He is giving the students and his junior colleagues an appalling example of irresponsibility.

Rather than resorting to gossip, however, the other instructor should inform Absent of the students' feelings and urge that Absent to modify his practice. If Absent's no-show behavior continues, the matter should be brought to the attention of the department chair. (See also 3-14. See 11-1 for missing office hours.)

Discussion Questions

1. What should Absent's colleague do if she provides Absent with feedback about his behavior and Absent tells her that his behavior is none of her business and persists in missing classes?

2. Suppose that when Absent's colleague confronts him, he replies that the class has had an average attendance rate of less than 50% and he is simply trying to show them what it's like to be stood up for class. He says he intends to make his point explicit at the next class session. Are there any ethical implications attending Absent's "lesson"?

3. If an instructor knows she will be absent on a particular day and informs her class of it in advance, need she explain the reason for her absence to them? To what extent does the reason for the absence (e.g., a professional meeting or a medical appointment) affect what she tells the class?

Case 3-16. Dress Code for Instructors?

> **Professor Sloppy teaches his classes in a sweatshirt, tattered jeans, and dirty tennis shoes. Some students think it's "cool" and others make jokes about it. Is this an ethical matter?**

The learning environment is best nourished when students feel comfortable and the overall ambience allows focus on academic matters. The instructor's appearance is one of many situational variables that can have an impact on the classroom climate as well as how students focus their attention. However, as long as Professor Sloppy does not dress in a way that would offend the sensibilities of the academic community, he is not directly violating any *ethical* principle. Some schools have dress codes for students, faculty, or both. But, generally speaking, clothing is not an ethical matter.

Whereas latitude in acceptable faculty dress and style is usually quite broad, we do believe that most academic communities are enhanced by a professional-looking teaching faculty and administrative staff. Clean and mainstream (or reasonably close to it) attire in good repair limits distractions while teaching and communicates an image of persons who take their professional position seriously.

Discussion Questions

1. What might be faculty attire that could offend the sensibilities of the academic community? Body piercing? Offensive or multiple tatoos? Women who do not shave their body hair? Are cultural issues to be taken into consideration here?

2. A female instructor wears low-cut dresses that show plenty of cleavage. Another wears extremely short skirts. Are these outfits appropriate? Are there implicit standards for professional attire that differ for women and men? Are double standards acceptable?

3. Is there an expectation of good bodily hygiene on the part of faculty? What if an instructor had habitually pungent body odor, or is habitually unkempt, or wears clothes that are always dirty? Are these examples anybody's business?

4. How important is the nature of the course being taught? That is, would you make differing judgments about acceptable work clothing for philosophy, business, art, theater, and gymnastics instructors?

Case 3-17. Requiring the Use of Technology

Professor Tekjock relies heavily on computer technology in his classroom teaching. His syllabus is available only on his web page; he notifies his students via email of upcoming events and changes in the course schedule. His office hours are conducted online. His justification is that students must be computer literate to prepare them for employment demands. Some students complain about this system. The commuters do not have easy access to the computer labs or their computers are too outdated. Others describe themselves as computer-phobic. Still others feel that Tekjock's practices are too impersonal and that they prefer more face-to-face interactions.

Faculty members are increasingly being called upon to integrate technology into the classroom. Many universities mandate that every course syllabus includes a description of the ways in which the course will help students become more computer and multimedia literate. Some universities even require every student to own a personal computer. The expectation that students become educated about the use of technology in their discipline mirrors expectations in the workplace. In this context, Tekjock's practices seem not only justified, but also preferable.

However, Tekjock needs to consider whether his course is accessible to all students and to recognize the diversity of students' needs as he makes plans to increase their computer literacy. Problems may arise if Tekjock relies exclusively on technology in his interactions with students, especially if these practices routinely disenfranchise them. (See also 6-2.)

Some students still enter college with a very limited technology base and with great insecurity about their ability to acquire basic computer skills. With minimal effort Tekjock can desensitize his students who are computer phobic by scheduling a class period in a computer lab. He might provide support for these students by offering help sessions on the use of email, accessing a web site, or by providing a step-by-step set of written instructions for use in computer labs.

Other students may not own or be able to afford a personal computer. Or, some may have employment schedules or family obligations that do not permit them to spend time in university computer labs before or after class. Tekjock should provide alternatives for these students. Posting messages outside the classroom is an easy-to-implement alternative to e-mail. He may want to help commuters without adequate computer setups at home locate work stations close to home (e.g., the public library) that would enable Internet access to the course web page.

Online office hours, although a great time saver for faculty and students, do depersonalize the student–instructor relationship. Besides the fact that this practice may deny some students access, some issues are difficult to manage by an online discussion. For example, some discussions require back-and-forth input to be adequately resolved. Sensitive matters often arise that the student does not feel comfortable expressing online. In addition, rapport with students may be compromised if students perceive disinterest from a instructor who does not want to meet them face to face. (See also 3-18 and 6-2.)

Discussion Questions

1. To what extent are the level and the content of the course considerations? Are Tekjock's practices more appropriate for senior-level courses than for an introductory level course?

2. Does Tekjock have an *ethical* responsibility to provide support for those students who are computer naive so that they can develop the skills needed to use technology effectively in his class?

3. Is it ethical to require assignments requiring access to technology when the institution does not support such access? For example, what about an assignment to hand in printed copies of certain web pages when a student does not have an Internet connection at home and the lab computers block downloading capabilities to prevent viruses?

Case 3-18. Reluctance to Change With the Times

Professor Standup, a senior member of the department, has had years of success using traditional teaching methods centered on classroom lectures and face-to-face interactions with students. Standup is becoming disheartened because contemporary students seem restless during his lengthy, albeit enthusiastic, lectures. Standup's student evaluations criticize his teaching for the absence of multimedia and other new technologies (e.g., electric grade reports, use of Power Point presentations. Furthermore, Standup is disin-clined to

> use email to communicate with students because he
> believes that personal conversation is the appropriate
> way to relate to people. Professor Standup is aware that
> his colleagues make considerable use of technology in
> the classroom, but remains convinced that he is the most
> effective when he does his work "the old fashioned
> way."

Standup's primary responsibility is to his students and their success in meeting the learning objectives of his course. Although he may excel as a lecturer, we believe that Standup should consider broadening his repertoire of techniques, especially if technical support is readily at hand. He need not abandon his lectures, which appear to be done with care and zest. But, perhaps he can interject an occasional display of a web page or video clips. Standup should consider the possibility that some of his material can be more effectively presented using the new teaching tools that are increasingly available.

We applaud Standup's desire to relate directly with students. One of the main differences between distance education and the traditional institution of higher education is that students and instructors can have direct interactions. However, the technology that allows students easy access to their educators and access to their progress in the course is extremely helpful to those students.

In sum, we certainly do not view Standup as behaving unethically, but he may be depriving his students of technological benefits that he can easily learn to master. We still find colleagues who admit to an underlying technophobia that weakens their motivation to learn new teaching technologies. However, we have also found that those who have mastered them enjoy teaching them to colleagues who have not, and that most of the techniques are far easier to learn than one expects. (See also 3-17.)

Discussion Questions

1. Is there an ethical responsibility to learn new teaching technologies? If so, which ones? If not, why not?

2. An invited lecturer to our campus delivered his entire speech with scant notes. Afterwards, an audience member thanked him for giving a brilliant presentation without resorting to any bells and whistles. The rest of the audience applauded. Is the true measure of a good presentation the ability to perform without props?

3. Is it risky to develop teaching technologies to the point where live instructors are superfluous?

4

Required In-Class
Learning Activities

College and university teaching have shifted from an exclusive reliance on the lecture format to an increased emphasis on a variety of active learning strategies. The current focus on engaging learners in the discovery process has resulted in a smorgasbord of in-class exercises intended to stimulate student interest, improve critical thinking skills, and develop the ability to apply knowledge to real-world problems.

This chapter deals with the ethical issues surrounding the selection of appropriate in-class learning activities. Major themes include effectively balancing the need to involve students in the learning process with the need to protect student dignity and privacy, defining the boundaries of pedagogically sound classroom teaching techniques, and incorporating controversial activities that may cause some students distress.

Case 4-1. Role Playing in Class

In teaching Techniques of Counseling and Psychotherapy 438, Professor Impersonate uses role playing regularly as an educational tool. Several times he has asked female students to play the role of a therapist while he portrays the role of a client who is sexually attracted to the therapist. Some of these role-play sessions involve graphic expressions of the "client's" feelings and fantasies toward the "therapist." Some students are uncomfortable with this activity and doubt that such in-class exercises with their instructor will help them respond to similar situations that could crop up in actual therapy sessions.

Role playing is a common teaching technique in counseling training, speech, and theater courses, and when done properly can be a stimulating way to practice and learn. However, the behavior of the instructor in this case is ethically questionable and may even constitute sexual harassment. The students' discomfort suggests that Professor Impersonate may be misusing his authority in the classroom. There is also reason to suspect that his motives are not entirely professional. (See also 3-8, 4-3, and 4-8 for other risky class presentations.)

Discussion Questions

1. Would the circumstance be judged differently if a male student (rather than the instructor) was asked to volunteer to be the "therapist"?

2. If the instructor warns students before beginning the session and emphasizes that anyone who chooses not to participate may decline without penalty, does this effectively minimize ethical concerns?

3. What if the instructor wants to demonstrate sexual harassment using role playing techniques? Is this an activity that can be ethically justified as a classroom exercise? How might such an enactment be done in an ethical manner?

Case 4-2. Films as Surrogate Teachers

Approximately half the time in Professor Cinema's class is spent showing videotapes and films. Some students and colleagues believe that Professor Cinema is lazy and that his students are not receiving the experiences they should expect from a college-level course.

The ethical issue revolves around the purpose for which the films are shown. If they are critical to teaching the course, illustrate points from the textbook or other material presented in class, or stimulate or focus class discussion, then a valid educational function is probably served. If, instead, the media are used to avoid preparing for class or to fill in time, then the course is unlikely to be providing adequate educational experiences for students. It does appear, at least *prima facie*, that 50% of class time spent viewing films is excessive. (We are assuming, of course, that the class is not about visual media.)

If large numbers of films pertinent to a course exist, instructors should be selective about what they show and might consider putting the others on a viewing list analogous to a reading list. These movies might be viewed outside of class time with several showings so that all students could attend. Some college and university audiovisual services have facilities for individual and small group showings on a walk-in or appointment basis.

Discussion Questions

1. With the growing use of teaching technology, the classroom is increasingly becoming multimedia experienced. Does the daily use of "canned" presentation programs or selected Internet viewing present the same problem as do videotapes and films? Why or why not?

2. What if Professor Cinema is a fine scholar but a poor lecturer? Assuming that the films are appropriate to the subject matter of the class, are students better off seeing films half the time?

3. What are your criteria for selecting a film or video worthy of class time?

Case 4-3. Sensitive Visual Images

> An explicit videotape about child abuse upset a number of students. Several complained that they should have been warned in advance that bruised and broken babies' bodies would be exhibited on a large screen.

Videotapes and other teaching technologies have revolutionized educational capabilities, and instructors cannot be expected to foresee every student's vulnerability. However, we must strive to be empathic with our less-experienced and more sensitive students by reviewing films and other media with the potential for creating undue student distress.

In planning research, scholars are obligated to balance the value of the knowledge to be acquired against any anticipated distress or other adverse experience for the participants. The same guideline can be applied to planning a course. Does the educational benefit of a potentially seriously distressing experience (such as the child-abuse film) outweigh the distress itself? If not, we believe that the film should not be shown in class, although it could be put on a "recommended viewing" list accompanied by an appropriate content warning.

If the educational value of a film that might upset students outweighs the possible distress, we see an obligation to minimize the distress by warning students about the nature of the film by:

1. discussing the film with the class, explaining both its purpose before showing it and its meaning afterwards;

2. encouraging students to talk privately with the instructor about the film and their reactions to it; and

3. informing students, whenever an image has a high risk for adverse reactions, about campus support services for those who have strong adverse reactions.

It would probably be best to give the content warning at least one class period before the film is shown to allow students who expect a severe adverse reaction to meet with the instructor and perhaps arrange an alternative assignment. Or, the film day could be optional.

It can be argued that making a big point about an upcoming class experience, and allowing students who would be upset to leave or not come to class, could have the unintended consequence of identifying vulnerable students to their peers, perhaps causing speculation among the other class members. Or, students who would prefer not to attend (or to leave) class might be coerced to attend from fear that others might talk among themselves about a departure or absence.

A student came to one of us after an excused film day to explain, in overdone detail, why missing the class had absolutely nothing to do with the film. This incident prompted a survey on the topic, asking students themselves how they would prefer classroom instructors to handle the matter. The results revealed that almost all students appreciated fair warning, but most would not be interested in why one of their peers was not there that day, even if they bothered to notice. "We miss any particular class for hundreds of different reasons," said one respondent. It appears, at least from this sample of almost 100 students, that they are not particularly concerned with what choices their classmates make. (See also 3-8, 4-1, 4-4, and 4-5 for risky class presentations.)

Discussion Questions

1. Have you had any experiences with adverse student reactions to a classroom experience? If so, how did you handle it?

2. What if the upsetting classroom experience is also one that is vital to the topic of the course? For example, a biology laboratory may require animal dissection. Should students who do not wish to participate be allowed to do alternative projects?

Case 4-4. Animal Demonstrations

> Using aversive conditioning to teach rats to learn is required in Professor Mammal's comparative psychology class. Two students express strong objections to the assignment and refuse to do it.

Mammal's case raises two ethical issues. Is it proper for students to conduct aversive conditioning experiments *solely* for the purpose of a class exercise? If so, should students be required to undergo a distressing experience? The 1992 ethics code of the American Psychological Association, states, "A procedure subjecting animals to pain, stress, or privation is used only when an alternative procedure is unavailable and the goal is justified by its prospective . . . educational . . . value." Although classroom aversive conditioning experiments have educational value, alternatives *are* available through videotapes and interactive computer programs that simulate conditioning experiments.

In situations for which such alternatives are not available, the second issue becomes relevant. If the course is not required of all students, providing advance notice of any potentially upsetting elements planned for inclusion in a course would allow vulnerable students to avoid distress. The beneficial applications of aversive conditioning (or other procedures in courses requiring that procedures be performed on live animals) could be presented, and student participation in the procedure could be made optional.

There comes a point at which engaging in learning activities that may be distressing to students (e.g., advanced biology courses) is required to master critical material. Some students may have to opt out of certain majors because they are not emotionally suited to the discipline. Instructors and advisors can avoid many types of difficulties if they ascertain that their students understand the full array of major requirements as early in their studies as possible. (See also 4-3 and 4-5.)

Discussion Questions

1. What if a student's personal values are strongly held, but seem "quirky" by common social standards? For example, a student explains that she cannot handle any sub-mammalian species because they house demons that make trouble for whomever touches them. What obligations, if any, does an instructor have to respect these values?

2. What obligations, if any, does a department have to provide courses with

alternative content for those students who cannot accept the procedures used because they violate personally held values or because they are too emotionally upsetting?

Case 4-5. Unusual Classroom Demonstrations

> To demonstrate the fallibility of eyewitnesses' memories for specific details, Professor Shakemup stages a mock theft in his criminal justice class. He arrives a few minutes early, deposits his notes and a book on the desk, and leaves. Just before class is about to start, and after most students have arrived, a confederate slips into the room, takes Shakemup's book from the desk, and quickly departs. Shakemup returns momentarily and creates a loud scene about the "stolen" book. Two members of the class have been tipped off in advance and volunteer erroneous information about the "thief's" appearance. Shakemup conducts class as usual. Ten minutes before the end of the class session he stops, explaining that he is still very bothered about the book theft and that he has decided to make a report to the authorities. He asks all of the students to write down everything they remember about the incident and turn in their lists to him. He waits until the following week to explain what really happened and to provide a summary of the class data about the thief's appearance.

The choice of classroom demonstrations must always take into account the relative importance of the message to be conveyed, the risks to students as a result of exposure to the demonstration, the availability of alternative methods for effectively conveying the point, and, when appropriate, the timing and quality of the "dehoaxing." In addition, when students become part of the demonstration, as were the uninformed classroom observers in this case, it is preferable that they do so voluntarily and with their informed consent. If deception is used in the course of a demonstration, uncovering the deception should always take place in a timely fashion. Some would argue that the benefit of deceiving one's students for the purpose of making a point is rarely worth the risks, which include subsequent mistrust of the instructor. In this case, even the "thief" could be at risk if a student recognized him on campus during the week and called the police!

We believe that Shakemup had an ethical obligation to uncover the deception *before* the end of the class period. There is no justifiable educational value in allowing students to leave the classroom anxious or distressed about events they believed to be real. Or, Shakemup could have chosen alternative procedures to convey information about problems with eyewitness demonstrations such as a film or a "flash card" demonstration. He might have achieved a similar educational goal without deceiving his students or causing them undue anxiety.

Instructors are frequently challenged by the need to enliven lecture material to stimulate student interest. Innovative techniques that carry minimal ethical risks are valuable contributions. Nonetheless, demonstrations that are selected solely for their shock value, and without consideration of the potential for negative consequences, simply turn the classroom into a side show and ultimately neglect a primary responsibility of instructors to create an environment that enhances student learning. (See also 4-3 and 4-4.)

Discussion Questions

1. What are some other types of classroom demonstrations that raise ethical concerns?

2. Have you attempted an innovative classroom technique that captured students' attention? What was it and how did it go?

3. What if Shakemup content analyzes the student's reports and publishes a study based on these notes. What may be additional ethical problems?

Case 4-6. Requiring Students to Disclose in Class

> The assigned grade in Professor Share's health class depends partially on students' disclosure during class discussions of personal habits (e.g., masturbation practices) and bodily functions (e.g., flatulence rate). Some students feel very uncomfortable about revealing what they consider to be their private affairs and only minimally participate. These students receive low grades on that component of their course grade.

Instructors should respect the privacy of those with whom they have professional relationships, including students. Requiring students to disclose highly personal information in class is a violation of this ethic. (To appreciate this, instructors need only imagine how they would feel if required to share similar personal details about themselves with students or a group of their peers). If a required disclosure results in embarrassment to a student, or is spread by gossip, additional harm accrues. The latter considerations also probably obligate us to attempt to head off voluntary, inappropriate disclosures and, privately, to advise effusively self-disclosing students to moderate their comments during class. (See 2-3.).

If self-examination of personal behavior or experiences is a pedagogically defensible course goal, students could be required to keep journals or write essays on particular topics. If these are turned in for review, the instructor has a strict obligation to maintain confidentiality. If such assignments are graded, the grading process should be based on the quality of the self-analysis, not on the depth of disclosure. Above all, the instructor should give careful consideration to the necessity of such assignments and allow alternatives, such as the analysis of another person (e.g., a fictional, historical, or public figure).

There may be some courses in which the public disclosure of personal information is appropriate (e.g., group supervision of advanced counseling graduate students). If so, students should be informed in advance of the nature, breadth, and depth of the required disclosures. In addition, specific ground rules must be established concerning what can be disclosed voluntarily and about respecting others' right not to disclose information even if it falls under the purview of the course.

Discussion Questions

1. Do ethical problems apply if personal information from students whose identities are known to the instructor is shared anonymously with the class as a whole?

2. What should an instructor do if a student's written assignment reveals a particularly disturbing or dangerous situation?

3. What are the boundaries between appropriate disclosures and inappropriate disclosures, and how do we help students recognize these limits?

III

Assessment of Students

III

Assessment Strategies

Testing and Other Academic Evaluations

Fairness on the part of their educators is very important to students (Rodabaugh,1996). Two primary areas of concern are the establishment and enforcement of rules for grading (the topic of this chapter) and the equitable assignment of grades (the topic of chapter 6). Although some members of the academic community question the value of testing and grading or other means of assessing student performance, evaluations remain an integral part of the educational system.

We doubt that many college and university instructors purposely set out to engage in unfair evaluations; nonetheless, such unfairness might arise as a result of other factors. The cases in this chapter present a number of issues that instructors often face in designing and using evaluation instruments that raise issues of fairness and ethics. These include the proper use and timing of tests and quizzes, the appropriate content of tests and other assignments, reusing tests and assignments, and make-up policies.

Case 5-1. "Weed-Out" Exams

Professor Sergeant administers a rigorous exam during the third week of classes as a way of encouraging weak and lazy students to withdraw before the deadline.

The ethical status of Sergeant's practice depends, to some extent, on its purpose. If the test accurately reflects the difficulty level of the course, he may be doing the students a favor. Even students who are not lazy may overestimate their abilities and remain in a course that is beyond their current capabilities. In such cases it would be appropriate for Sergeant to explain his reasoning in the course syllabus and call the class's attention to this aspect of the course during the first meeting.

On the other hand, if Sergeant's exam is unreasonably difficult or given primarily to reduce the size of the class or his workload, an ethical problem certainly exists. It is inappropriate to deprive students of an opportunity to learn. An excessive reduction in the course enrollment also short-changes Sergeant's institution. (See also 6-6.)

Discussion Questions

1. Suppose there are other sections of this course taught by other instructors. Should Sergeant and the other instructors attempt to make their respective sections as similar as possible (e.g., with respect to timing and difficulty of exams), or should they allow the sections to vary and encourage students to "shop" for the one that seems best for them?

2. Is it actually good ethical practice to give students a *fair* exam before the drop period?

Case 5-2. The Professional Note-Taker

> **Candy Noshow hires a professional note-taker to come to class in her stead. Candy shows up only to take exams. The instructor grades Noshow down for nonparticipation, noting the section of the syllabus indicating that classroom attendance is expected. Noshow counterclaims that nothing in the syllabus indicates that any part of the grade would depend on her attendance.**

The instructor should have looked into school policy as soon as he saw what Noshow was doing. It is probable that the regular attendance of unenrolled students in the classroom is disallowed unless specific permission is granted (e.g., note-takers for disabled students). In the absence of such a policy, and if the syllabus policy is sufficiently ambiguous with regards to a clear statement of penalties for not attending class, Noshow has a point. Assuming that Noshow is performing acceptably on the academic criteria (exams, papers, and so forth), she would likely prevail if she complained about her lower grade.

Although instructors typically accept that some students have a legitimate need for note-taking, many may resent students who can afford to pay someone to go to class for them. Something inherently irksome surrounds the notion that students (or their families or taxpayers) pay the tuition to take courses and then pay for someone else to attend them.

Furthermore, professional note-takers are available only to more advantaged students. We have heard of fees up to $20 per class session.

For instructors who want to avoid this problem, we suggest making attendance requirements clear in the syllabus, including precisely what penalties will accrue if there are deviations from the policy. (We do argue for flexibility in specific instances in other cases in this book). Putting copies of class notes on file in the library or on a web page would render note-taker services superfluous and be more equitable, but may also encourage absenteeism.

This case raises the larger issue of whether, assuming there is no required attendance policy, a student should be able to earn academic credit for just sitting for exams. It can be argued that if students can pass a course by coming to class only on exam day, more power to them. On the other hand, we might ask ourselves how it could be possible to succeed in our classes if we are, indeed, making valuable use of class time.

Discussion Questions

1. Should we control how students decide to go about learning in our courses?

2. Students often take notes for each other as a favor. How would you feel if the *paid* note-taker was also enrolled in the course?

3. How would you feel about a student who hires note-takers for his overload courses? (There is an actual case of a student, with the assistance of a paid note-taker, who completed 30 credits in one term!)

4. Would it be possible for students to pass your courses by showing up only for exams? If so, is this acceptable to you? If not, why not?

Case 5-3. Unannounced Evaluations

Professor Bushwhacker gives pop quizzes at irregular intervals. The combined quiz score is worth half of the course grade. A missed quiz counts as a zero, and no make-ups are allowed. Students complain that this feature of the course keeps them anxious, discriminates against students with genuine infirmities or other emergencies, and allows contagiously ill students (who drag themselves to class to avoid missing quizzes) to infect everyone else. Professor Bushwhacker contends that the classroom should prepare students for the outside world that goes on with or without them.

Considered from one perspective, Bushwhacker's policy encourages students to develop self-discipline by requiring them to live up to their role obligations of attending class and always being prepared. Whereas other instructors (e.g., 6-1 and 6-6) inflict harm on students in the form of undue stress, one could argue that any harm that comes to Bushwhacker's students comes from their own voluntary inaction.

But what of students who are absent because of circumstances beyond their control? They must either accept a lower grade than their accomplishments deserve (through zeros on missed quizzes) or withdraw from the course (if the missed quizzes are early enough in the term) to avoid the lower grade. By promoting these outcomes, Bushwhacker's policy harms students and shows a lack of concern for their welfare.

This policy could also discriminate against students who have chronic illnesses or disabling injuries. A temporary relapse or a necessary medical appointment (e.g., for dialysis) could make an absence unavoidable. The Americans with Disabilities Act upholds the principle of "reasonable accommodation," which could apply in this case, and most colleges and universities have policies that require provisions for students in certain circumstances. But, if these students are to be accommodated, is it ethical to exclude others with legitimate but less predictable reasons for absence (e.g., child care), or does such exclusion constitute reverse discrimination?

The potential for harm and discrimination is largely avoidable if Bushwacker allows one or two make-up quizzes or drops the one or two lowest quiz scores. The latter policy would remain consistent with Bushwhacker's desire to model the world of work, in which employers allow a certain number of sick and personal days off from work before docking their pay.

If Bushwhacker chooses not to make any accommodations, then he has an obligation to inform students of his policy early enough in the course to give them an opportunity to transfer to another section or to substitute another course. However, if Bushwhacker is teaching the only section of a required course, we believe that students are being forced to accept an unreasonable condition.

Discussion Questions

1. Would the ethical problems disappear if the combined quiz scores were worth considerably less than one half the course grade?

2. Bushwacker wants his class to operate as the outside world does. To what extent are expectations in the classroom the same as in the outside world, and in what ways are they necessarily different?

Case 5-4. Play It Again, Sam:
Reusing the Same Tests

> Professor Repeat uses the same exams each semester. She does not return them to the students, except for a brief period in class. Students who want to spend more time reviewing their exams must come to her during office hours. Some students would like to spend more time reviewing their exams, but their schedules preclude meeting Repeat's office hours.

Typically there is no requirement that instructors allow students to keep their exams. Because other instructors may use the same textbook or test bank items or share test items, instructors have reason to maintain a degree of security. Furthermore, retaining items that show validity based on statistical analysis of results from previous classes has merit. However, students should be given sufficient opportunities to review their exam performances. If Repeat does not want to use class time, she may hold one or more special meetings in which she (or her teaching assistant) goes over each item and answers students' questions.

Using exactly the same items from semester to semester does pose potential problems. Unless heroic prevention methods are implemented, copies can be procured and passed around to give some students an unearned advantage. For example, a student can leave with the crowd in a large class, carrying an exam, and later show up for a make-up. Organized groups (e.g., social clubs) have been known to assign "memorization items" resulting in a reasonably complete set of exam questions. Finally, exams in most fields eventually become stale and can benefit from rewriting, recasting, and introducing fresh material. (See also 5-5. See 19-1 for a case about giving the same lectures year after year.)

Discussion Questions

1. Assume that Repeat establishes a system that allows students ample opportunity to review their exams and receive feedback on how to improve their performance. However, only students who are doing well on the tests show up at these sessions. Does Repeat have an obligation to require or otherwise induce (e.g., by offering extra credit) poorer performing students to review their performances?

2. What about a situation in which an instructor makes an entire test bank available to students for study, but selects only a relatively few questions from hundreds of items to ask of the exam. Are there ethical problems here?

3. A student claims intellectual property rights to his answers on essay exams and insists on keeping them. Does this student have a legitimate request?

4. What is your policy on reusing exam items?

Case 5-5. Same Assignments Every Term

> For the past 15 years Professor Sluffoff has assigned the same term paper project, an analysis of the same two books. A colleague asks him if he is concerned that current students will simply hand in friends' old assignments. He shrugs and replies, "What could I do about it if they did?"

Sluffoff dismisses his colleague's concern about possible plagiarism too casually. Students should be evaluated on their actual performance with respect to course assignments, and instructors should act in ways that encourage ethical behavior by students. The circumstantial possibility that current students may submit, as their own work, papers based largely or entirely on others' efforts is serious enough to warrant concern.

Thus, Sluffoff needs to do more than simply shrug off the potential for plagiarism. At least three options are available. If he wishes to maintain the specific assignment in question, he should do more to reduce the likelihood that current students will use previous students' work inappropriately. For example, Sluffoff can explicitly warn students that using the work of others on this assignment is plagiarism and, if uncovered, will be dealt with as such. At some schools, an honor code requires students to sign a statement that the work they are submitting is their own. Although this practice is no panacea, it would at least put students on record as claiming the work as their own and deter those who do not (or claim not to) know any better. Sluffoff might also require students to meet with him about their papers as they work on them, thus giving him an early peek of their personal efforts on this assignment.

A second option is to retain copies of all past papers (and let students know of the existence of this collection). In this way, plagiarized papers could be detected, although the process of doing so would be laborious. Sluffoff hardly gives the impression of a person who would use this safeguard.

A preferable option is to change the assignment in ways that automatically reduce the usefulness of earlier students' papers and, therefore, boost the chances that they will learn something on the assignment. For example, assigning different books each year would require a more effort on Sluffoff's part but might also make his students' work more interesting for him to read. Sluffoff could also try a less structured assignment. Writing assignments and other projects providing some latitude for individuality allow students to participate more actively in shaping the final product. An alternative to a less structured assignment would be for Sluffoff to use the same books, but have a more structured assignment that changed from year to year. (See also 5-4. For more cases about academic dishonesty, see chapter 10.)

Discussion Questions

1. Laboratory assignments that illustrate basic principles should always provide the same results, especially in the natural sciences. How can an instructor prevent or detect plagiarism or answer-copying in this situation?

2. The extent of admitted plagiarism among today's college students on anonymous surveys is quite high. Some instructors have responded by not requiring any written assignments. What are the ethical implications of such a policy?

3. With the increased availability of computers, word processors, and image scanners, how can an instructor prevent students from modifying a previously created work or detect such modification?

Case 5-6. Harsh Make-Up Policies

> No make-up exams are allowed in Professor Stalwart's class. She reasons that students are given fair warning and can plan their lives carefully, including taking reasonable precautions to maintain good health. A missed exam receives no points. No exceptions. Stalwart also records zero points to any term project that is handed in after the beginning of the class hour on the due date published in the syllabus. She reasons that students have a full term to work on the project and that no excuses, even an emergency during the previous week, are valid.

This case offers two examples of inflexible policies regarding deadlines for important assignments. Although both examples involve the strict observance of clearly announced deadlines, the dissimilar nature of the two assignments leads us to somewhat different ethical analyses.
Instructors are expected to show fairness and respect for students,

to devise policies that avoid or minimize harm, and to base evaluations on actual performance rather than extraneous conditions. Stalwart's absolute policy of no make-up exams seems unfair, to at least some students (e.g., a student whose final grade was reduced because of a zero although his or her overall performance was otherwise outstanding) and discriminates against those with excuses involving unavoidable circumstances. Setting strict limits on the permissible reasons for missing exams, requiring advance notice and written verification, offering limited make-up opportunities, and other similar regulations are ethically acceptable methods of reducing the size of the make-up exam pool. However, zeros are usually damaging beyond repair to a student's overall grade. We believe that an opportunity to make up for an unavoidable absence should always be made available. Stalwart's exam policy seems to make class attendance more important than learning.

Stalwart's refusal to accept term papers that are even 1 hour late would lower the overall grade of virtually all students who did not turn in their term projects on time. It is possible that this result could be harmful and discriminatory for some students, but many instructors believe that subtracting points or letter grades for varying degrees of lateness results in greater fairness to all students, especially when the deadlines are announced well in advance.

In the end, firm deadlines are indeed a part of everyday life, and failing to complete a project assigned 3 months before its deadline is far less likely than missing an exam to be the result of an emergency or bad luck. Thus, in this second instance, concern for the best interests of all students does not preclude strict adherence to an announced deadline. Most of us have experienced unavoidable delays or complications in completing our own work, but we may also believe that firm deadlines actually promote fairness and respect for the efforts of students who turn work in on time. Even with term projects, however, instructors might want to be sensitive to the student who has a verifiable emergency that either precluded finishing the project (such as a lingering illness) or a last-minute emergency that made it impossible to arrange for the paper to be turned in. (See also 1-4, 5-3, 17-3.)

Discussion Questions

1. Stalwart establishes a fixed scale of punishment. What if a varying scale is used? What criteria can be used to establish such a policy? Are there ethical problems related to varying punishment scales?

2. How do you handle students who turn in their assignments late?

Case 5-7. Variable Make-Up Policies

> Tom says he missed an exam because he was in a car accident. Sue says she missed the exam because she said she had the flu. Bill thought the exam was scheduled for the following week. Jane claims her alarm clock did not go off. Tom and Sue were allowed to take make-ups, but Bill and Jane were not.

Bill and Jane were punished for their honesty. And, for all we know, the instructor did not seek verification from Sue and Tom. They may have been rewarded for prevarication.

To avoid discriminatory effects or appearances, verification of excuses should be required of everyone or of no one, although the latter increases the risk of duplicity. Other systems, such as dropping the lowest score for each student while not allowing any make-up exams, can also be implemented. In all instances, policies should promote fairness and minimize the extent to which a student's grade inadvertently comes to be based in part on factors other than actual performance.

In our view, the key issues are having a clear, specific, publicly announced make-up policy and applying this policy uniformly to all members of the class. The course syllabus should include a statement regarding the instructor's make-up policy including whether make-ups are allowed, and if so, the general categories of reasons that are allowable as well as any that are not. This policy should be reiterated in class as needed. (See also 1-4, 1-5, 1-6, and 17-3.)

Discussion Questions

1. What if the instructor's policy differs significantly from that of colleagues in the same department? Is there merit in establishing make-up policy at a department level?

2. What if an instructor allows a make-up, then later finds out the excuse was a lie? Should the credit for the exam be withdrawn? Should the student be dealt with as having committed an act of academic dishonesty?

3. Because research findings suggest that about 50% of the excuses students give for failing to complete a class requirement in the manner specified are untrue, should educators simply ignore excuses all together?

Case 5-8. Testing on Material
Not Discussed in Class

> Professor Tester does not review the material from the assigned readings during lecture, but does include questions from this unreviewed material on his exams. Students complain that he is unfair because the material could not possibly be important if it was not covered in class. Tester replies that the purpose of lectures is to supplement the readings, not to summarize them. Furthermore, he says, college students should be capable of reading and understanding readings on their own.

We agree with Tester's view of the role of lectures, and we also generally agree that students should be capable of understanding well-selected readings. However, not all textbook material is easily understood by students, and, guided by his experience, Tester should certainly cover any reading material that students are likely to find difficult, either during class or special review sessions.

Tester's test-construction policy also appears to be overlooking an important perception on the part of some students that can arise from time to time, namely the assumption that if something is not covered in lecture it is not important enough to read about. Professor Tester should, therefore, include in his syllabus a clear statement that the contents of all assigned readings are subject to testing. It would be wise to reiterate that policy during a class meeting prior to each exam. He should also ensure that students have the opportunity to ask questions about readings not covered in class by periodically inviting such questions. He could also periodically remind students to visit him during office hours with their questions and encourage them to utilize any available tutoring services. (See also 5-13.)

Discussion Questions

1. A possible solution to Tester's problem would be to craft the exam questions so that students who came to lectures but merely skimmed the textbook and those who memorized the book but frequently skipped classes could achieve C grades, but only those who both attended class and studied the text could achieve grades of A or B. Under what conditions would this be an ethically defensible testing policy, or is it completely indefensible?

2. How can one draw the line between an appropriate amount of assigned

reading and an amount that is so heavy or difficult that ethical questions of fairness could be raised?

Case 5-9. The Resistor

> Professor Sorry learned that an exam had been stolen before the test was given. He explained the theft to the class and announced that if the culprit would come forward, the rest of the class would not be penalized. No one came forward. He apologized to the class, but because he did not know who took the exam he had no other choice but to require everyone to take a new exam. Sue Balk informed Professor Sorry that she was not willing to take a second exam on the same material. Sue explained, "I was not the one who cheated. I would never do such a thing, and I refuse to take another exam. My schedule is so busy, I just don't have time to study for this exam again."

Professor Sorry is attempting to resolve a terrible dilemma. Whereas he feels that he cannot simply let the matter drop because it would reinforce dishonest behavior and be a disservice to honest students, his solution also penalized students who had no preknowledge of the questions. Sorry has no idea who stole the exam or how many students were involved. Even Sue Balk could be deceiving him.

Unless Sorry does not count the exam at all (still risking the ire and resentment of students who studied long and hard), we conclude that Sorry has no recourse but to actively attempt to convince Balk that she must take the exam. Perhaps Sorry can reassure all of the students by making the test a bit shorter and more general than the original, on the assumption that the person or persons who stole the exam had not studied for it. In any case, the decision must be made swiftly and the second exam given as soon as feasible to maximize students' ability to recall what they had previously studied and to minimize the opportunity for the cheater(s) to learn the material.

This matter should also be fully discussed in class on the day that Sorry publicly announces his grim discovery. Sorry should allow students to express how they feel. He might even ask what they would do if they were in his predicament. Such a discussion may help students such as Balk empathize with him. Sorry should not be afraid of expressing his profound disappointment and hurt, although his anger should remain controlled. Sorry should also state how badly he feels about having to penalize honest students. Students may feel, at the very least, resigned to the notion of retaking an exam if they fully understand all of the ramifications of what devastation the test thief has caused.

This problem is not unusual. The authors' department endured two such incidents in a 1-year period. In one case, the instructor left his office door open and empty for less than a minute to get coffee. In another case, the instructor was tipped off by students about the stolen exam, but she was not able to determine how it was procured. The best solution, of course, is prevention. It is difficult for most of us to imagine that students would steal exams from us, and taking precautions to protect test security makes us almost feel guilty for being so suspicious. However, exams should be locked up at all times. Exams should not be left, unless encrypted or password protected, on computer hard drives. These simple steps can save instructors from facing Sorry's difficult situation and the stalemate with Balk. (See more cases on academic dishonesty in chapter 10.)

Discussion Questions

1. What if the stolen exam was the final exam? How would you handle such a situation?

2. Should students be asked to vote on possible solutions? Would Professor Sorry be bound by a majority vote?

3. Does Sue Balk have a legitimate point? After all, we would not tolerate such a penalty in our legal system (e.g., convicting everyone in a company whenever someone embezzled money).

Case 5-10. Equivalent Tests for Nonequivalent Sections

> Professor Sametest teaches two sections of the same course, one on M-W-F for 50 minutes per session and the other T-Th for 75 minutes a session. He uses the same exam for each section. MWF students complain that they are at a time disadvantage, especially because the instructor plans to use the same grading curve for both sections.

This testing dilemma is not uncommon. Professor Sametest is trying to make the two course sections equivalent in terms of assessment techniques. However, sticking with his wish to operate this way, he could give each section an exam designed to take no more than 50 minutes, and find some other way to use the 20-25 minutes left over in the T-Th section. Although admittedly awkward, he might lecture or otherwise conduct an abbreviated class session, meet informally with students concerning projects, papers, or other aspects of the course (which he would also do with the MWF students, just not on the day they take the test), give the students an out-of-class library or computer lab assignment designed to take 20-25 minutes (which, again, the MWF students would also do), and so on. Alternatively, instead of exams designed to take an entire class period he could give more shorter exams or quizzes (each to be completed within 15-20 minutes) and fill in the time left over in a similar fashion in both sections.

Some instructors would not worry about making the two sections so precisely equivalent. Despite one's best efforts, these two classes will inevitably be different in some respects, and for this reason we think a separate grading curve for each section is more appropriate. (See also 6-4.)

Discussion Questions

1. What other ethics-related risks pertain when the same exam questions are used in two or more sections?

2. What ethical risks pertain when one attempts to create two very different exams for two sections of the same course?

Case 5-11. Unusual Class Assignments

Professor Relevant requires students in his Contemporary Social Issues course to complete a term project from a list of several possibilities. All options involve visits to actual sites where contemporary issues are "happening," such as a gay bar, an Alcoholics Anonymous meeting, a militant political group gathering, and a homeless shelter. Students write a paper about their experiences. Many students find the assignment exciting. Some students, however, are extremely uncomfortable because they are afraid to go to any of the approved sites. Some students believe that they would be exploiting or invading the privacy of the groups, whereas others believe the project is not appropriate for an academic exercise. Some students admit to being frightened by the assignment. Professor Relevant, however, insists that college students need to "get out on to the front line of life if they ever aspire to understand it."

The classroom is not necessarily the best place for students to learn everything relevant to a course. Blending classroom learning with the kind of educational experiences that result from direct participation in relevant off-campus settings can be educational and enlightening. Relevant's enthusiasm for unsupervised, off-campus assignments may ultimately translate into outstanding teaching effectiveness.

To be defensible pedagogically, however, off-campus assignments must be integrated into the overall content and process of the course, and the expected benefits from completing the assignments must outweigh the potential risks. In the present example, the issues include the pedagogical soundness of the assignment as well as concern for the rights, dignity, and welfare of students and those persons they are observing. Furthermore, the settings in which the assigned experiences occur are not under Relevant's supervision and some are, indeed, potentially unsafe.

Professor Relevant would be well advised to check his institution's insurance policy and ask students over the age of 18 to sign waivers of liability. Minors who are not legally emancipated likely require parental permission. He should also describe and clearly explain the nature of the controversial assignment in the syllabus. Those doing the standard assignment should have some choice with respect to the setting they will visit and should prepare for their forays in advance, such as by reading about the setting, interviewing people already familiar with it, and knowing how to "bail out" if their discomfort threshold is reached. In addition, Relevant should be relatively accessible to students (e.g., by telephone) during the hours they are in the field.

Ethical concerns are minimized somewhat if the students have choices. Students should have the opportunity to complete alternative assignments without penalty. However, even with safeguards, Relevant must recognize the liability (including potential legal liability) he may assume for untoward incidents or emotional reactions, and the possibility that students, parents, and colleagues may criticize his judgment. (See 3-8, 4-3, 4-4, 4-5, and 4-6 for related issues.)

Discussion Questions

1. Is there less ethical concern about Professor Relevant if the students aspire to a profession that requires interaction with the groups assigned for observation?

2. How might students gain experiences about people different from themselves and avoid the ethical problems inherent in Relevant's assignments?

3. Would it make a big difference if Relevant personally accompanied small groups of students on these off-campus excursions?

Case 5-12. Requiring Personal Disclosures in Assignments

> Professor Reveal requires students in her composition course to write essays about their personal lives, including "your most traumatic experience," "what shamed you most," and "intimate encounters." Students who submit stilted or superficial essays receive lower grades.

Using assignments that help students learn by using the already-familiar as the basis for new skill-building is a popular educational strategy. However, a line may be crossed that produces counterproductive results, such as discomfort, embarrassment, emotional trauma, or fear of exposure. According to Swartzlander, Pace, and Stamler (1993), "Every day in college classrooms and faculty offices across the country, students receive writing assignments requiring inappropriate self-revelation" (p. 00). These authors believe that personal turmoil and intimacy should not be the basis of course content unless it can be pedagogically justified and even then, only if the students are given sufficient warning so that they can attempt to find an alternative course should they wish not to participate.

We believe that students generally should not be required to write about deeply personal and intimate material. Aside from ethical implications, faculty members may find themselves enmeshed in situations that they are unprepared to handle, such as dealing with a very upset student who, upon confiding to the instructor in an assignment, expects the instructor to become involved as a counselor or confidant. Students have been known to complain about instructors who get too involved in commenting on their personal lives, and, in at least one case, the professor was fired (Wilson, 1997). (See Case 4-6 for a discussion of requiring personal disclosures in class.)

Discussion Questions

1. What if an instructor requests that students simply write an essay about "a childhood event" of their choice. One student details a serious event involving an unsolved crime. How would you respond?

2. In a genetics class, the instructor requires students to create a family tree going back two generations, detailing certain phenotypical characteristics such

as eye color and height. Why might some students find such a seemingly straightforward assignment upsetting?

3. Are advanced clinical or counseling psychology courses exempt from the admonition against requiring students to reveal intimate information about themselves in class discussions or assignments?

Case 5-13. Reading Assignments: Amount and Cost

> Professor Heavy requires two 500-hundred page textbooks and one smaller paperback book for his 3-credit undergraduate class. Students complain that this is too much reading, Further, the books for this one course cost more than $200. Several students claim discrimination because they cannot afford to buy the books.

If all three books can be defended as necessary for the course, we see no ethical problem. The students' financial outlay could be lowered if Heavy put copies of the books on reserve at the library. To the extent that the necessity for the books decreases, however, an ethical problem emerges because students are being required to bear unnecessary expense as well as being burdened beyond what is necessary to complete the goals of the course.

Generally, the amount of reading assigned in a course is not an ethical issue unless a requirement to read irrelevant or marginally relevant material distracts students from pertinent material, or unless the reading requires the typical full-time student to spend so much time that the ability to prepare for other courses is jeopardized. Professor Heavy's reading requirements do, however, seem excessive for an undergraduate class.

Discussion Questions

1. What is the upper limit on reading hours that an instructor should expect for a three-credit undergraduate course?

2. Is the amount of money a student must spend on books or other assigned materials an ethical issue? If so, under what circumstances?

6

Grading Methods

Just as testing and evaluation can be challenging aspects of teaching, the assignment of grades presents perturbing dilemmas. Final course grades become part of a permanent record that can affect students' lives well past graduation and, therefore, have an ethical dimension. The cases in this chapter describe issues surrounding the grading process, including the appropriate criteria for determining grades, consistency in grading, and the proper use of the "I" (incomplete) grade.

Case 6-1. One-Shot Grading

Professor Emcee administers one 200-item multiple choice final exam. The entire grade is based on the score earned on this single measure. Students complain they are frustrated all semester because they do not know if they are studying and learning the material in a way that will meet with success. Furthermore, they believe that a single multiple-choice exam does not allow them to demonstrate what they have learned. Dr. Emcee assures the students that if they know the textbook and attend class every day, they will have all the information needed to succeed in his course.

Generally speaking, Emcee's testing policy is questionable for use in undergraduate education. Students receive little or no information about their progress in the course until it is over. As a result, they do not have an opportunity to change their study approaches to meet course requirements. For instance, is Emcee interested in the students' ability to comprehend information, apply principles, analyze problems, synthesize information, evaluate courses of action, think critically, or some combination of these? If any of the alternatives are of concern, his evaluation is insufficient to assess all but the ability to take in facts and recognize them among an array of incorrect options.

Although making representative questions available to students early on could give them an idea of the content of the final exam, such samples would not give much feedback on why students made mistakes. The uncertainty is likely to provoke considerable stress. The anxiety might also lower the validity of the final exam by masking the students' true performance levels. Although it could be argued that uncertainty and the resultant stress are part of life, and that all exams are anxiety provoking, Emcee could mitigate unnecessary anxiety by giving more tests.

Emcee's evaluation method gives him insufficient information on student progress during the term. He cannot adjust the course's content or process to fit students' needs or to diagnose the source of any problems. He does not know if the learning objectives of the course are being met. For example, perhaps an early test assessment would show that students can learn the basic principles he teaches, but cannot apply them. Perhaps Emcee does not even care what students are or are not learning, and giving only one exam is the result of his disinterest or laziness.

Circumstances may exist in which Emcee's evaluation procedure is acceptable, though not likely ideal. Graduate-level professional training programs (e.g., law schools) often give only a single exam at the end of the term. Or, a single exam might be adequate in an advanced, small seminar where the instructor is in tune with student progress through class discussions, opportunities for students to ask questions, and individual consultations. (See also 6-7.)

Discussion Questions

1. Would it be different if a student's entire grade is based on a single project or paper over which the student has considerable control and for which the student receives feedback prior to submitting it for a final grade?

2. If Emcee is giving himself too little opportunity to evaluate students, can the opposite, namely too many exams and assignments, also be an ethical issue?

Case 6-2. Term Project Format Versus Substance

Professor Font openly acknowledges that handwritten and poorly typed or printed papers are graded lower than are cleanly printed papers. Students complain that content should be the only grading criterion and that Font's demands discriminate against students who have insufficient clerical skills or who do not have easy access to quality computers or the means to hire assistance.

Although a primary theme of this casebook is the welfare of students, Font's case reminds us that students also have responsibilities. It could be argued that one of those responsibilities is competence in skills related to the role of being a college student. In this age, those skills include the ability to produce typed or computer-printed documents. Research has demonstrated that the appearance of a paper plays a role in its evaluation, even though the evaluator may not be consciously aware of the influence. Therefore, all students are probably subject to this bias. Professor Font has simply incorporated a control for this into the class requirements.

Because typewriters and computers with word-processing programs (both mainframe and desktop) are easily accessible to most college and university students without a fee, availability is an increasingly rare problem. The skills required to operate these machines and programs are easily learned, so it is not necessary for students to pay someone to do the work. And, just as students should not have to strain to see what an instructor has written on the board or take an exam that has been duplicated so poorly that the questions are difficult to read, instructors should not have to struggle unreasonably with sloppy handwriting or a faint printer.

There may, however, be cases in which students can neither afford word-processing equipment nor have access to cost-free equipment (e.g., child-care responsibilities prevent the student from being on campus when computer labs are open). If such circumstances can be documented, Font should make an exception to his policy. (See also 3-17.)

Discussion Questions

1. What is your policy, if any, regarding the approved appearance of assignments? What latitude, if any, is allowed and for what reasons?

2. What if Font's assignments require graphs, tables, or other figures? Is it fair to expect computer-created quality for more complicated presentations?

Case 6-3, A & B. Strict Curve Versus Easy Grading

Students complain that Professor Stringent adheres to such a strict grading curve that only one or two students in a class of 40 earn As. Most get Cs. Students argue that his system is out of line with that of other instructors and that he hurts their chances for the future.

Professor Lax gives most of the students in his classes As, and no one gets a grade lower than a B. He

> defends his position on the grounds that students will
> be less anxious and better able to learn and enjoy the
> subject matter.

Instructors are obligated to grade students on the basis of the their actual performance according to established criteria. Therefore, to the extent that Stringent and Lax have established grading criteria, regardless of the degree of strictness or laxity, it could be argued that they have committed no ethical violation.

However, a grading system that is overly strict in the sense of under-representing students' true performance levels harms students. Rigid curves unrelated to students' actual mastery of the material are questionable on ethical grounds. Overly narrow and inflexible percentage-based curves assume both a normal population and exams with normally distributed scores. It is unlikely that Stringent can justify his proposed distribution of grades empirically. Because eligibility for financial assistance, admission to graduate school, and other benefits are allocated at least partially on the basis of grade-point average, Stringent is potentially limiting students' ability to compete fairly for these benefits.

Lax presents another interesting situation. Although nothing in ethics codes prohibits us from overbenefitting students by awarding them higher grades than their performance justifies, most educators would consider such behavior improper. It can be argued that giving *all* As and Bs harms truly high performers by devaluing their grades through inflation, although it may be difficult to demonstrate the actual harm. Students' belief that they know more than they actually do could backfire on them at some point. Students could also be so secure in their position in Lax's class that they give it limited attention, further minimizing the amount that they learn. Too much leniency appears to be a situation that many see as a problem, but one that is not generally addressed in ethics codes.

A preferable system may be to set grades based on competence attainment. It is possible, for example, that a bright and very motivated class could earn all As and Bs if they attain the instructor's thoughtfully prepared set of standards. (See also 6-6.)

Discussion Questions

1. Should the level of the course (e.g., introductory/survey, senior seminar, graduate seminar) influence an instructor's decision concerning the grade distribution?

2. It is not uncommon for instructors at highly selective colleges and universities to award no grade lower than B. This practice seems to be based on the assumption that these "better" students deserve special consideration because these are the grades they would earn in less selective institutions. Thus, the higher grades reflect the students' performance relative to all college students, not just those at the selective institution they attend. Are there any ethical implications of this practice? That is, should students be evaluated relative to a generalized (and vague) national standard or should more selective schools establish and enforce higher criteria for each grade?

3. It has been argued that grade inflation imposes serious penalties on the very best and most deserving students. Do you agree? Why or why not?

4. Do you feel ethically comfortable with your grading criteria? Why or why not?

Case 6-4. Major/Nonmajor Grading Curves

> Professor Twogauge admits to some of her frustrated students that she has two grading curves: one for philosophy majors and one for nonmajors. Her standard for philosophy majors is higher than that for nonmajors. She argues that majors should know more about philosophy and be better able "to think like a philosopher" than students who are not majoring in philosophy.

Using two grading curves is unethical because it misrepresents the performance of one of the groups, making the reasonable assumption that there is no mark on each student's transcript as to whether a major or nonmajor curve is used to compute the grade. This tactic also lowers class morale and could encourage manipulation, such as taking Twogauge's course *before* declaring oneself as a philosophy major.

Students who want to study in a discipline other than their major might consider taking the class credit/no credit. Students need not then worry that majors will easily outdistance them, resulting in a lower grade despite considerable effort. On the other hand, some students may not exercise this option to broaden their knowledge base because of a concern that "credit only" courses may be viewed unfavorably by employers or graduate school evaluators. Perhaps it would be wise for all of us to encourage evaluators to admire rather than discourage students who venture outside their majors.

Sometimes departments solve this dilemma by offering separate versions of certain courses, tailoring them to the special needs and competencies of majors and nonmajors. If such a procedure is used, we believe that the different versions should have separate course numbers to reflect the difference in expectations. (See 9-1, 9-4, and 9-5 for other cases dealing with differential grading.)

Discussion Questions

1. What if Twogauge used the same grading curve but required majors to do an additional or different term project? Would that diffuse the ethical dilemma?

2. Consider the situation in which a senior-level undergraduate course also enrolls for graduate credit first-year graduate students who have not previously taken the course. Should a more stringent grading standard be applied to the graduate students despite the fact that they have almost the same background in the subject as the undergraduate students?

Case 6-5. Grading Essay Exams

Professor Orderly always arranges essay exams in alphabetical order by students' last names before grading them. Students with names beginning with letters early in the alphabet complain that this practice is unfair because Orderly appears to grade the earlier exams more strictly than the later exams. In a similar vein, students with names beginning with letters later in the alphabet complain that Orderly's practice is unfair because an unusually good answer by someone earlier in the alphabet creates a contrast effect that leads Orderly to grade their answers lower than he otherwise would . Orderly reasons that no system is perfect and that because everyone is dissatisfied, his system must be all right.

Both groups of students have reason to be concerned. Sometimes our a priori grading criteria are too strict and we might be overly hard on some students until we get a feel for the "average" answer to a question. We might also unwittingly use an unusually good answer as an inappropriately high standard. The issue of grading order may be a problem especially when there is no single right answer to a question, as when students are asked to evaluate, reflect, or critique.

Possible solutions add a little work, but they probably increase the fairness, or at least students' perceptions of the fairness, of the grading process. We offer the following plan:

1. Shuffle the exam papers into a random order.

2. Read all the answers to the first question, sorting them by quality and getting a feel for the average answer.

3. Grade the first question for all students before grading the next question.

4. Reshuffle the papers, grade the second question, as outlined above, and continue the process for all the questions.

Although this solution does, as we noted, require more time than sequential grading, sometimes instructors find they have to go back and change scores when they realize they have been grading too strictly. Similarly, sometimes students interpret a question differently than the instructor had intended, and only after grading a number of exams does the instructor realize, "Aha! That's why they answered it that way!" In both cases, it would be necessary to go back and repair some exam scores. Therefore, grading exams a question at a time rather than a student at a time might not add much time in the long run.

Discussion Questions

1. Consider the situation in which an instructor gives a test consisting of both multiple-choice and short answer or essay questions. Does knowing a student's score on the multiple choice questions bias the instructor's evaluation of the student's responses to the other questions? Because some students perform much better on one type of exam than the other, what could be done to prevent such bias?

2. Because how much an instructor likes (or dislikes) a student may bias the grading of essay or short answer exams, should some procedure be instituted to prevent identities from being known during grading? If so, what might those procedures be?

Case 6-6. Unfair Grading: Too Hard

> **Professor Indolent begins his first class by informing the class of his grading policy; "A is for God, B is for me, and C is for the good student." The students are**

> panicked and ask others who have been in Indolent's classes before if he really means it. They find that Indolent often has a final distribution of grades that includes no As. Many students attempt to transfer to another section.

Indolent's grading policy violates the intent of his institution's grading scale, which is far more stringent than a grading curve based on actual student performance. A grade of A is intended to indicate excellence on the part of college-level performers, *not* perfection.

Indolent's remarks also reflect an arrogance that is inappropriate for the classroom setting. Rather than sharing his knowledge in an attempt to make his students better, Indolent appears to have a intense need to maintain his feelings of superiority. It is likely that he will drive away many excellent students. Those who are trapped because they need Indolent's class are especially disadvantaged.

Professor Indolent should be made to understand that the grading policy he uses has far-reaching consequences. Not only will there be an immediate impact on his students, but the severity of his scale will affect awards, honors, graduate school admission decisions, and other subsequent activities of many of his students. (For other cases dealing with stringent grading practices, see 5-1 and 6-3.)

Discussion Questions

1. How much should an instructor consider the long-term effects of the grading when setting the standards for a particular class?

2. Indolent's case is, obviously, an extreme. Should colleges and universities have policies in place that prevent this kind of radical grading scale? If so, who should monitor individual instructors' actions?

Case 6-7. Unfair Grading: Too Little Data

> Professor Lazee gives only two short exams during the entire term. Her students realize that very small point differences can change their grades considerably. They protest that Lazee cannot make meaningful distinctions based on such limited information.

There are problems and many possible negative effects associated with Lazee's method of grading. Unless the course has very little to offer to begin with, two small exams are certain to be inadequate assessments of students' learning. Moreover, the failure to provide a number of opportunities to determine how well students are learning the materials may lead many to employ incorrect study techniques for a large portion of the class.

When a point or two may determine the difference between receiving a B and a C, overall grade point averages can be affected significantly. Such large grading distinctions based on very small differences in assessment jeopardize a valid measurement of student abilities. Assessment procedures and the grading scale should be established in ways that ensure fairness to all students. (See also 6-1.)

Discussion Questions

1. What is the ideal "evaluation package" of a 3-credit course with 30 students? That is, how many and what kind of exams and other assignments provide a fair basis for assessing what students have learned?

2. Can there be too many graded assignments in a class?

Case 6-8, A & B. Grading Students Down for Attitudes

> Carl Caveman is a student in Professor Suffra Jet's course in Women's Political History. Carl is an active participant in class and gets good grades on the objective tests and quizzes. However, he frequently interjects rude and blatantly sexist comments in his essay exams. Some of Carl's remarks seem like deliberate attempts to offend and antagonize Jet. Professor Jet is considering assigning Carl a lower grade as punishment for the tone of his essays.
>
> Neil Natsi is a student in Professor Normandy's World War II seminar. During class discussions, Neil promotes his beliefs that the Holocaust is exaggerated propaganda and his view of "Aryan racial superiority." Professor Normandy and Neil's classmates resent this proselytizing, but Neil claims his right to express his views, arguing that they are related to the course content. Professor Normandy detests Neil and is bent on grading him down.

Policies that govern students' moral and ethical behavior, including provisions for the instructor's response to immoral or unethical behavior, are unclear. Thus, it is left to the instructor to decide how to deal with a wide range of behaviors of the sort we see in Carl Caveman and Neil Natsi. In most circumstances, however, an instructor would be ill-advised to consider immoral or inappropriate behavior in the assignment of a grade. Grades should not be used as punishment because they are almost always mandated to reflect academic achievement.

Does this mean that instructors are forced to tolerate uncivil, offensive, or disruptive comments by their students? Many instructors include in their course syllabi explicit ground rules for written work and class participation that include guidelines for courtesy, respect, and both the quality and quantity of participation. These guidelines often state the instructor's right to direct (or redirect) discussion or respond to inappropriate oral or written comments. If the course syllabus includes a policy statement, an instructor would certainly be justified in dealing forcefully and directly with offensive and nonproductive contributions. Most academic institutions have provisions for removing students from a class, although these are legally complicated.

Caveman and Natsi should be given early feedback concerning the inappropriateness of their inputs so that they have an opportunity to modify their behaviors. Although instructors have the latitude and the obligation to address offensive commentary from their students, coercing students to change their attitudes by holding a grade hostage is likely to result in additional problems. (See also 1-1 and 6-9.)

Discussion Questions

1. How does an instructor decide the point at which one student's academic freedom or civil rights violate those of other students?

2. To what extent should civility be actively taught in academic settings?

3. Is it more ethically defensible to grade a student down for interjecting disagreeable attitudes in an essay exam than deducting points from a classroom discussion grading component? Why or why not?

4. Have you dealt with this kind of problem? If so, what did you do, and what were the results?

Case 6-9. Grading Students
Down for Unethical Acts

> Beanie Thief is a student in Professor Wallstreet's
> finance course. Wallstreet requires students to write
> short response papers to articles they have read in
> investment periodicals. Students must also submit a
> photocopy of each article with each reaction paper.
> Street is appalled when he sees that Beanie has
> submitted original articles that he has torn out of the
> library's periodicals. Professor Street assigns Beanie an
> F based on his destruction of library resources. Beanie
> objects, reasoning that he should be graded on his
> scholarship rather than on an unrelated behavior.

This case raises the issue of whether a student's unethical behavior outside
of class should be considered in the assignment of grades. If destruction
of library property appears in the institution's academic honesty code as a
form of cheating, it can be argued that Beanie's act can be dealt with in
accordance with institutional policy. The F on the assignment may be within
the allowable sanctions that instructors can assign on their own for
committing academic dishonesty. Or, it could be argued that assigning
Beanie a lower grade can be defended on the technical grounds that he
did not follow the assignment directions that clearly stated that a *duplicated*
copy was to be handed in.

But, what if the institution does not explicitly include destruction of
library resources as a form of academic dishonesty? In this instance treating
the behavior as an academic performance issue could be problematic.
Beanie's instructor would have difficulty arguing that a grade should be
lowered. This is not to say that such behavior should be ignored. Beanie
needs to be sensitized to the gravity of his action. He needs to be reminded
that defacing resources deprives everyone in the university community
for years to come, that replacement is often extremely costly, and that other
students find his behavior reprehensible.

We also believe that the instructor should do whatever it takes to assure
that Beanie also pays for restoring the journal to as close to its original
status as possible. Beanie should, at the very least, be sent over to the
library with the severed article and present it to the appropriate staff
member. (See also 1-1 and 6-8 for grade penalties for actions not related
to academic performance. See chapter 10 for more cases dealing with
academic dishonesty committed by students.)

Discussion Questions

1. What would you have done with Beanie?

2. Can a grade ever be used as punishment for unethical behavior? If so, what might be an example?

Case 6-10, A & B. Use of the Incomplete Grade

> Roger Roundball is in a bind. He is failing Calculus 396. However, he needs to maintain his GPA to remain on the basketball team. He asks Professor Softtouch if he can miss the final exam and take an I (incomplete) so that he can retain his athlete standing.
>
> Grace Goodmoney works full time and takes a full class load. She has a student loan that requires her to maintain a passing GPA each term. If her GPA falls below the standard, she loses her financial aid. Grace also asks Softtouch if she can take an I in the class, even though she has no hope of passing. She reasons that she can do extra-well next semester to keep her GPA above the cutoff point.

Most faculty members have encountered students who are struggling to manage multiple demands while attempting to maintain good academic standing. Student athletes, students who are employed full- or part-time while taking classes, and students who have full-time family responsibilities may find themselves overextended toward the end of the semester, with grades and financial support in jeopardy. It is tempting to give these students a break, especially when they have been making sincere efforts to pass.

Roger and Grace, however, are asking Softtouch to consider falsifying their records to alleviate their difficult situations. Neither student appears to have any hope of passing the course, even if given extra time. In fact, Roger wants to deliberately miss a course requirement.

The legal implications of honoring such requests can be far-reaching. For example, students may be prosecuted for fraud under the terms of some federal loan programs. A student's athletic eligibility may be endangered, which, in turn, could have effects on a team's standing within its athletic conference. Instructors who collude with students may be held liable as well.

Just as any other letter grade is an official record of a student's performance in a course, the I grade is used to indicate that the student has not completed some of the course requirements. Although the I grade may be open to interpretation, the spirit of incomplete policies is to cover situations in which a student needs additional time to complete an assignment or exam due to illness or other unusual circumstances that resulted in extended absence, not to cover a failing performance. (See also 17-1.)

Discussion Questions

1. Are there ever circumstances in which Softtouch might be justified in giving Roger or Grace an I?

2. Are there circumstances where instructors might agree to an I grade for reasons other than its typical purpose? If so, what?

3. Should any student be attempting a full-time job and a full-time college-level course load? Is it the faculty's responsibility to accommodate any problems caused by such an overloaded student schedule?

4. How do you perceive the purpose of the I grade?

Case 6-11. Grading Group Projects

In Professor Team's advanced classes, students collaborate on group projects worth 25% of their final grades. Groups submit a single report. All group members receive the grade assigned to the group report. However, some students complain that this grading system is unfair because some members contribute more to the project than do others. The upset students contend that students should be graded on their own work only, even if that means doing away with group projects. Professor Team responds that students often learn more when they work together. In addition, Team reminds students that they must get used to collaborative work and its attendant advantages and disadvantages because work groups, such as committees, task forces, and design teams, are commonplace in the workplace.

Group projects are gaining popularity because, as Team notes, the world of work is becoming increasingly collaborative. It is therefore quite reasonable to assign group projects when they are appropriate to the content and goals of a course. Nonetheless, people in positions of authority, such as instructors, should endeavor to make their students' lives as fair as possible. We believe that instructors can simultaneously enhance the fairness of grades assigned for group projects and the educational value of the projects themselves in several ways.

First, instructors should fully explain the importance of individual contributions to group work. Students may not understand what peer collaboration involves, especially if they have never participated in this type of project. An effective way to accomplish this end is to meet with each group to clarify individual and collective roles and responsibilities. These meetings could culminate in a written group contract that specifies each member's contributions. (See Dyer's [1995] chapter on "Developing the Temporary Team" for some techniques that can facilitate this process.) It can also be useful to have periodic follow-up meetings with the groups to check their progress and to encourage the airing of any group dynamic issues, with the instructor taking the role of discussion facilitator. These meetings will not only assist students in understanding their roles, but will also help them better understand group processes.

If different parts of group reports are prepared and written by different students, two grades could be given to each student, one for the report as a whole and one for the student's section, perhaps with more weight given to the latter. Alternatively, one could have each student submit an individual report based on the group's work. In conjunction with either of these approaches, group members could rate the contributions made by the other members and incorporate these ratings into the individual grades.

Students may be reluctant to make peer ratings, but the instructor can make two points. The first is fairness. The only people who have accurate knowledge of each group member's contribution are the group members themselves. The second point is experience. When people work together on a job, they are frequently required to rate their coworkers' contributions to the final project. Therefore, peer ratings mirror practices that students will encounter outside of the classroom.

Student objections to peer ratings can also be minimized if the ratings do not contribute excessively to the grade and if the students are allowed to rate their own contributions to the group. These self-ratings can also be factored into the project grade. The instructor could also give credit for effective problem solving within the group, such as ways the group kept itself cohesive and productive.

Discussion Questions

1. Given that any class is likely to be composed of individuals with different levels of knowledge, skill, and motivation relevant to a given group task, how should student groups be formed? Should students be allowed to form their own groups, which might lead the more able and better motivated students to choose each other while the less able and unmotivated students are left with each other. Or, should the instructor construct groups that contain a mixture of more and less skilled students? The second approach has the potential to improve the learning environment for the less able students, but might hold the better students back. To whom does the instructor have the stronger duty, the better or the poorer student?

2. A problem that can occur in work groups is that of the slacker who procrastinates or does an incomplete or inadequate job. Given that one goal of group projects is to deal with actual group dynamic problems, how should the responsibility for dealing with a slacker be divided between the instructor and the other students in the slacker's group? If the group seems to be doing an inadequate job of handling the problem, at what point and to what extent should the instructor intervene?

3. How can one tell the difference between a slacker and a student who is less competent, stressed, or troubled?

Case 6-12. No Extra Credit

> **Students complain that Professor Stern offers no opportunity to earn extra credit points. These students feel that they deserve an opportunity to do better.**

Students seeking opportunities to enhance their performance are usually those who need points late in the term to bolster sagging grades. However, instructors are under no obligation to offer students extra credit options. The offer of extra credit options raises the concern that irresponsibility and procrastination could be reinforced (Norcross, Horrocks, & Stevenson, 1989). Instructors should encourage students to seek assistance early enough to address any problems they are having with their academic performance.

Instructors should also be available to students seeking a better performance on the remaining assignments. When students' grades are based on several assignments spaced throughout the term, and their nature and weight and any extra credit policy is made clear in the syllabus, the likelihood of misunderstanding is reduced. (See 6-13 for a case dealing with too much extra credit.)

Discussion Questions

1. Is extra credit fair to the best students?

2. Should there be limits on the extent of the impact extra credit can have on the final grade?

3. Do extra credit opportunities reward procrastination?

4. What is your policy regarding extra credit?

Case 6-13. Plenty of Extra Credit

> Professor Splat gives students multiple ways of earning extra credit. Some are fairly traditional, for example, a book report. Others are more unusual, such as adopting a pet or giving blood.

Just as there is no obligation to offer extra credit opportunities, there is nothing inherently troubling about offering them. However, instructors must justify why extra (as in "outside") credit is appropriate. In addition, these opportunities should be pedagogically sound. Good deeds, while having a laudable place in one's personal moral commitments, are not proper assignments for academic credit unless they are related directly to the course. (See Hill, Palladino, and Eison, 1993 for an interesting discussion of the ethics of extra credit. See also 6-12.)

Discussion Questions

1. A very civic-minded colleague tells you that he gives his students considerable extra credit for volunteering to work three hours a week in a local adolescent care program. He is in the Department of Mathematical Sciences. What would you say to him?

2. Should departments develop policies regarding the type and extent of allowable extra credit? Why or why not?

3. Some academic programs require volunteer field service. Failure to complete the activity jeopardizes grades, completion of the degree program, or special recognition. Is it fair to require students to volunteer time?

Feedback
to Students

Part of an instructor's obligations is to promote learning, not just in what they do in class but also by "closing the loop" with each student by providing constructive feedback on the student's work. Ethical feedback is that which respects students' dignity and their development as learners. In this chapter we offer examples involving feedback that include inappropriate or demeaning criticisms of student work and responses to student work that are public and risk embarrassing students. Instructors need to be sensitive to the power they wield over students' emotional attachment to learning and social standing with their peers. In addition to these examples, we include cases concerning feedback that is insufficient in quantity and timeliness.

Case 7-1. Written Feedback to Students

> When students attempt to write essay exams without a full grasp of the information, Professor Bovine draws a little cartoon of a bull flying through the air on their blue book covers. A student complained that the drawing insulted and embarrassed her and that she was doing the best she could. Professor Bovine defends his cartoon by asserting that students should learn that attempting to pull a scam on experts is a bad idea. He views his technique as a harmless yet effective way to teach this valuable lesson.

The problem with Bovine's teaching-a-lesson defense is that it is often impossible to distinguish between true "bull" and an honest, but incompetent, answer. The only surefire way to avoid falsely accusing a sincere student's effort is to make appropriate remarks on the work that are relevant to the content. This feedback can be candid without resorting to mean-spirited silliness.

The impact of Bovine's cartoonish statement depends to some extent on the visibility of the drawing. If it is inside the blue book, and so cannot be seen by others, perhaps this behavior is more an example of poor taste than of poor ethics. If the drawing is visible to others, the resultant humiliation is more damaging to the student. In either event, Bovine's behavior fails to respect the dignity of his students.

Finally, although instructors do not appreciate student attempts to pretend to know what they do not (and pray to go unnoticed), it can be argued that students should feel free to give every challenge a try. The line between an attempt to put one over on us and giving something a try in the hopes that it hits the mark may not be that easy to draw. Humiliation may only serve to repress a willingness to stretch. (See also 1-3.)

Discussion Questions

1. When does bad taste become bad ethics? For example, if Bovine had warned his class early in the term about his little slinging bull figure, is his practice less disrespectful?

2. What if the majority of the class enjoys Bovine's jibes? Does embarrassing only a small minority of recipients matter?

3. What might be an example of negative feedback to a student's strong and apparent attempt to fake an answer that is also ethically and professionally appropriate?

Case 7-2. Oral Feedback to Students

> Professor Expose makes audible remarks as he hands back students' exam papers. To the best students he says, "great work" or "good going," and to the poorer students he says, "need to spend more time studying," or "better come see me about this." His smile is wide as he hands back the best papers, and his brow is slightly furrowed as he delivers the exams with low scores. He defends his practice as a way of rewarding the best students and motivating the poorer ones to do better next time.

Student performance results are confidential by law, and although Expose's tactic is not quite the same as reading grades aloud or posting them on his office door, the effect is similar. Professor Expose is also revealing faulty logic. Not all high-scoring students experience public disclosure as rewarding, and the poor students may well experience their publicly revealed failures as demoralizing rather than motivating. If Expose has comments that he would like to share with his students, he should speak to them in private or put his notes on an inside page of the exam.

Expose may want to consider how he would feel about public revelations of his teaching evaluations, merit pay review, or evaluations of his professional writing. For example, would he want his work evaluated in a department meeting? (See also 1-1 and 20-6.)

Discussion Questions

1. What circumstances might warrant public praise of identified students in class?

2. Are there circumstances when public criticisms in the classroom can be justified?

3. Is it ethical to have other students help pass back tests or papers to their classmates?

Case 7-3. Minimal Feedback to Students

> Professor Nofeedback assigns a grade to the term project without further comment. Students are unhappy because they cannot ascertain the basis of his grading. Nofeedback contends that there is insufficient time to make comments on each of seventy papers. He believes that he should be commended for even requiring a writing assignment and for his willingness to read them all himself.

In an era when academic reformers are calling for more writing assignments and fewer "bubble-in-the-answer" assessments, Professor Nofeedback is to be commended for assigning term papers in a relatively large class. For most students, the act of writing bestows learning benefits independent of any feedback or evaluation. Moreover, it is common to find that some papers are so good that a few-word accolade is all there is to say. Others are done so poorly that one does not know where to start with commentary. However, the students' frustration is understandable. An analogy might be the journal editor who rejects our submission of a scholarly paper with no rationale or further comment.

Reactions to writing style, ability to organize thoughts, and development of arguments are among the critical purposes of such assignments. Therefore to provide no additional feedback may not be unethical, but it constitutes a poor pedagogical practice because students do not learn as much as they could from the writing exercise. If Professor Nofeedback does not have the time or resources to give careful, individualized feedback, compromises should be considered. These might include:

1. giving students a list of common errors and positive features, each with a number, and inserting the numbers in the margins of each paper;
2. giving general oral feedback during class, explaining the grading rationale and noting frequently occurring problems and solutions to them;
3. assigning shorter papers, thus allowing extra time that can be spent offering individual feedback;
4. assuring that students are given very specific grading criteria in advance so that they can better understand the grade received;
5. including at least a few words on the face page that summarize the basic reaction (e.g., "some good ideas, but presented without sufficient documentation"); or
6. inviting students who want more detailed feedback to confer during office hours.

Finally, the power of margin notes such as "good point" or "excellent writing skills" cannot be overestimated. Positive remarks, when indicated, are all it takes to profoundly reward the sincere student's efforts.

Discussion Questions

1. Sometimes a paper is so poorly done that it seems impossible to know how to create critical feedback. What should one do in such a situation?

2. Nofeedback reads his own papers, but some instructors assign teaching assistants to grade written assignments. Do ethical problems exist here? If so, how can they be minimized?

3. Is it appropriate to provide access to samples of excellent term papers from prior classes? How should this material be made available? Are there drawbacks to this practice?

Case 7-4. Untimely Feedback to Students

> Students are disgruntled because Professor Dilatory takes 3 to 4 weeks to return exams. Students claim that they are made overly anxious and that this interferes with their ability to study the next set of materials. Professor Dilatory retorts that it takes considerable time to read essay exams but that this is a better way to assess students as compared to multiple-choice exams. He feels that students should be more appreciative and understanding.

Essay exams are far better for many purposes than are objective (multiple choice or matching questions) exams that can be graded more quickly. The predicament is less severe than in the case of Emcee (6-1), because Dilatory's students do, eventually, receive feedback on their progress. Although Dilatory should not be dissuaded from essay testing, he should be more sensitive to the students' distress. Solutions to Dilatory's problem include giving shorter but more frequent exams that could be graded and returned more promptly, or giving combination multiple-choice and essay exams.

Discussion Questions

1. What is a reasonable amount of time in which to provide students in a class of 40 with feedback on exams and written assignments?

2. Are there other kinds of delays that are equally problematic, such as providing a promise to find the answer to a question raised during class? How long should the student wait for an instructor to "I will get back to you about that"?

8

Writing Reference
Letters for Students

Most students fail to realize that the dispensing of grades can be the *second* most powerful influence that faculty have on students' educational and career advancement. Letters of recommendation can make— and even more easily break—a student's success in obtaining additional training or employment. As a result, many students fail to realize that missed exams, coming to class late and misbehavior in class may come back to haunt them later. However, whereas instructors have considerable latitude in choosing whom to support and what to include in the letter, ethical conflicts often arise. Often enough we have to make an agonizing choice between being completely honest or glossing over shortcomings of otherwise worthy students, knowing full well that complete candor will likely foreclose on our students' quests for graduate school or a job.

This chapter covers issues such as conflicted loyalties, the inclusion of negative information, sharing letters with students, and confidentiality.

Case 8-1. Biasing in the Service
of Helpfulness

> Nikki Nice is an extremely pleasant, generally hard-working and sincere young woman who aspires to becoming a school teacher. Nikki asks Professor Pearl for a letter, and Professor Pearl agrees. Pearl has observed Nikki's patience and interest in helping other students in the class. However, Pearl has a few concerns. Nikki's assignments are often a day or two overdue. She usually gets to the 8 a.m. class a few minutes late because, as she explains, "I have a hard time getting out of bed." She earned a B, just barely, in Pearl's class. Pearl, convinced that Nikki can do better, does not mention

Nikki's dilatory behavior patterns in his letters to potential employers.

This situation probably arises often. Research suggests that including a negative statement in a letter, despite other positive characterizations, drastically reduces the students' chances of acceptance into graduate school or offers of employment (Keith-Spiegel & Wiederman, 2000). Why? Because most letters contain no negative commentary whatsoever. This situation, sadly, creates a "Catch-22" for instructors who sincerely believe that, despite some weaknesses, the student will likely succeed. For the personal reference system to work as it should, every letter should be truthful. It is unfortunate that being less than completely candid may be the only way to protect a worthy student from probable rejection in favor of one of the majority of "flawless" applicants.

As for Nikki, Pearl should highlight her strong points and attest to his belief that Nikki will be a fine teacher. If time permits, he can warn Nikki of the problems he sees and suggest that if there are immediate, consistent changes, he will not have to describe these patterns in the letter. However, we also believe that there is such a thing as being *too* kind. If a student is recommended who is unlikely to succeed, the student is disadvantaged and the referee's ability to accurately judge students is called into question. This could reduce the chances of future applicants recommended by a referee whose earlier students failed to live up to expectations.

Pearl could express his concerns directly to Nikki and note that he is considering characterizing her as slightly immature and irresponsible at this point. Nikki may then choose to withdraw her request for a letter. (See 9-2. See 8-2 and 8-3 for opposing situations.)

Discussion Questions

1. What if Pearl did warn Nikki at the beginning of the semester, noting that her behavior would be unacceptable in a work setting. She then came to class on time more often and her assignments were only rarely late. But the negative pattern was still there, albeit in a much weaker form. What, then, should Pearl do when Nikki asks for a letter?

2. How can an instructor determine that an irresponsible behavior is an ingrained pattern as opposed to an exception to the student's usual mode of operating? For example, if a class has four exams and a student needs to take one make-up, most of us would not think much of that. But what about two or three make-ups?

3. Do we enhance our students' probability of failure by withholding information about them that employers and others will find unacceptable?

Case 8-2. The Bomb Letter

> Professor Bashem agrees to write a reference letter for a student he neither likes nor respects. The letter reads, "Regarding the application of Joshua Vreeb to your PhD program, save yourself trouble and burn his file now!"

Regardless of the legitimacy of Bashem's disdain, this type of letter about a student should never be written. Its effect on the candidate is likely to be devastating, but no clear basis for it has been offered. For all we know, it is Bashem who is unstable or holds some grudge based on personal or personality characteristics unrelated to Vreeb's intellectual and moral fitness as a graduate student.

It is not unethical to include damaging information about a student in a recommendation letter. However, the facts upon which a conclusion is based should be spelled out in concrete, behavioral terms, and they must be truthful. When an opinion is being offered, it must be clearly labeled as such and carry no implication of a factual basis. For example, if Bashem also adds, "It is my distinct impression that Vreeb cheats on exams," he implies that facts may be available but does not cite them. If this statement could be shown to be untrue, it is arguably defamatory.

Should Bashem have agreed to write a letter for Vreeb in the first place? We can assume that Vreeb had no idea the letter would be so disparaging. As a general suggestion, we believe that faculty members should let students know when a letter would have to reveal more than a very minor weakness. This gives the student an opportunity to find another referee. (See 8-6 for an exception to this advice.)

Discussion Questions

1. What do you say to a student about whom you hold many reservations when a letter of recommendation is requested? How honest should you be? What are the variables that would influence your decision?

2. Say a student requesting a letter appears to be arrogant. For example, this student cuts conversations short, does not maintain eye contact, and appears to be self-absorbed and snobbish. Others appear to actively avoid this student. You

have had conversations with this student in your office and realize that the student is actually very shy. Once the student relaxes—and that takes a while—a very pleasant demeanor is revealed. What would your letter say?

3. Say that a student is very bright and performs near the top of the class. But, your personalities clash. She rubs you the wrong way. What would be the appropriate course of action should she ask you for a letter of recommendation?

4. Is a student at fault for not picking up signals that an educator will write a negative letter? That is, is the student largely responsible for the consequences?

Case 8-3. Instructors' Hurt Feelings

> Professor Hurt overhears Roger Loud in the men's room refer to him as a "pompous dork." When Roger, a brilliant and popular student, asks Professor Hurt for a letter of recommendation to graduate school, Hurt declines without further comment.

It might be argued that Professor Hurt is overreacting and that Roger's negative characterization does not deserve such extreme retribution. However, the basic issues are more straightforward. Instructors have been given the ethical responsibility to assist in the professional development of students they can support, but they are not required to write letters of recommendation for every student who asks. Letter writing is a privilege earned by the student, and Roger's outburst obviously risked his status with Professor Hurt. Indeed, Professor Hurt is in a position to gain massive revenge by writing a scathing letter, and it is to his credit that he did not elect that option. Because research reveals that negative evaluations usually ensure dropping applicants from consideration, Roger's career could have been derailed.

However, Professor Hurt could and perhaps should have made the incident a learning experience for Roger rather than leaving the rejected student completely in the dark. At the very least, Hurt should have told Roger the reason for his decision. It is even possible that an open discussion could lead to a reconciliation that would be satisfying to both parties. (See also 9-2.)

Discussion Questions

1. In the foregoing case, Roger has made a judgment about Hurt's personality style. What if Hurt had overheard Roger refer to him as "a burned-out fraud," thus attacking Hurt's competence and character. How would you now react to

Roger's request? How would your response be different, if at all, from the main case?

2. What if, instead, Roger did not acknowledge Hurt in the hallways or occasionally came to class a few minutes late or disagreed with something that Hurt said in class? Are students' common behaviors that are not necessarily a personal attack legitimate grounds for refusing to write letters for students? That is, at what point can we say that an instructor is being unfair or overly sensitive when the student's nonacademic behavior is used as a major factor in agreeing to write (or not write) a letter?

3. Is the degree to which we like or dislike a student, for whatever reason, a legitimate factor to reveal itself in a recommendation letter?

Case 8-4. Recommendation Letters
and Previous Information

> Professor Consultant's student in his abnormal psychology course is the same woman on whose case he reviewed (with the client's consent to bring in unnamed experts) during her hospitalization for depression a couple of years ago. She had made previous suicide attempts, one while in the hospital. The student does not know that her instructor was one of the specialists, and asks Consultant to write her a letter of recommendation to law school. Questions about emotional stability are specifically asked on the referee form.

It is probably more common than we realize for instructors to have additional information about their students. Academic and professional communities interact in many settings, especially in smaller cities. As revealed here, those associations can cause intense and complicated ethical issues related to confidentiality and the determination of loyalties.

The student's current level of functioning and class performance should be the primary criteria upon which an evaluation is based. However, Consultant does have information that surely colors his views to some extent. He cannot directly describe his knowledge about the student's previous difficulties because that would be a breach of confidentiality. But, his letter could be short and unhelpful, or reflect a general or diffuse concern that any evaluator would detect.

If Consultant remains concerned about the student's suitability to the profession, does he owe it to the student to reveal his role in her life and openly discuss what effect it might have on his letter? This seems awkward, but it may be the most fair course of action. Such a discussion should help both the student and Consultant decide how to proceed. The student might wish to withdraw her request. Consultant might decide not to write a letter or, if he does, explain to the student how the letter might be damaging. Or, all concerns may be removed as a result of the discussion, at which point Consultant can confidently recommend the student based solely on her role as a student.

In this case, there has been a 2-year lapse during which the student may have improved markedly. However, what if only 6 months had passed? Or what if, rather than a mood disorder, the student had been violent or engaging in abusive or antisocial behavior? At this point, an instructor faces a more acute dilemma. Instructors may certainly refuse to write a letter, but some may believe that they are abandoning their responsibility to the profession by failing to warn a graduate program or employer about the unsuitability of certain applicants. A negative letter will almost always result in an applicant's rejection in a competitive program or job opportunity. However, the insidious element here is that the student is completely unaware of the instructor's knowledge and was, therefore, blindsided.

Should an instructor, then, confront a student about whom he or she has grave concerns, especially if the student is unaware of the instructor's prior knowledge? Assuming that the instructor simply cannot write a letter no matter what, the decision becomes a matter of personal conscience. If the student could conceivably be helped by the disclosure, it should be considered. However, when ethical dilemmas become this complicated, and contain some legal or extant policy issues, seeking legal counsel before proceeding is recommended. (See Chapter 20 for additional cases involving issues of confidentiality.)

Discussion Questions

1. Should the student's career plans influence Consultant's decisions about how to proceed? For example, would it matter if an emotionally labile or depressed student was pursuing a history or mathematics degree versus a career in teaching or law enforcement?

2. Suppose Consultant has the impression that the student's difficulties are under control, but does not have enough information from his limited contacts to make a comfortable determination. Would Consultant ever be justified in attempting to verify that the student had been successfully treated? Why or why not?

3. Suppose Consultant had not been directly involved as an expert in the student's case, but had been visiting someone else in the mental hospital and recognized the student sitting in the ward. How does this change the nature of Consultant's options in dealing with this ethical dilemma?

Case 8-5. Recommendation Letters and Second-Hand Information

> Gyp came to Professor Privy for a letter of recommendation. Gyp had been a fairly good student and was pleasant and charming. Normally Privy would have written a positive letter. However, Privy's colleague, Instructor Tellall, told Privy that Gyp had been caught cheating in class and that Privy should watch out for him. Privy never saw any evidence of dishonesty in his class and is perplexed over how to proceed.

Relying on first-hand information when writing letters of recommendation is a good general rule of thumb, but is too easy an answer in this case. Damage to Gyp's image has likely been done because the information divulged by Tellall cannot be completely ignored no matter how hard Privy might try to put it out of mind. As seen in Case 8-4, the letter will be influenced in some way, especially if credibility is heightened because Tellall is a highly respected member of the department or Privy's close friend.

This case is especially difficult because it involves potential legal complications, especially if Privy decides to open up the matter by confronting Gyp with the story. Confidentiality rights pertain to students in some situations, but it is not usually clear whether cheating is one of them. And, if the student has denied all charges, slander may be at issue.

Privy might attempt to get more detailed information from Tellall. What does "caught" mean? What was the evidence? Was the student confronted? What was the result of an inquiry? If Tellall did not follow through with a complaint, why not?

One must not lose sight of the fact that Gyp should not be put aside without considerable reflection. It would be easy for Privy to dismiss the matter by telling Gyp that he does not know him well enough, or to write a brief or non-helpful letter that evades the issue. Taking the easy way out, however, deprives Gyp of the consideration every student deserves.

Discussion Questions

1. What weight should be given to first-hand versus seemingly reliable second-hand information?

2. Suppose Gyp decides to go ahead and write a favorable letter for Gyp. However, Privy is later caught cheating in Privy's class. Should Privy contact the recipients of the letter and ask that it be withdrawn?

Case 8-6. Reference Letters:
To Whom Is One Loyal?

> **Slick applied to several medical schools and asked Professor Purple for a letter. Purple felt torn because she could not support this student. At the same time, she has just been given an opportunity to ensure that Slick never practices medicine. Considerable evidence coupled with numerous opportunities for direct observation has unmasked Slick as manipulative and devious. He is arrogant and disliked by faculty and students alike. He openly declares that his sole reason for selecting a premed program is the wealth he intends to accumulate from performing plastic surgery on "old, saggy, rich women." The faculty is not convinced that his manifestations are simply due to immaturity.**

In these more extreme cases, legitimate loyalties openly compete. Slick's personality style appears to be deep and pervasive to the point of possibly rendering him unfit to offer health services. Purple can simply refuse to write a letter. It appears that Slick will have trouble getting a letter from anyone in the department, and Professor Purple's personal and immediate dilemma might be solved in this way.

Would it be appropriate for Purple to agree to write a letter, and then recount *detailed, verifiable, behavior-based* observations of Slick (as opposed to a string of negative adjectives)? Although this option should be exercised only after considerable soul-searching, protection of the public—especially when the student will be entering a position that will confer power over vulnerable consumers—can be a compelling reason to act in favor of the public good. (See 8-2 for commentary regarding the impact of negative information.)

Discussion Questions

1. What if Slick was merely arrogant, but the other alleged acts were unsubstantiated rumors? How would this alter your approach to a request for a letter?

2. Would you feel comfortable in telling Slick directly that he was not currently suited to practice medicine? What would be the advantages and disadvantages of being very honest with students about nonacademic assessments?

3. Would you feel differently about recommending Slick if he was planning to become a businessman? That is, does a student's future plans (including the possible sensitivity of that position) have any bearing at all on what we say about students in letters? Why or why not?

Case 8-7. Sneaking a Peek at Reference Letters

Graduate programs increasingly request that applicants collect the letters of recommendation themselves and include them with the application packets. Envelopes are usually provided with instructions to the referees to seal the envelope and sign it across the back before returning it to the student, thus ensuring confidentiality. Professor Wary has learned about a practice whereby students give instructors a graduate school recommendation form for a program to which they will purposely not apply. They then open that letter to view its content. This allows the students to either eliminate any letter that is not positive or select only the best ones to include with their serious applications. Professor Wary feels a loss of trust and is now reluctant to supply any letters for students. His students do not understand why Wary turns down their requests for a reference.

Loss of trust issues are difficult to resolve. Such a practice is dismaying to say the least, but we must remember that not every student is deceptive. We must also understand (without having to agree with) the underlying motivation for such deceptions.

Professor Wary can minimize victimization while still meeting an obligation to assist students with their educational and career development. Wary can inform the students of what kind of letter he could write and express openly any concerns that he may have when a student first requests a letter. Wary can inform students for whom he cannot write a positive or helpful letter, and he can refuse to write letters for students he does not know well enough or who he cannot support.

There are many ways for students to be deceptive, and the method described earlier is only one of them. If we shut down because some students may attempt to betray our trust, we will become jaded and, as a result, less effective overall as teachers and mentors.

Discussion Questions

1. Are there other ways to defuse the "extra letter ploy"? Should referees, for example, query students about the seriousness of their choices?

2. Might submitting recommendation letters by e-mail solve a host of problems, including this one? What new problems could arise?

Case 8-8. The Demand to See Reference Letters

> Moxie Galore demands to see the letter that Professor Withhold wrote for her. "It is our inalienable right," says Moxie, "for us to know what someone is saying about us, especially when what you say may determine the course of our lives." She adds, "Even if we sign a confidentiality waiver, that does not mean that you cannot show us a copy." Professor Withhold responds that he wrote a mostly positive letter for Moxie, and verbally summarizes the contents, but refuses to show her the actual letter. He believes it is up to his own discretion as to whether a student sees a letter. Moxie replies, "I think you don't really care about students," and storms out of the office.

After such an encounter Professor Withhold may well be tempted to recall his letter, and may even to add a negative comment to it. Moxie's behavior seemed overbearing, inappropriate, and unappreciative. Moxie reveals a side that Withhold had not previously observed.

There is, however, reason to be sympathetic to Moxie's point, even though her approach revealed uncultivated social skills. The fact remains that Moxie's fears are realistic, and many students probably have them even though they remain unspoken. The student has a great deal riding on applications for advanced training or employment, and recommendation letters are a major factor in the recipient's decision making. As considerable research reveals, even one negative comment in an otherwise positive letter is often enough to disqualify the applicant from further consideration. Research also reveals that when the applicant has waived the right to see the letter, the letter is more likely to contain negative comments than are letters without a waiver. (It should also be noted that letters without a waiver are, however, taken somewhat less seriously.)

Whereas Moxie has openly stated what many students feel, an instructor is not required to show any student the letters written about her or him. We recommend that students who the instructor cannot support be informed of that up-front. The usual reason is that instructors feel that they do not know the student well enough. If a letter would be unhelpful, it is to the student's advantage to know that, even if the student does not appreciate it at the time. For students who the instructor can support, any policy about sharing letters should be disclosed at the onset. Professor Withhold's willingness to simply summarize the letter to students who ask is an acceptable policy as is never or always sharing letters. We suggest deciding on a policy and, except for unusual circumstances, sticking to it. (See 8-7 for a devious way students can review reference letters.)

Discussion Questions

1. How would you have responded to Moxie?

2. What if Moxie had been very polite and far less assertive? If she had said something like, "These letters have such a great impact on our futures. Might you be willing to show me the one you wrote for me?" Would you have shown her the letter?

3. Is it acceptable to share "good letters" but never share letters with neutral or unglowing commentary? What are the possible consequences of this double standard?

Biased Treatment
of Students

Biased treatment of students is a problem with ethical dimensions that every instructor is likely to face at some point. This chapter looks at playing favorites, giving breaks to special student groups, revealing a bad attitude toward all students, and making individual compensations for certain students when others are not offered the same treatment. Special emphasis is placed on the concept of impartiality, for when advantages are extended to some students, unintentional harm may befall the others.

Case 9-1. Differential Evaluation of Students

> Randy Promise was able to discuss clearly and accurately every facet of the course material during Professor Support's class discussions and informal office hours. Support was very impressed with Randy and believed he could have a successful future in the field. However, Randy performed C level work on exams. When Professor Support queried Randy about the discrepancy, Randy responded that he never did well on tests. At the end of the semester Professor Support assigned Randy a grade of B because of the strong belief that his informal assessments of Randy's potential were more accurate than Randy's scores on four multiple-choice exams.

We have all taught this sort of baffling student at one time or another. However, selecting one student for a special appraisal is not equitable. It is appropriate to attempt to evaluate the reasons for the seeming discrepancies in such students and to search for appropriate mechanisms that may align the performance in one setting with that in another. For example, Randy may have text anxiety. Or, he may manage his study time poorly. The instructor can encourage Randy to take advantage of services available to work with such problems. Support could also initiate a willingness to write a reference letter for Randy, stressing his very strong points.

If an instructor finds that it is not uncommon for seemingly gifted students to perform poorly in the class, a review of student evaluation measures is in order. Specifically, Professor Support should assess his use of four multiple-choice exams as the sole source of the performance-of-record. (See also 8-1 and 9-2.)

Discussion Questions

1. What if Professor Support's syllabus clearly states that part of every student's grade is based on attendance and the quality of class participation? Would Support's decision to give Randy an advantage be more justifiable in such a case?

2. Can an instructor ever be justified in using a different form of evaluation for a selected student such as Randy Promise? If so, under what conditions?

3. Are we ethically obligated to assess students in a variety of ways to ensure that students with different learning styles and performance strengths have an opportunity to shine?

Case 9-2. Enhancing the Evaluation of Likeable Students

> Several instructors, chatting openly one day, admit to each other that they allow how much they like (or dislike) a student to influence the grade the student receives, especially when the student's grades are on the borderline.

A national survey (Tabachnick et al., 1991) indicated that favoring liked students when grades are assigned is a common phenomenon among college and university faculties. Most respondents also acknowledged the inappropriateness of allowing likability to influence their evaluations. Only a few respondents indicated that they *never* let such considerations influence their evaluations.

Perhaps this bias reflects our mere humanness, yet ethically it is an urge that teaching professionals must constantly fend against. Except for programs in which personality plays a legitimate part in students' evaluation (e.g., a supervised nursing or teaching practicum), students should be rewarded for their academic performance whether we like them as people or not. Our mission is to teach and then to evaluate what has been mastered by our students, not to match or mismatch our personal selves with theirs.

For faculty members who have trouble remaining objective, the "blind" reading of writing assignments should be considered. Having a colleague review an assignment of a particularly liked (or disliked) student may be appropriate in more extreme cases. (See also 8-1, 8-2, 8-3, 9-1, and 9-3.)

Discussion Questions

1. No doubt students believe that if an instructor likes them they are more likely to receive a more favorable evaluation. They may behave differently toward instructors than is their nature. Do you think that students who ingratiate themselves to instructors are behaving unethically?

2. If a student appears to be disliked by both faculty and peers, should the instructor address this problem directly with the student? What are the potential risks and benefits of such an involvement?

3. How do you handle the grading phase when you assign the final grade to a student you particularly like or admire and one you dislike?

Case 9-3. Choosing Favorites

> Students complain that Professor Prefer is much friendlier to some students than to others and that only the students he likes are invited to collaborate on his research projects. Prefer's response to a confrontation is that he, indeed, does like some students better than others, but that this is simply human.

As long as Prefer's grading is done fairly, selecting well-liked students as collaborators on outside research projects is probably ethically defensible. Research *is* a time consuming and intellectually intimate working relationship. The tendency to work with people with whom one is comfortable is easily understandable.

However, assuming that the research experiences Prefer provides are useful learning experiences (or lead to a professional paper or journal article), it is hoped that affability is not the sole criterion for selecting student-colleagues. Such a criterion prevents well-qualified students from having the chance to improve their credentials. In the interest of scientific integrity, top priority should be given to students with the requisite skills, high levels of responsibility, and commitment to excellence.

Research conduct aside, Prefer may want to be less obvious about whom he likes best or he may want to make himself available to all students in some sort of open forum setting. As an example, one of our colleagues eats lunch at the same time and table in the student center every day. All of his students have been told that anyone is welcome to join him. In this way more students who want to know him have the chance and concerns about favoritism are blunted. (See also 9-2.)

Discussion Questions

1. Does it make a difference, ethically speaking, if Professor Prefer's likes and dislikes are based on academic rather than personality traits?

2. Would you ever chose to work with a student who was talented but who you did not particularly like? If yes, under what circumstances?

3. What are your criteria for selecting student collaborators on research or other pet projects?

Case 9-4. Compensating for the Needs of Certain Students

> Marcia, a student in Professor Soft's class, is a single parent and often misses class because of her children's frequent illnesses. Marcia performs extremely well on exam questions taken from the required readings. She does poorly, however, on questions from the lectures she misses. Soft, therefore, gives those lecture questions less weight in determining Marcia's grade than he does for other students.

Should special consideration be given to the unique problems commonly faced by re-entry students? Returning students are potentially rich resources, and instructors should be sensitive to the particular needs and unusual schedules that many of these students must juggle. However, special grading standards based on atypical life situations are, in principle, just as discriminatory as those based on race or gender. Any action that diminishes the rights of more conventional students to the grade to which they are entitled (in this case, evaluation of a classmate based in part on conditions extraneous to actual performance) violates the principle of fairness.

Nowadays, even in a small class, Marcia is not a unique case. Athletes, musical or theater performers, long-distance commuters (especially those dependent on public transportation), students with physical or mental disabilities, and numerous others also must cope with scheduling conflicts that are not under their direct control. In fact, every student's situation is at least a little bit different, and once we open the door to singular grading scales, where does it end? Course instructors cannot compensate for all of life's complications, and grading standards that are not applied uniformly cease to be standards. Thus, we consider Professor Soft's ad hoc approach ethically problematic and would recommend instead that Soft help Marcia take maximum advantage of all those forms of assistance that are available to students in general, such as help during office hours and notes from classmates, lecture taping, negotiating additional time to complete an assignment when appropriate, or extra credit for which everyone is eligible. (See also 6-4, 9-5, and 9-7.)

Discussion Questions

1. How much extra help is appropriate to give students like Marcia? For example, is the instructor ethically obligated to take the time necessary to review with her what material she missed in class?

2. Should the amount of help an instructor provides vary depending on the severity or intensity of the student's problem or disability?

3. What if, instead, Soft agreed to give Marcia an extra assignment to make up for her exam performances? Is this any different from an ethical point of view? (Assume that this option is not extended to other students who performed poorly.)

4. What if it was Marcia herself who was ill for several weeks. Would you look at the situation differently?

Case 9-5. Giving Breaks
to Special Student Groups

Professor Boost firmly believes that the available methods of classroom evaluation underestimate minority students' knowledge relative to that of Anglo students. He, therefore, routinely elevates each of his minority students' final grades (e.g., a C+ becomes a B-).

Can this version of affirmative action be justified? Does an ethical mandate exist for individual instructors to do something to help compensate for the inadequacies in some students' academic and social experiences? Sensitivity to diversity is one of our professional responsibilities as teachers, and feedback that is appropriate is given in an atmosphere of trust and respect. However, in the end the paramount concern is the recipient's educational benefit.

A distinction must be made between Boost's judgment that existing evaluation measures may underestimate minority students' knowledge and the singular step he takes in acting on this belief, in this case, "race-norming" his class's final grades. We believe that Boost's procedure constitutes reverse discrimination against nonminority students, some of whom may also be disadvantaged in other ways. All students are entitled to receive the grade they deserve. For some, such as those seeking admission to highly competitive graduate programs, top grades are a necessity.

Boost's practice could even, inadvertently, harm the efforts of his minority students. All students benefit most when they are challenged. Boost's grading is condescending to minority students and misrepresents their actual performance, perhaps giving them a false perception of their actual abilities. Inflated grading may cause such students to question the validity of all grades they receive. Race-norming of standardized test scores such as the General Aptitude Test Battery (GATB), while highly controversial, at least has the advantage of being based on large and well-validated databases, information that a single instructor is very unlikely to have about his assessment measures.

Boost's procedure begs several other questions. For example, who qualifies as minority? Background, first or last name, and even physical appearance do not offer fool-proof criteria. Some of those who qualify for Boost's bonus are probably advantaged in other respects than students he has defined as mainstream. Furthermore, if there is no way to measure the exact amount of bias because no instruments are free of it, how can Boost know that one third a letter grade is an appropriate adjustment? Does Boost explain his procedure in advance to avoid the confusion that may result when identical performances result in different final grades?

If Boost's practice is truly appropriate, there is no reason to keep it a secret. If it became public knowledge, however, other students would certainly make strenuous objections and prevail in grade appeals.

What can Boost do instead to assist any higher risk students? Before final grades are determined he could provide extra help to any students who seek it, refer students to any and all additional support services (e.g., learning resource centers, private tutors), and model, shape, and reinforce competent performance. After final grades are processed, he can offer educational or career information and affirmative letters of recommendation. (See also 6-4, 8-1, and 9-4.)

Discussion Questions

1. What if Boost applies his grade adjustment only occasionally and only at the lowest end of the scale, such that what was originally a D minus becomes a D? Suppose, further, that this policy directly affects only one or two students. Is this more acceptable? Why or why not?

2. Do any special circumstances exist (e.g., students with disabilities, or those who are avid learners but whose English is poor) where grade adjustments such as Boost practices might be defensible? For example, could an instructor modify the criteria for just a portion of the overall course grade in special cases (e.g., the portion based on class participation for students whose spoken English is poor, or the gymnastics performance required of a student who has a physical disability)?

Case 9-6. Stifling Multicultural Perspectives

> Students who ask questions in Professor Local's class about the cross-cultural implications of various theories and research findings are told, "Time doesn't permit discussion of those issues," or "Those issues aren't really relevant to today's topic." When students from other countries or geographic locales attempt to interject their culture's point of view into class discussions, they are ignored. When a student says, for example, "In my country we do it another way," Local dismisses the student by saying, "I'm sure that is very interesting, but we have to move along."

Diversity of expression in the classroom can be an enriching, energizing experience for the students as well as for the instructor. Many educators and policymakers are calling for increased attention to multicultural educational experiences for very practical reasons. Students are often woefully lacking in a global perspective, yet occupants of the planet are increasingly interdependent. In many academic areas, multicultural applications of theory and research are integrated into textbooks and ancillary materials. In some disciplines, an entire course or some degree of integration of multicultural applications are required in the major.

Local may be reacting, at least in part, to his own knowledge-based insecurities by suppressing students' interest in information that he has not mastered. This does not absolve him of the responsibility for becoming acquainted with relevant multicultural applications. Ethical guidelines require instructors to take necessary steps to remain current in their disciplines.

Professor Local sends a contrary message to his students, namely that "different" is not important enough to warrant a forum. Local apparently neither understands nor accepts that students can sometimes be as much an educational resource for him as books, journals, or his peers. He has made the poor decision that pertinent other-cultural commentary is neither productive nor germane. This message may undermine the self-confidence of some students or reinforce the biases of those with very restricted viewpoints. (See also 1-2.)

Discussion Questions

1 Suppose that Professor Local refuses to incorporate multicultural issues in his course, arguing that forcing him to do so violates his academic freedom. Is this an appropriate argument? If not, how should colleagues in his department respond?

2. What risks are associated with requiring faculty who are unsympathetic or insensitive to multicultural issues to cover these topics in their courses? How might these risks be minimized?

3. Should the inclusion of multicultural perspective be integrated into *every* course? What kinds of courses would be exceptions?

4. How do you integrate multicultural content into your courses? If you do not do so, why not?

Case 9-7. Use of Word Definition Assistance During Exams

> English-as-a-second language (ESL) students in Professor Webster's classes are allowed to use English dictionaries during exams. A student has complained that native-born students are disadvantaged because they also have an occasional need to know word definitions to fully understanding an exam question.

All students should be evaluated on the basis of their actual performance rather than on extraneous conditions. The question, then, is the extent to which limitations in English vocabulary, by both English language and ESL students, are extraneous. Because the technical vocabulary of the course is obviously relevant to the mastery of the subject matter, students should not normally have access to special assistance when the meaning of a word or term is fair for testing. However, most abridged dictionaries (either definition or translation) do not include the technical vocabulary. Hence, access to them typically gives students no special advantage. By contrast, ignorance of nontechnical words could artificially lower exam scores.

Access to nontechnical definitions could be provided by allowing all students to bring small (abridged) dictionaries, providing dictionaries in the exam room, or telling students that they can ask for definitions during exams. The last two provisions have the advantage of preventing less-than-honest students from hiding crib notes in dictionaries. ESL students should be conversant enough with English to understand an exam monitor's explanation of unfamiliar words. Ways to minimize the problem from arising during an exam are to use the most common appropriate wording when constructing exams and to include brief definitions in the exam itself for more difficult or less-familiar words. (See also 9-4 and 9-5.)

Discussion Questions

1. How much help with the English language should an instructor be expected to provide to ESL students? What are the students' responsibilities?

2. Should instructors allow extra time for ESL and other disadvantaged students who do not make special arrangements for their exams with the appropriate office (e.g., Office of Disabled Students)? Why or why not?

3. Are there nontechnical words that every college-level student should know, at least when in the context of an exam question? For example, if a student asks for a definition of "pervasive," are we obligated to define it?

4. Have students who have mastered better vocabularies earned an advantage on exams? Does providing word definitions for some students unfairly neutralize that advantage?

Case 9-8. Penalizing the Honest Student

> Professor Scorer returned the first test of the semester to his students. Ann Tegrity approaches him after class to inform him that an error in addition he awarded her three too many points out of the 100 points possible. Scorer tells Ann that she can keep the three points because it is his policy to reward honest students who report errors in their favor. Other students waiting to

> speak with Scorer overhear this conversation and protest
> that his policy is unfair because it gives a student points
> that she did not earn. Scorer agrees that honest students
> get extra points, but it balances out because students who
> do not report such errors in their favor also get points
> that they have not earned.

Although all instructors should encourage honesty in their students, we do not believe that Scorer's approach is the best way to do it. Although, as he says, dishonest students can receive unearned points by concealing advantageous errors, his actions do not honor other students whose exams were scored correctly. Also, if Scorer assigns final grades based on the average class score or some other norm-referenced criterion, Ann's extra points could conceivably lower other students' grades.

We recommend that Scorer reduce Ann's test score by the three erroneous points. We take this position for two reasons. First, as we have noted, it is the fair thing to do for honest students. Second, it appears to be what Ann expects to happen, given that she brought the error to Scorer's attention. At the same time, Scorer can reinforce Ann's honesty by expressing his admiration of it. If relevant, he can even point out to her that these are the kinds of situations that come to instructors' minds when they are writing letters of recommendation because they are clear indicators of the student's integrity, a trait about which graduate, professional schools, and prospective employers often ask referees.

Such errors should be avoided. Double-checking hand scored papers takes very little time.

Discussion Questions

1. How should students who reveal a high sense of integrity be rewarded?

2. How would you handle Ann's revelation?

Case 9-9. Instructors With Bad Attitudes About Students

> "Narcissistic," "uninspired," and "lazy" are some of the
> terms that Professor Lunk constantly uses to describe
> the contemporary college student. He often tells his
> classes how much they disappoint him and how he worries
> that they are too "soft-headed" to make it "out there."

Professor Lunk's demeanor extends beyond impatience and a healthy concern for his students' performance and future. Lunk is abusing his position of trust. He is a poor role model to boot, because generalizing these pejorative labels to all students creates an exaggerated stereotype that is no more accurate than saying that today's college-level faculty are narcissistic, uninspired, and lazy. Negative feedback to students should reflect relevant comments about their overall performance on a specific piece of work, not in reference to them as members of a generic group. (See also 1-3, 3-1, and 7-2.)

Discussion Questions

1. What are some ways that negative feedback can appropriately be handled when most students in the class perform especially poorly on an assignment? Should instructors ever openly express extreme disappointment in their students? Why or why not?

2. What is the appropriate venue for college-level educators to express what they see as disturbing, general trends in contemporary students? Can this be done in the classroom? Under what circumstances?

3. Some information, despite its negativity, may actually help students gain insights into their behavior or futures. How does one draw the line between passing along useful insights and inflicting insults?

Academic Dishonesty

Dealing with students who cheat is one of the most stressful aspects of the teaching profession (Whitley & Keith-Spiegel, 2002). Some instructors are known to ignore even strong evidence of cheating, perhaps because it is too onerous to deal with or perhaps because pursuing the issue is difficult if students deny the charges. To ignore evidence of cheating, however, is unethical because it harms honest students and subverts the purposes of higher education.

Teachers often feel personally violated and mistreated by their dishonest students, reacting with feelings of anger and disgust (Johnston, 1996). These feelings may make it difficult to respond thoughtfully to suspected cases of academic dishonesty, leading to the ironic possibility that an instructor might respond to an unethical act in an unethical manner. In addition, instructors are faced with the problem of deciding whether an act of academic dishonesty has occurred and, if so, what to do about it. Evidence is often not clear-cut or easily verifiable. These issues are addressed in this chapter.

Case 10-1. Impermissible Collaboration

Professor Webmeister assigns his class members to independently complete and print the results of an information search on the Internet. Although Webmeister stipulates that the assignment is to be done independently, two students turn in identical printouts. These students are friends who often sit together in the classroom, and Webmeister suspects that they collaborated. As a strong believer in the benefits of collective decision making and egalitarian learning

environments, Webmeister decides to bring the matter to the entire class and ask them as a group what she should do about the fact that two (unnamed) classmates turned in identical products on the assignment.

Even though the students are friends and might have collaborated inappropriately, before jumping to any conclusions Webmeister should first have spoken to the students separately to learn how they created the assignment and if they collaborated. If they deny working together, Webmeister can ask each student to explain (or demonstrate at the computer) what key words and search engines were used, and what other decisions she made. It is possible that by following identical "default" steps (same search engine, same links) these students could have generated identical outputs independently. If the students insist that such identical products were simply a coincidence and Webmeister finds no "smoking gun" to contradict this claim, their work should be accepted as submitted.

For future reference, instructors should make absolutely sure that students understand the procedures entailed in an assignment and the opportunities and expectations it provides for them to demonstrate their creativity and originality. In a case like this, instructors should point out that printouts are unlikely to be identical and review in class what constitutes plagiarism on the Internet. Students could be required to submit a journal or diary detailing the decisions and procedures they used in completing the assignment. Another lesson here is that instructors need to have more than a minimal amount of experience and understanding of technical materials and procedures (like navigating the Internet) when they assign (or allow) students to use these resources. Instructors must have some basis to backtrack through a procedure and understand what results were more and less likely to have happened by chance. Some students are very sophisticated about these technical procedures, and instructors need to understand these methods well enough to evaluate the integrity of students' work.

We have serious reservations about Webmeister's decision to involve the class in resolving this situation because it reverses (or at least confuses) the roles and responsibilities of the instructor and the students. The pair suspected of cheating will be extremely uncomfortable with this process, and their identities may eventually become known. Most or all of their peers will be uncomfortable being placed in the role of grand jury and will probably wonder, "Why is the instructor asking us what she should do?" Agreeing in advance to abide by the class's decision is risky. The only specific suggestions may be trivial at one extreme, draconian at the other, or not permitted by school policy. Rejecting such solutions, however, would make a mockery of the idea that the class is directly participating in solving the problem. Private discussion with colleagues would be an excellent way for a hesitant instructor to decide what to do.

Discussion Questions

1. What if this or any other form of suspected academic dishonesty occurs at the very end of the term, and there is no opportunity to speak with the students before grades must be turned in?

2. Students differ markedly in their computer and Internet access and experience. To be fair, should an alternative assignment that does not involve Internet access be offered to students? Or are Internet literacy and use required skills in this age?

3. Most students may rely on the Internet as their primary source of information. Do educators have a responsibility to create assignments that require consulting print media and library resources?

Case 10-2. Cheating or Not?

> Professor Hesitant notices that Cribby Note spends considerable time glancing around during an exam. Afterwards a student informs Professor Hesitant of her suspicions that Cribby appeared to be looking at a little piece of paper on the floor. However, because it could not be proven with certainty that Cribby cheated, Professor Hesitant did nothing.

Without harder evidence, there is probably nothing that Hesitant can do about Cribby, although one wonders why Hesitant did not watch Cribby more carefully once he started "glancing around." Because Cribby's accuser could be mistaken, it might not be proper to confront Cribby directly, even in private, with an unsubstantiated accusation.

Hesitant can take some action at this point, however. He should remind the class about the ethics of cheating and the institution's policy about it. He can point out that certain behaviors (e.g., looking around the room) could give the appearance of cheating and lead others to doubt one's integrity. At a minimum, Hesitant should monitor exams more closely. Hesitant should also explain to the accusing student why he cannot take direct action and what he intends to do in the future. It takes courage for a student to come forward, and such acts should receive an affirmative response.

Instructors are obligated to evaluate students on the basis of their true performance levels. The duty becomes stronger if Hesitant uses relative, rather than absolute, grading criteria because an artificially high grade of a student pushes other students' grades down. Prevention is the best means of minimizing the distress of dealing with the possibly dishonest student. Stating one's stand on academic dishonesty, defining academic dishonesty in concrete terms relative to the class, assuring that academic evaluations and grading practices are fair, changing exams and assignments each term, and monitoring exams carefully are among the techniques that reduce the incidence of cheating. (See also 10-6.)

Discussion Questions

1. How "hard" need the evidence be before one accuses a student of cheating? What are some examples?

2. Should Professor Hesitant have informed Cribby of his and the other students' observations? What are the advantages and disadvantages associated with sharing one's mere suspicions with the student suspected of cheating?

3. If you are suspicious of a particular student early in the term, what appropriate precautions can you take to help ensure that the student will not cheat, or at least will not go undetected?

Case 10-3. Protection Against Cheating Students

> On exam days in his large lecture classes, Professor Guard creates three versions of his multiple-choice tests, checks the student's photo ID cards as they enter, requires all carry-in items to be left at the back of the room, and arranges for two additional monitors to pace the aisles. Any student who appears to be looking at another's paper has the exam removed on the spot and must appear in Guard's office for discussion and disposition. Students he judges to have cheated are given Fs in the course.

Cheating is mentioned consistently in reports on the status of contemporary higher education as a crisis on college campuses. Furthermore, faculty and administrators are increasingly criticized for failing to detect and follow through on instances of suspected cheating. Thus, Guard cannot be faulted for his careful attention to a serious problem. It is an ethical responsibility to curb academic dishonesty. But, has Guard created an environment that hampers students' ability to perform adequately on examinations? We have concluded that, with two exceptions, Guard's tactics do not cross any ethical or legal boundaries.

The point at which Guard removes a student's paper raises a serious question. If seats are crammed together, then peeking is more likely. However, it is also more likely that normal movements of human heads may cause false judgments against innocent students. If an innocent student protests and demands a hearing, as an innocent student should, and the student prevails, Guard himself can be penalized for not allowing the student to complete the exam.

Regarding the removal of the exams of suspected cheaters, to be fair as well as self-protective, the exam paper should be confiscated only if there is very strong and tangible evidence of cheating, such as crib notes in the student's lap. Otherwise a possibly innocent student would be unable to complete the exam.

Classes held in huge auditoriums pose a special dilemma because seats cannot be moved apart. Using multiple versions of the exam is recommended in such situations so that those attempting to cheat will likely copy useless information. In smaller classes, monitoring by one person who is not engaged in another task is usually sufficient to dissuade peeking. Because students cheat more often when the monitor is a student, it is recommended that instructors be in the room, ideally slowly scanning the test takers. Caps with bills should be disallowed during exams because students can look down and view neighbors' papers (or anything else in the area) without being detected.

We also recommend against a faculty member independently assigning a grade of F in a course, based on academic dishonesty, even if the institution allows it. Review boards are increasingly viewing faculty members as competent to impose penalties when cheating occurs on a specific piece of work (an academic matter) but not to impose a broader penalty (e.g., an F in a course). Such severe penalties are disciplinary in nature, and faculty members are not the authorized agents of discipline. Check your institution's policy before handling any case of suspected academic dishonesty on your own.

Professor Guard's tactics create another potential problem. Students who would never consider dishonest acts are subjected to a system that appears to assume otherwise. Guard should discuss his anti-cheating methods with the class and assure honest students that his system is designed to protect their efforts, not to insult them. (See also 10-4.)

Discussion Questions

1. What about the opposite situation, in which the instructor informs the class that he trusts them and then leaves the room for periods of time during exams? Is this a responsible practice?

2. Some institutions allow instructors to handle cases of suspected cheating on their own, without referring the cases to a formal hearing board. What are the advantages and disadvantages of this policy?

3. Do you believe that the presence or absence of an honor code at the institution make a difference? How so, or why not?

Case 10-4. No Exit: Preventing Cheating

> **Professor Hold does not allow students to leave the classroom during exams because they might cheat. Once a student with a chronic health condition was forced to leave the room permanently before she had finished the exam. Another time, a student with a bad cough disrupted the entire class for almost 15 minutes because he did not want to fail the exam by temporarily removing himself from the room.**

Like Professor Guard (see Case 10-2), Hold has instituted a strict policy to prevent cheating. However, this case more clearly illustrates how too-rigid policies harm innocent students. Students with legitimate special needs should be able to take an exam in an environment that does not threaten their class standing. Professor Hold should be sympathetic to such students' needs even though it may mean extra work for him, such as finding an alternative testing situation for a student with a health-related need. And, whereas it is appropriate to remind students to use the bathroom facilities or get a drink of water before the exam, he should realize that his policy can unfairly penalize a student with a compelling urge who is forced to turn in an exam prematurely. (See also 10-3.)

Discussion Questions

1. If you wanted to institute a policy similar to Hold's, but with some exceptions, what would those exceptions be? Could the legitimacy of a requested exception be determined?

2. This case and Case 10-2 deal with some extreme measures for preventing cheating. What other less drastic measures can prevent and detect cheating during exams?

3. How do you monitor your exams?

4. What do you do when you see a student who is behaving suspiciously during an exam?

Case 10-5. Handling Suspected Plagiarism

An undergraduate student's paper is flawless and sophisticated. Professor Load is suspicious that someone other than the student created it. However, it could have come from anywhere, and the already busy Load has no idea where to start looking. He decides to give the paper a C grade because that is the grade the student received on all of her exams. Load assigned her final grade without ever expressing his suspicions directly to the student.

This type of suspicion is both common and, indeed, frustrating. Professor Load reads a paper exemplifying the best of what he is looking for only to suspect that a student's product of this quality is improbable. Load must somehow reconcile two very different performances by the same student. The problem of insufficient time to get the full story before final grades are due (or, if ever) complicates his decision-making process.

Although some students perform better on papers than on exams, a very large disparity does raise a red flag. Nevertheless, this student must be presumed innocent until Load seeks out more information to confirm his suspicions. Students must be evaluated on their actual performance on course assignments, and that means, at this point, that Load has no basis for assigning a C grade to work that would normally receive a grade of A. Ethically, Load is required to get to the bottom of this awkward situation *before* assigning a final course grade to this student. If insufficient time is available, the student could be assigned an Incomplete until Load and the student resolve the matter.

If Load asks the student how the paper was researched, including some questions about the content, the matter could be quickly resolved. It is unlikely that anyone who plagiarized an assignment would be able to intelligently discuss the content. Students often confess to their inappropriate appropriation of content at this point. The course syllabus could note that students *may* be called in to discuss the content of their writing assignments. This could even help reduce temptations to plagiarize as well as preventing students from feeling singled out if ever called in to discuss their papers.

Finally, just as the Internet has provided a quick way for dishonest students to create papers, it also provides a means of detection. Sometimes plagiarized papers can be readily identified by entering in a short string of words, using a search engine, such as GOOGLE. Or, for a reasonable fee, academic institutions can purchase access to services that are reasonably successful at tracking down plagiarized content posted on the Internet. (See also Case 10-6.)

Discussion Questions

1. Assume that Professor Load calls the student in to discuss the paper. The student says that the ideas are hers, but that she had a friend rewrite her first draft because her writing skills are poor. The student provides evidence that the ideas are hers (e.g., research notes in her handwriting, the first draft of the paper) and can answer questions about the content of the paper. Has the student provided a good case for a lesser penalty? Would it be a sufficient penalty to have the student rewrite the paper herself for regrading?

2. Should Professor Load's reaction be different if the assistance came from a writing clinic established by the institution? Does Load have a responsibility to discuss with the writing clinic staff the kinds of assistance he considers to be appropriate?

3. What if the student is not a native speaker of English? It is permissible for the student to arrange for extensive editorial help with writing assignments?

Case 10-6. The Plagiarized Thesis

Gary Goniff gives what he describes as a draft of his undergraduate honors thesis to his thesis advisor, Professor Danno, a month before Goniff is scheduled to graduate. When Danno reads the thesis, it reminds him of an earlier, unpublished doctoral dissertation. Danno obtains the dissertation in the university library and finds that Goniff copied large sections verbatim without indicating that these passages are quotations and without citing the dissertation as a source. When Danno confronts Goniff, Goniff denies that he plagiarized anything. Rather, he says, he was just using

the dissertation as a guide for organizing his thesis and
was going to paraphrase the copied sections and cite the
dissertation as their source when he created the final
draft. Danno is unconvinced by Goniff's explanation,
but unsure about how to handle the situation.

This case raises two ethical issues: Goniff's apparent plagiarism and
Danno's supervision of Goniff's work. Although many first-year college
students do not understand what plagiarism is, seniors should already be
fully aware of the nature of plagiarism and how to avoid it. Should Danno
file formal plagiarism charges against Goniff with the university's judicial
board? That depends on the circumstances. If Goniff appears to be truly
ignorant of what constitutes plagiarism, then admonishing Goniff to
rewrite the thesis properly may be appropriate, although advanced
students' denial of the meaning of plagiarism is rarely credible. Of course,
if university rules require that all suspected cases of academic dishonesty
be pursued through formal judicial procedures, Danno should follow the
university's procedures.

If the plagiarism appears to be intentional, Danno should file a formal
charge of plagiarism and tell Goniff that he is doing so. Any other course
of action would reinforce Goniff's dishonesty. Again, however, we must
include a caveat. If the university's definition of plagiarism states (or
strongly implies) that plagiarism occurs only when assignments are
submitted for credit, the argument that what Goniff submitted was "only
a draft," even if only a quick but devious response to the accusation of
dishonesty, could be persuasive to a formal hearing board. In that case,
Danno should consult with his department chair or the administrator who
oversees judicial procedures for advice on how to proceed.

In any case, Danno should retain a copy of Goniff's draft as evidence,
should that ever be necessary to disclose. This particular incident might
have been avoided if Danno had provided more intensive supervision for
Goniff, such as requiring outlines, bibliographies, and drafts of the various
sections of the thesis as they were completed. We believe that instructors
have an obligation to educate their students not only in the content of
their areas of expertise, but also in academic and professional ethics. This
ethical education should include informing students of what is expected
of them and continuous monitoring to ensure that they carry out these
responsibilities in an ethical manner. (See also 10-5.)

Discussion Questions

1. We suggested different actions depending on whether Danno believed

Goniff's plagiarism to be intentional or based on ignorance. How does one decide whether plagiarism, or any other ethical lapse by a student, is intentional or unintentional?

2. We indicated that instructors have a responsibility for the ethical education of their students. How do you communicate information about plagiarism to your students?

Case 10-7. Cheating on Homework Assignments

> To give students practice on the skills being taught, Professor Homer assigns many graded homework assignments. Several students complain that other students cheat on these assignments, using such means as getting answers from organizational files, sharing answers, and getting unauthorized help from reference librarians. Homer acknowledges that cheating is probably occurring, but claims that there is no way to control it.

Cheating on homework is endemic among students. But, contrary to Homer's view, quite a bit can be done to control or at least diminish its impact on honest students.

First, the problem of organizational files can be dealt with by frequently changing the assignments. Although this process can be laborious, it is also effective, and honest students will benefit from the instructor's extra effort. In addition, changing assignments facilitates the detection of cheaters who (as happened in one of our classes) copy answers from files without checking to see if the questions had been slightly changed in a way that would render the file answers incorrect. Homer could watch for unauthorized collaboration by being alert for answers that are suspiciously similar when some variation is expected. He could also keep file copies of submitted homework and make students aware of his file by requiring them to turn in two copies of each assignment. In addition, Homer can inform the reference librarians about the types of assignments that require library use and what kinds of assistance are and are not permitted. This procedure not only reduces the likelihood of unauthorized help, but it also protects the library staff from being caught in the middle of a dispute.

Professor Homer could also encourage students in advance to complete the work themselves by including the skills practiced on the homework assignments in tests and informing students that such questions will be on the tests. Students who do not do the homework themselves will be less likely to pass the equivalent portions of the tests. Homer can also try to ensure that the homework assignments are meaningful and, importantly, *perceived* by the students as meaningful rather than mere busy work. Finally, in computing final grades, Homer might give appreciably more weight to tests and in-class assignments, thereby reducing the impact of points based on homework on final grades. (See also 10-1.)

Discussion Questions

1. The chances of getting caught for cheating on homework assignments are very low. For this reason, some of our colleagues hold the opinion that those who copy miss out on learning and let it go at that. Given the difficulties in monitoring how homework is done, is this an acceptable argument?

2. Copying homework is seen by most students as a very minor discretion. Do you agree?

Case 10-8. Detecting Bogus Student Excuses

> The day before the big midterm exam, Professor Bump receives a message from four students explaining why they will not be showing up to take it. Gus says his grandmother just died, Tylena says she has a migraine headache that will likely last for several days, Pally announces that he must rush to the side of his best friend from high school who has been in a terrible automobile accident, and Otto claims his car broke down that and he cannot get it fixed in time to get to the exam. Professor Bump dislikes giving make-up exams, but he also does not want to punish students who offer legitimate excuses. He decides to excuse only those students who can provide definitive proof that their reasons are factual. All four students complain that Bump is being punitive, heaping additional problems upon them during difficult times.

Perhaps Professor Bump has read the survey research suggesting that over 50% of student excuses are bogus (Caron, Whitbourne, & Halgin, 1992). Instructors should be concerned about this form of deception for three reasons:

1. Students are attempting to deceive them;

2. Successful deceit reinforces dishonest behavior; and

3. At least some other students would have welcomed extra study time, and perhaps benefitted from it, had they decided to be dishonest.

Whereas we do not advocate the elimination of make-up exam options (see 5-6), we do encourage faculty to take the excuse dilemma seriously. We do not view Professor Bump's actions as unduly punitive. Gus can turn in a funeral card. Tylena may have more difficulty proving the existence of this particular headache, but she could show the instructor a prescription or a note form the doctor that she does, indeed, suffer from migraines. Pally can provide documentation that such an accident occurred, and Otto can show Bump the car repair bill. Even though such verifications can also be forged, this policy probably cuts down on the number of bogus excuses offered in the first place.

In any event, every instructor should put their policy about missed exams and assignments in the syllabus. Prewarning about the requirement for required validation of absences may actually help prevent bogus excuses. Furthermore, holding students to a high level of responsibility facilitates their maturity. (See 1-5, 1-6, 1-7, and 1-8 for other cases dealing with excuses for absences. See 5-6 for a case about strict make-up policy.)

Discussion Questions

1. How do you handle students' excuses for requesting more time to accomplish course requirements?

2. What if Gus forgot to get a funeral card, Otto's parents threw away the repair bill, Tylena does not have a documented history of headaches, and Pally says that the two parties in the accident simply agreed to fix the very minor dents in their own cars. How far are you now willing to go to verify the excuses?

IV

Outside the Classroom

Availability
to Students

Although instructors have a duty to make themselves accessible to students at times other than before and after class, this chapter explores how this is to be accomplished in a fair and ethical manner. Such considerations may be particularly important in our growing technological age because the kinds of interactions students expect may be changing rapidly. Several of the cases have to do with reasonable accommodations for students with the instructor's chosen office hours and the availability of the instructor through telephone or other electronic means. Also considered is whether unintentional bias may result from what happens during more casual, out-of-class interactions.

Case 11-1. Failing to Meet Office Hours

> Professor Empty's students often find a little note saying "No Office Hours Today" taped on his door. When confronted by a student about the difficulties in making contact, Empty replies that most of the time no one comes by, and he has lots of other things to do.

Most postsecondary institutions set policies for the minimum number of weekly office hours that instructors must hold. Empty's practice is neither acceptable to his institution nor his students. If circumstances arise that prevent an instructor from keeping office hours (e.g., the only time available for a medical appointment conflicts with posted hours, or an important committee meeting intervenes) students should be informed in advance, if at all possible. An announcement could be made in a class meeting before the canceled office hours. If feasible, such announcements could be supplemented with electronic mail or an electric bulletin-board posting. Canceled office hours should normally be made up by scheduling additional hours that day or week if students have needs to see their instructor. Or perhaps a special effort (e.g., telephone appointments) can be arranged to provide alternate times for students who planned to come in the day of the cancellation.

We haveheard from many colleagues that office hours for undergraduates are the loneliest time of the day. But, when we ask students why they do not avail themselves of opportunities to discuss academic matters in private, many say, "Instructors are always so busy. I feel like I am interrupting them." The fact still remains that students need opportunities to see instructors privately. And, we might add, what differentiates campus-based educations from distance learning is the personal connections we are able to make with our students. We can encourage students to take advantage of office hours. We recommend informing students that whereas we do take care of pending matters if no one is waiting, as soon as someone comes by our attention will shift over to their needs. (See also 11-2.)

Discussion Questions

1. If one finds that office hours must be altered substantially and permanently from the hours that appear in the syllabus, what is the best way to go about doing this?

2. How does one handle the student who abuses office hours? This may be the student who seems insensitive to the fact that several other students are waiting or who comes by very frequently wanting to discuss off-task topics.

3. What is your practice regarding making time available for your students?

Case 11-2. Inconvenient Office Hours

> Professor Dawn Twilight holds her office hours from 6 to 7 a.m. on Tuesdays and Thursdays, and from 5 to 6 p.m. on Mondays and Wednesdays. If anyone mentions that her hours are inconvenient, she reminds them that she holds more office hours than are required by campus policy and that if students are sincere about meeting with her, they can.

Assuming that the institution does not have policies about the times of day that office hours are to be held, Twilight is within her rights to hold odd office hours. However, her spirit seems disagreeable, and her underlying motivation appears to involve a desire to avoid students.

Office hours are of no value to students if they cannot get to them. Although we are not required to accommodate every student's schedule, attempts should be made to arrange times when most students are likely to be around. (See also 11-1.)

Discussion Questions

1. Must instructors hold office hours in the evenings if they teach evening classes?

2. How much effort should instructors make to accommodate students who cannot meet their regularly scheduled office hours?

Case 11-3. Refusing to Return Students' Messages

> A student complains to a department chairperson that Professor Nocall never responds to numerous phone and email messages. The student believes that ignoring a student's request for a response to a matter related to the class is a breach of academic responsibility.

Instructors have a responsibility to be available to students for regular time periods at reasonable times during the day. Once that criterion has been met, however, instructors have no further *ethical* responsibility to respond unless, perhaps, some compelling condition exists (e.g., a student in the hospital requests information about reading assignments). Many instructors, however, are very accessible and promptly return telephone calls or e-mail messages. Some even allow students to call them at home. This student may have had experiences with instructors with generous policies and may believe them to be normative.

Returning phone calls from students who are often unavailable to answer the phone is frustrating, and we do not fault instructors for failing to make multiple attempts. However, email is an easy way to fulfill student needs that are focused and require a brief response. Professor Nocall would not have been unduly inconvenienced by hitting the reply function and providing his student with the information she needs. If it is not feasible to respond by email, he could ask his students to come by during office hours.

Misunderstandings about how one is willing to respond to phone calls or email messages are easily precluded by including policies about student-instructor out-of-class contacts in the course syllabus and presenting them during an early class session. Periodic reminders may be necessary.

Discussion Questions

1. Should instructors be required to attempt, at least once, to return a student's telephone call?

2. Should departments establish policies regarding responses to student inquiries? Why or why not?

3. How do you handle messages from students that request a response from you?

Case 11-4. Rights of Working Students

Working students complain that they cannot complete their chosen major in a timely period because core classes are not held during the evening hours. These students assert that offering evening courses is an ethical responsibility of every department.

Teaching evening or weekend classes is unappealing to many faculty members. However, the assumption that education is a privilege around which students must accommodate the rest of their lives needs to be balanced by the reciprocal notion that educational opportunities should be accessible to those who need (and are paying for) them. It asks too much of otherwise qualified students that they give up their jobs (or a full paychecks) to be able to take a required class. We believe that higher education has an obligation to serve the entire spectrum of eligible students, not just those whose lives are uncomplicated enough to permit easy scheduling.

For their part, employers are often willing to accommodate employees' educational needs (e.g., with flexible work hours). Similarly, we conclude that postsecondary educational institutions have a responsibility to rotate required courses into evening and other "off-peak" hours over a reasonable period of time (e.g., offering each one at least every 2 years) so that working students or students who are relieved from child-care responsibilities when a spouse comes home after work can complete their degrees eventually. Instructors who volunteer to teach a core course during less conventional hours might be offered some additional considerations (e.g., choice of courses and teaching hours otherwise).

Discussion Questions

1. To what extent must other related services (e.g., instructor's office hours, practice studios, or laboratories) be provided during evenings or weekends for students in the classes that meet during those times?

2. Because the burdens of offering courses at irregular times fall more heavily on smaller departments, should these departments receive any recompense?

3. With more adult learners opting for the "virtual university" marketplace and private "certification" programs, should traditional institutions of higher education position themselves to compete with any of these alternatives in terms of convenience, cost, and curricular offerings?

Case 11-5. Spending Fun Time
With Students on Campus

> Professor Fresh is 27 years old and well liked by the students. In his first year of teaching, he has become one of the most popular instructors on campus. Three or four students are usually in his office, often talking about rock groups, sports, and other nonacademic topics. Fresh can often be found around lunchtime at a crowded table in the student cafeteria. Some of Fresh's colleagues believe that he is overstepping the boundary between faculty member and friend.

Professor Fresh and Professor Nocall (Case 11-3) are at opposite ends of a continuum. Assuming that Fresh's classroom lectures are pedagogically sound, that he is fulfilling his other academic duties, that he is open to all students that come by (as opposed to a favored in-group of students), and that the traditional office hour purpose is served as needed, Fresh is not acting in an unethical manner. One of the reasons that Fresh is an effective teacher may be that he is in touch with what interests his students. His colleagues might benefit from incorporating some of his openness to interaction with the students rather than complaining about his behavior.

We are assuming, however, that Fresh has a personal life independent from his students. Examples have been brought to our attention involving instructors whose social lives consisted entirely of student interactions on (and off) campus. This situation is not a healthy for an instructor, and it is potentially precarious for the unwitting students upon whom such instructors are emotionally dependent. (See also 9-3.)

Discussion Questions

1. Suppose Professor Fresh's rapport with his students becomes such that they invite him to their parties or to the local bar. What are some of the danger zones that Fresh might anticipate in socializing with students off campus and after hours?

2. What are the limits of faculty conversations with students? For example, are there topics that should be avoided?

3. Do educators like Fresh create a backlash effect? That is, do students become critical of those who maintain traditional, formal relationships with their students? Would such comparisons show up in students' teaching evaluations of the more traditional instructors?

Student–Faculty Interactions

What ground rules should guide instructor-student interactions outside the familiar confines of the classroom or laboratory? For example, how much latitude do we allow ourselves to enjoy unscripted, after-hours contact with students? The specific cases in this chapter involve responding to inappropriate student behavior outside of class, contact with students on "their turf," hosting students on "our turf," and sharing mutual interests with students after hours. The symmetries across this collection of cases offer a useful reminder that outside of our structured academic world we can be as unsure of ourselves as students are of us, and yet it is nearly always our responsibility to observe the boundaries that define our relationships with them.

Such situations can raise profound ethical issues. Even though instructors are encouraged to view out-of-class opportunities as a way of enlarging the teaching and mentoring role played in students' development, it is important to keep in mind that transgressions could have untoward effects, not just on a student or instructor but also on third parties.

Case 12-1. Handling Prejudicial Statements Made by Students Outside Class

> As Professor Norman and his students were leaving his classroom, he overheard one White student whisper to another, "That [racial slur label] in the back row wore the same ugly shirt yesterday."

This type of disturbing scenario is somewhat difficult because the remark was not made during class time and was most probably meant to be a private communication. The instructor might choose to ignore it. But because the instructor was not purposely eavesdropping, and because freedom of speech can be argued as applying to people who hear others exercising their free speech in a public setting, the instructor could not be faulted for reacting to the remark. The instructor might say, right then, "Please do not use that language around me. I do not find that characterization of other human beings acceptable." If it is appropriate to the course, the instructor might take time in an upcoming class period to discuss language choice and its social effects on the user and others.

Instructors do serve as exemplars, whether or not they welcome that status. This kind of situation provides an opportunity to exercise strong, in vivo ethical leadership by having the courage to speak up. (See 2-10 for making prejudicial statements in class.)

Discussion Questions

1. Some prejudicial remarks would probably be judged by most to be more offensive than others. Suppose the instructor had overheard, "That tub of lard . . . ," or "That redneck . . . ," or "That ugly chick . . . ," or "That boozer . . . ." What determines whether a response seems very much in order?

2. In general, do instructors have an ethical obligation to speak out whenever a remark that unfairly stereotypes a certain group is made on campus?

3. How would you have responded to the scenario presented in this case?

Case 12-2. Attending Students' Social Events

Professor Gregarious is popular among students and is frequently invited to their parties. He often attends them.

University communities encourage faculty/student interactions during and after hours. There is nothing inherently unethical about attending student social events unless this association in some way leads to advantage in a class for some students as opposed to others. However, Gregarious must adhere to standards of good taste and decorum, avoiding any situation or behavior that is illegal or inappropriate.

Gregarious and all colleagues are less exposed if the parties they attend are sponsored either by a department or some student group, such as a campus club, or a special activity associated with events that mark student achievements such as a senior recital or research paper presentation. In addition, the old saw about safety in numbers applies here. Attending a party where other colleagues are present is preferable to being the only faculty member at a strictly social student party. (See also 11-5, 12-3, and 14-7.)

Discussion Questions

1. Suppose Gregarious finds himself at a party in which he observes underage drinking? How should he respond? Does he have legal or ethical obligations? Should he simply leave?

2. What about situations in which students invite all department faculty to an off-campus party, but Gregarious is the only one who shows up? Based on the "safety in numbers" principle, should a faculty member always determine if colleagues will attend beforehand?

3. Are there limits on faculty-student socializing? Suppose Gregarious decided to invite all of the students in his small seminar to his home for dinner or to his boat for the day. What are the advantages and disadvantages of *initiating* private, social interactions with students?

Case 12-3, A & B. Shared Interests After Hours

> **Professor Love plays tennis every day. His student also plays tennis every day. They decide to play tennis together every day.**
>
> **Professor Birdie, an avid golfer, has a student in his class who works at Birdies country club. Birdie and the student often leave after class and head for the course where they play nine holes together before the student starts work.**

We waffle a bit on these two cases, primarily because we cannot expect either instructors or students to desist from engaging in their favorite outside activities on their own time. They will likely be in the same space at the same time anyway, especially if they are in smaller communities. In both situations, however, the *preferable* arrangement is to find other partners, especially if the students are undergraduates in the major.

To further evaluate these cases, we need to know whether the participants reach a level of intimacy that would create favoritism for the student or a disadvantage for other students in the class. Other students, if they know of such a steady arrangement, may feel resentment, even if the instructor attempts to remain scrupulously objective. Or, what if the student makes a remark that is objectionable to the instructor during their recreational sessions? Or, what if a highly competitive instructor is constantly losing to the student? Is the student placed at risk of some form of retaliation when it comes to assigning grades?

What if the student is at the graduate level? It is well known that instructor-student relationships often become increasingly more collegial as a graduate student progresses through the program, and the nature of the relationship often expands. However, caution is involved because as relationships become more complicated, so does the potential for conflict. (See also 11-5, 12-2, and 13-8.)

Discussion Questions

1. How close are these scenarios to dating a student?

2. How much does the sex (or sexual orientation) of the student-instructor pair matter?

Case 12-4. Students at Professional Meetings

> Professor Hilton takes a group of students to the regional professional meeting every year. They dine together in the evenings and often proceed to a party or go sight-seeing.

Facilitating students' attendance at professional meetings is a positive endeavor. It is an excellent way for students to make valuable contacts that may serve them well in the future, to learn directly from scholars in their discipline, and to gain experience with this particular facet of professional life. Because the setting is usually a nice hotel or convention facility and far from home-base, interactions between instructors and students are likely to be less formal. Liquor is usually available during organization-sponsored social hours.

Hilton must retain an appropriate role with his students, ensuring that what happens at the meeting in no way jeopardizes his professorial relationship with them. Hilton has an excellent opportunity to model for students how to conduct themselves in a professional manner in ambiguous circumstances. It can also be noted that this experience is a good way for Hilton to learn more about the students' expectations, needs, and interests than he can ever learn in the classroom. Such information could improve Hilton's teaching. (See also 11-5, 12-2, and 12-3.)

Discussion Questions

1. Should Hilton always make sure that he is with a group of students rather than just one?

2. What if the students, after having a couple of drinks and feeling very relaxed, begin to talk about Hilton's colleagues in personal and sometimes demeaning ways? How should Hilton respond?

3. Some instructors who used to take students to professional meetings have ceased the practice for fear of sexual harassment or other complaints. How real are these dangers, and how can their occurrence be minimized?

4. Should students under the age of 21 be excluded from instructor-organized trips or professional meetings?

Case 12-5. Off-Campus Class Sessions

> Professor Homegather held the last seminar meeting in her own house. She served punch and cookies. Although the discussion was a bit more informal than usual, the nature of the final examination was described and questions about how to study effectively for it were answered. While walking toward the door, a student tripped over the edge of a carpet and fractured his foot. The student sued Homegather, charging that the carpet was not properly secured and that lighting was insufficient.

Many of us who attended smaller liberal arts colleges have fond memories of informal classes held in our instructors' homes. Some institutions still encourage this practice. This scenario, adapted from an actual incident, throws a wet blanket on a type of event that some instructors are willing to provide for their students.

We see no ethical problems with the practice of holding informal classes off campus as long as institutional policy does not prohibit it. Because important information (i.e., final exam hints) was imparted, however, Professor Homegather does have the obligation to ensure that every student has a way of getting to and from her home or that students can promptly get hold of the information some other way.

The litigiousness rampant in today's society certainly poses a risk that must be considered by faculty members as well as by the institutions themselves when students are required or requested to leave the campus compound. Field trips and volunteer or off-campus study programs, although often offering enriching opportunities that cannot be simulated on campus, may run the same risks of liability. We recommend consulting the university's policies or legal counsel before planning off-campus events.

Discussion Questions

1. Assume that Homegather's institution encourages such gatherings and provides liability coverage for them. Do any other problems remain?

2. Do you see a problem with meeting a class on a special occasion in an off-campus restaurant or coffee house?

V

Relationships in Academia

Relationships in Academic

13

Multiple Role Relations and Conflicts of Interest

Among the most difficult situations to navigate in any professional setting occur when faced with multiple-role relationship conflicts. Multiple-role conflicts exist when the demands and obligations of the primary role are compromised by the demands and obligations of one or more additional roles. College and university campuses are fertile ground for multiple-role relationship conflicts.

Like in other professional settings, explicit hierarchies exist in which some members are supervised or evaluated by other members. Conflicts arise because the power imbalance appropriate to the primary relationship may be inappropriate in the context of the secondary relationship. The dynamics of these mixed roles are complex, and their impact can have negative influences at many levels.

Complicating the matter further is the implicit mandate that instructors should be actively involved with students beyond the role of teaching content. Postsecondary educators are also expected to facilitate students' socialization into their adulthoods and the world of work and to model good citizenship. To accomplish these roles, it is necessary to spend time getting to know students as individuals and to interact with them outside the classroom. In other words, instructors are *expected* to engage in multiple roles! The challenge, then, becomes how to act as teachers, advisors, mentors, confidantes, and role models to students while maintaining appropriate boundaries in the process.

The cases in this chapter highlight the many ways that multiple-role relationships between students and instructors can occur in the campus environment. Our commentaries focus on ways to avoid risky multiple-role relationships, ways to extricate oneself from inappropriate multiple-role situations that inadvertently arise, and ways to manage unavoidable multiple-role relationships that carry a risk of harm.

Case 13-1. Look Who Showed Up in Class!

> Professor Buddy is surprised to see that his best friend's daughter, whom he has known since she was a baby, enrolled in one of his classes. She smiles widely as he speaks, calls him by his first name, and, he suspects, has told the other members of the class stories related to their preexisting relationship.

The circumstances Professor Buddy faces create a problem if favoritism leads, even without Buddy's full awareness, to unequal evaluation performance. The same dynamic could exist with students Buddy knows and likes from previous classes, students who have served as baby sitters in his home, or students who were close friends of Buddy's daughters or sons. Indeed, such occurrences are common when many local students attend postsecondary institutions in smaller towns and cities.

Buddy's simplest solution is to attempt to convince the student to enroll into a different section of the course. If that cannot be accomplished, ground rules need to be created that minimize any appearance of favoritism, not to mention any actual advantage for the student. Buddy must insist that the young woman call him "Professor," "Mister," "Doctor Buddy," or whatever is customary. He needs to discuss the relationship complication with the young woman and insist that her behavior conform to the demands of the appropriate roles while she is in class. However, Buddy should have foreseen his current dilemma and headed it off before classes began. (See also 13-2.)

Discussion Questions

1. Suppose Buddy and his family frequently celebrate holidays and birthdays with this student and her family. Should there be new, temporary ground rules for out-of-class contacts between Buddy and his friend's daughter?

2. What levels of familiarity between instructors and students are problematic when a prior relationship exists? That is, what are examples of potential (or easily perceived) conflicts-of-interest that would require a sharp limitation of the instructor/student role?

3. Most college-level teachers in smaller cities or towns or with a large local population of students have run into the kind of situation discussed in this case. If you have faced such a dilemma, how did you handle it?

Case 13-2. Friends Enrolled in Class

> Professor Pal's good friend Marci wants to take Pal's class. Marci tells Pal, "I've been hearing about your work for so long, and it's so interesting. I will have no problem getting an A."

Many adults return to take college level classes. This phenomenon is enriching for mature students as well as for instructors. However, when a good friend or other close relative wants to take a class, in most cases he or she should be discouraged.

Pal should explain to Marci that her presence could make things difficult for both of them. Marci has already waved a bright red flag, namely her expectation of receiving a top grade in the class. Pal should remain firm in dissuading Marci, even if Marci complains. Pal can help Marci find another class that she would find valuable.

The situation becomes more complicated if the friend or close relative is in a degree program that requires the course and only one person teaches it. If this dual-role situation is unavoidable special safeguards should be explored, such as conscripting an outside third party to help monitor the student's progress. (See also 13-1.)

Discussion Questions

1. Occasionally our colleagues from other departments want to audit or take one of our classes for credit. What unique problems does this pose for the instructor?

2. Suppose Marci is the spouse of a high-ranking university administrator or someone above you in the chain of command. What additional safeguards should be established for dealing with this awkward situation?

Case 13-3. Lending Money to Students

> Bob is a pleasant student who is down on his luck. His roommate left in the night with back rent due. Bob was laid off his job. Professor Kindly loaned Bob 500 dollars until Bob could get back on his feet.

It is easy to view Professor Kindly as a Good Samaritan. But Kindly's loan set up an ethically problematic bond between the teacher and student, one that could lead to potential coercion. Kindly might, for example, devalue Bob's work because Bob gets behind in his payments, or enhance his view of Bob's work if Bob is ahead with payments. Such biases might operate without Kindly's full awareness. Further, even if Kindly could be completely objective, any course evaluation of Bob could appear to reflect considerations other than Bob's performance.

Professor Kindly would be wiser to help Bob find emergency funds from the financial assistance office or from a commercial banking institution. As it stands now, Kindly has created an incompatible dual-role relationship as Bob's teacher and Bob's banker.

The size of the loan can also be an issue. Although a small loan (such as a quarter for parking) is unlikely to create any problem, even if the student forgets to pay it back, 500 dollars is a sizeable amount. It does not appear that Bob will be able to pay back Kindly's loan any time soon. How will Kindly react when he sees Bob wearing a new leather jacket or overhears Bob describe his new stereo to a friend? Might such resentment create an influence when it comes time to assign grades? Helping a student is rarely considered to be an ethical problem, but the creation of circumstances that might lead to disaffection or coercion is.

Discussion Questions

1. What if a student lost her purse and is hungry for lunch? The sympathetic instructor loans her 5 dollars. Three weeks pass and the instructor is rather irritated that the student has not repaid the loan, even though it is small and the instructor can afford to forgive it. How would you feel if this happened to you, and what would you do?

2. Is there ever a situation in which an instructor could borrow something from a student without creating an ethical conflict?

3. What complications can arise when colleagues make loans of money or other goods to colleagues? What precautions might preclude ethical dilemmas when loans among colleagues become complicated (e.g., money is not repaid as agreed upon or the borrower loses or breaks a borrowed object)?

Case 13-4, A & B. Gifts From Students

Professor Vogue compliments a well-dressed student of very average academic ability on her lovely outfits. The student tells Professor Vogue her clothes are from her father's store and that Vogue is welcome to come in and choose anything she wants at her father's wholesale cost.

> After the final exam, but before grades were submitted, Professor Likeable found a relatively expensive watch in his mailbox from an admiring student. A card praised Professor Likeable for making a big difference in the student's life through his encouragement and kindness.

We believe that the opportunity to shop at a considerable discount at a student's father's store should be declined while the student is in class, or if there is any possibility the student will be in another class at some time in the future. Anything other than refusal will lead to an appearance of impropriety.

Can Professor Vogue accept the offer at some later date? If the student has graduated, or if the offer is made not just to Vogue but to other faculty members as well, circumstances could permit an acceptance. However, even these criteria may still leave a question of indiscretion, especially if the student needs a letter of recommendation in the future. Vogue is wisest not to accept the offer.

Professor Likeable is in a similar situation. The gift is expensive, the timing is questionable, and the possible precedent could be a bad one. The gift should be returned. The instructor might write a thank-you note, declining the gift but reinforcing the thought that kind evaluations from students are much appreciated.

Small (inexpensive) presents are probably acceptable as long as they are tokens of appreciation at a suitable time (e.g., upon graduating). A predicament, however, is agreeing on what constitutes "small." A coffee cup, a little box of candy, or even the proverbial teacher's apple would likely meet the "appropriately small" criterion. Also, sometimes students make gifts especially for instructors (e.g., a needlepoint pot holder with the school logo). To refuse such gifts could be upsetting to the givers and cause more problems than would acceptance. If a instructor is unsure about a gift, consultation with colleagues is advised.

We should note that even a small gift could be inappropriate if it is too personal, although drawing that line can also be difficult. We heard of a student who gave her instructor a pair of boxer shorts sporting printed red ants. We do not know the motivation for selecting this particular gift (the instructor was *not* an entomologist), and it may well have been as simple as giving something cute to a favorite instructor. But, the student's choice was not appropriate.

Finally, it should be noted that sometimes students offer opportunities that lead to an educational advantage for an entire class or department. As an example, using a father's contacts to enable the class to take a special field trip would normally be appropriate. Even then, however, care must be taken to objectively grade the student who facilitated the opportunity. (See also 17-5.)

Discussion Questions

1. Would giving an instructor a bottle of cologne or a single red rose be examples of questionable gifts? What other determinants (e.g., the gender of student and instructor, nature of previous interactions) might make such gifts appropriate or inappropriate?

2. What if a student gives a gift that is unsuitable for any other recipient because it has been personalized? For example, what if a silver dish was engraved with the instructor's initials? Or a personal message was written inside a very expensive book? Should this change the response that the instructor might make? If so, how?

3. Do you have experiences with a student gift? If so, how did you handle it?

Case 13-5. Selling Goods to Students

> Professor Testerosa was finally able to buy the car of his dreams. His struggling student assistant wants to purchase his older but still sturdy automobile. Testerosa sells it to the assistant at "medium blue book."

A primary issue in this instance is good business ethics. As long as Testerosa offers the car at a fair price—which "medium blue book" is likely to be for a car still in good shape—there is probably no ethical risk. However, Testerosa should encourage the student to consult a mechanic or others to ensure that the transaction is fair. A professional inspection also protects Testerosa from any later complaints of pre-existing problems. Testerosa should not finance the purchase. (See 13-3.)

It is preferable to avoid any financial transactions with students currently enrolled in one's classes. We also do not recommend selling goods to students as the typical method of disposing of used items. If the student is ultimately dissatisfied with the purchase, the complications can be troublesome to everyone concerned. Difficulties are more likely with temperamental items that students might want to buy, such as automobiles, computer hardware, stereo equipment, television sets, and musical instruments. However, we recognize that it is sometimes to the students' benefit to have access to opportunities that instructors are able to offer, assuming that fair business practices apply. (See also 13-6 and 13-8.)

Discussion Questions

1. What if a student buys a television set that was working fine when it was picked up from the instructor, but a week later the student claims it doesn't work and wants her money back. The instructor knew it was in good working condition the day the student put it into her car and drove off. What should the instructor's response be?

2. Should instructors ever purchase items from students? What might the ethical complications be?

Case 13-6. Bartering Services With Students

> Clera is a student in Professor Trade's class. Trade provides consultation for Clera's parents' business in exchange for manuscript preparation by Clera. Clera's parents give Clera a break on her rent for her participation in this arrangement. Everyone seems happy.

Despite the current level of satisfaction with this three-way deal and the seeming arm's length between Trade and his student, bartering arrangements involving students can go awry and should generally be avoided. What if Clera's class or manuscript preparation performance erodes? What if Clera's parents become dissatisfied with Trade's advice? Would Clera's standing with her instructor then be jeopardized? Given that Clera is stuck between her parents and her instructor, could Clera afford to assert herself if she becomes dissatisfied with any aspect of this arrangement?

Clera is clearly the least powerful component in this multiple role relationship and she probably has the most to lose if any facet turns sour. We believe that Trade should have never become involved because Clera's vulnerability is obvious. Efforts should be made to minimize multiple-level relationships with students because the potential for exploitation is ever-present. (See also 13-5.)

Discussion Questions

1. Is there a way that the players could have remained the same, but the potential complications with ethical features greatly minimized?

2. Would it be markedly different if Clera was a student in Trade's department, but not currently in one of his classes? Or, if Clera was a student, but not in Trade's department?

Case 13-7. Asking Favors of Students

> The affable Professor Needy often and repeatedly asks
> students for favors such as driving him home when his
> car is not working (as it frequently isn't), taking his
> books back to the library, or picking up food from the
> cafeteria. His requested favors are usually small, not
> requiring students to go much out of their way. Students
> do not complain. In fact, they are often eager to help
> him out.

The words "often" and "repeatedly" are the key to this case. It appears
that Needy acts in a nonreciprocal manner, using his status and influence
to obtain services from students on a regular basis. Such a pattern is an
inappropriate use of the inherent teacher-student power differential. By
contrast, *occasionally* requesting small favors probably would not be out
of the ordinary and would not pose any ethical concerns. For example, if
a student says, "Well, I'm off to the library," it would not be unreasonable
for the instructor to ask if the student could also return his book.

True emergencies would also be an exception. A ride home is a favor,
but a ride to the hospital in an emergency situation is quite another matter.
Instructors could never be faulted for asking for help from anyone in the
immediate vicinity should a dire need arise.

Discussion Questions

1. Is it more appropriate to request small favors from graduate students than
from undergraduate students?

2. Say that Professor Needy asks one of his students to arrive at his office 10
minutes before class every morning and help him carry class materials to the room.
Would that be acceptable and, if so, under what conditions? Would it make a
difference if Professor Needy had asked for a volunteer (thus giving all students
an opportunity to respond) rather than approaching one in particular?

3. What if Professor Needy asks to borrow small amounts of money from
students for the food machines on a fairly regular basis, claiming that he "has no
change today." Assuming that he does pay it back promptly, is there a difference
between borrowing money and the types of "gofer" favors asked in the case text?

4. Do students in Needy's class realistically have an option to exercise
voluntary and informed consent to such requests? That is, could a student
comfortably decline Needy's requests?

5. For faculty members not raised during the "computer age," students are often in a position to be very helpful. Furthermore, students seem to get a kick out of helping their computer-perplexed instructors, and usually do so with enthusiasm and pride. Is asking our students to help us become more computer literate inappropriate or a win-win situation? What factors might determine the appropriateness?

Case 13-8. Businesses That Could Involve Students

> Professor Rent owns several houses close to the university and has converted them to student housing. Occasionally tenants will also be students in Rent's classes. This semester Tardy and Thunder are student-tenants. Tardy is always late with her rent, and neighbors often call Rent to complain about Thunder's loud stereo.

Educators are not prohibited from outside investments or commercial ventures. However, this case illustrates why conflicts of interest should be avoided if at all possible. Rent's difficulties with unsatisfactory student-tenants could transfer (or appear to transfer) to his evaluations of their work. The students may feel unable to consult with Rent about course matters because of their poor standing with their landlord. Also, students tenants may not feel comfortable complaining to their professor about any problems they are having with their living quarters.

Furthermore, suppose the problem is the opposite. The students are likeable and make excellent tenants, and Rent would very much like to retain them, but poor performance in his course is jeopardizing their prospects for staying in school. Might Rent be tempted to help them out with some extra generosity in their final grades?

The primary purpose of any relationship Rent has with students who attend his institution is the students' education. Whether he wants to or not, he is also expected to model for students how to handle professional relationships (student-teacher, tenant-landlord) in an ethical manner. Rent courts a conflict-of-interest by failing to institute measures that would have distanced his outside enterprise from the students. Even though outside management might decrease Rent's profits, this mechanism would defuse the problem. If it is not possible to create some form of reasonable arm's-length distance between instructors and students when a longterm, continuing conflict-of-interest may be at issue, we believe that the outside business opportunity should be avoided. (See also 13-5.)

Discussion Questions

1. How could Rent minimize conflicts?

2. Are the ethical problems reduced if Rent screens prospective tenants to minimize the likelihood he will ever have them in class? Is it fair (or even legal) for Rent to discriminate against students who need housing simply because he might evaluate him at some point in the future?

3. Suppose Rent owns a small business in town that sometimes employs students. What problems may result if Rent hires (or avoids hiring) students who are in his class or majoring in his department?

Case 13-9. Instructor–Student Love Relationships

> Linda Lovaprof, an undergraduate student, lives with Professor Shackup. Although she takes no classes from him, she often attends parties where Shackup's colleagues are present. Linda has classes with a few of these other instructors. Other students believe that Linda probably gets an advantage simply by the added social exposure.

The affair between Linda Lovaprof and Professor Shackup might put any of Shackup's colleagues in an uncomfortable situation. Case 13-10 deals with problems involved in dating one's students, an activity that is not recommended. Here we focus on the impact of such relationships on colleagues and other students.

The couple's attendance at faculty parties almost certainly creates dual-role problems for Shackup's colleagues. It is unlikely that Linda, because of her major study area, can avoid taking classes from Shackup's colleagues. Therefore, ground rules should be established to minimize the appearance of favoritism, although this matter is touchier because revealing Linda's relationship with the instructor may create more problems than it solves. In such circumstances, colleagues might do best to avoid Linda outside the classroom, by not inviting Linda and Professor Shackup to any social events, or by staying away from her if she attends.

This case reveals how dual-role relationships can be problematic beyond the individuals directly involved in a dual role. If Shackup is despised by one or more colleagues, how might this affect the young woman who is in this colleague's class? If Shackup is a powerful member of the department, what are the personal consequences of avoiding the young woman at parties and other events or of giving her other than a glowing grade?

When faculty members are married to students in the same department, similar problems can exist. However, this situation may be viewed as a more stable and acceptable, especially if the couple was married before the spouse enrolled in a program. Even when the couple is married, however, there may be dual-role concerns. One of our friend's provided an anecdote that reveals how uncomfortable colleagues can be with student partners. The colleague of our friend was married to a student who was not doing well in her class. The colleague brought his wife to the New Year's Eve party, hosted by our friend. The friend reported feeling ill-at-ease all evening and confided to us, "I'm not going to host another department party until that woman graduates." Thus, despite the marriage bond, if a spouse is in a colleague's class, the couple would do well to consider the awkward position in which they may place others, and proceed accordingly. (See also 13-10.)

Discussion Questions

1. Whereas Lovaprof and Shackup are presumed to be consenting adults, is Shackup himself at risk should the young woman later become dissatisfied with the relationship and press sexual exploitation charges?

2. What if Shackup and Linda effectively hide their relationship? Is this a recommended solution?

Case 13-10. Dating Graduate Students

> Professor Amore dates students provided that they meet all of the following criteria: (1) They are graduate students; (2) They are not enrolled in his classes; (3) It seems highly probable that they will not be in any of his future classes or under his supervision; and (4) They have initiated a clear indication of an interest in seeing him socially.

No matter how careful Amore might be, or what standards he establishes for dating relationships, potential danger lurks in dating any student in one's own department. The power differential that characterizes teacher–

student relationships can come into play and will continue to exist as long as the student is enrolled in the program, regardless of whether the individual is a student in Amore's classes. Moreover, other interactions the student might have, such as those with Amore's colleagues or even among the student's friends, may be affected by the relationship. (See 13-9.) The key is to avoid any conflict that might jeopardize this student's (or any other student's) opportunity to learn in an unrestricted environment.

We would also note that the academic level (i.e., undergraduate vs. graduate student) may be increasingly spurious. The growing numbers of re-entry, nontraditional undergraduate students may well be far more mature than many traditional (ages 21– 25) graduate students.

For mental health professionals in psychotherapeutic situations, there is to be no sexual contact with patients at any time during the therapy according to both ethics codes and most state laws. Some people believe that current students should be viewed in exactly the same manner as current psychotherapy patients. The admonition by the American Psychological Association (1992) is that once a patient has concluded therapy, an extended "cooling off" period should exist before any sexual contact. Adapting the flavor of this ethic to the teacher– student situation, sexual contact with should, at a minimum, wait until after the student graduates or otherwise finishes the program. The waiting period policy, however, fails to address any future need for a letter of recommendation or other form of support. Because dating relationships often break apart, usually not comfortably, a student risks losing a potentially important professional supporter for now and even into the future. This risk can be avoided if Amore finds his dating partners elsewhere.

Discussion Questions

1. This case deals with students in Professor Amore's department. Does the situation change if the student is from an unrelated department?

2. What if Professor Amore is not a faculty member, but a staff member (such as the department's lab coordinator, office supervisor, or equipment manager)? Amore is, nevertheless, invited to many faculty social gatherings. In this situation Amore feels free to date any students in the department regardless of their specific circumstances. Does this present a problem for the students he dates, the faculty, or other students from the department?

3. Are instructors fully capable of assessing clues that students are expressing a romantic interest in them? What other dynamics could be operating?

Case 13-11. Hiring Students From Personal
Funds for Nonacademic Jobs

> Professor Labor hires students he knows well and trusts
> to baby sit, stay in his home while he and his family are
> on vacation, and do gardening and repairs around his
> house. He often expresses to his colleagues how
> fortunate he is to have such a responsible but financially
> needy pool of workers so readily available.

This scenario is so common that it may surprise readers to see it in an
ethics casebook. Although such arrangements usually work out very well
for all concerned, ethical risks are ever-lurking and should be considered
whenever students are hired from personal funds to do personal work.

The scenario is not explicit regarding whether Labor's students are
currently in any of his classes. We recommend that students currently
enrolled, or likely to enroll, in our classes should not be hired to do work
in instructors' homes. Unfortunate outcomes can cause serious conflicts.
The student could fall down your stairs and break several bones. The
student's work performance could be subpar, causing an unpleasant
dispute when the student asks for payment. Something very valuable
could be missing from your house. The student could lose your dog while
walking it. None of these examples are fanciful. Each has occurred to
colleagues we know. Each caused difficulties that interfered with the
primary role instructors have to educate and objectively evaluate students.

If students attend the college or university but are in different
departments or highly unlikely to take the hiring instructor's course, the
ethical risks are markedly minimized. (Note: Tax issues may pertain and
are not covered here.)

Discussion Questions

1. Some students are so in need of funds that they will work for far less than
the job is worth. For instructors, is there an ethical responisbility to pay students
the going wage for what work they do, or is this situation just another perk? How
should the exact amount of the wage be determined?

2. Have you had experiences, either good or unfortunate, with hiring students
to do personal work for you?

14

Interprofessional
Relations

College-level educators have traditionally enjoyed considerable autonomy and often work   independently of one another. Yet, virtually all of us must have at least superficial relationships with our peers and other departmental and campus personnel. In what ways might loyalties or obligations, such as to a student on one hand and a colleague on the other, come into conflict? How can such conflicts be managed? This chapter depicts instances of overheated personal or professional disputes as well as faculty who refuse to participate with their peers on committees or other group tasks. Additional cases cover triangles involving two instructors and a student, being privy to information about unethical or embarrassing behavior by a colleague, and allowing stereotypes and biases to color our personal views of colleagues. As shown elsewhere in this casebook, the fallout from ethical problems like these is unpredictable and can radiate from the immediate situation to cause damage to others.

Case 14-1. Sour Grapevines

> Professor Bada suspects that Professor Bing voted against his internal grant proposal. So, when a colleague tells Bada that she heard from a neighbor who heard from another neighbor that Bing's wife was having an affair with the provost, Bada took notice. Bada had reason to doubt the story, but passed it along to other colleagues anyway.

Gossip, for better but often for worse, appears to be part of human nature. Good and bad news about the community is passed along, and the more fascinating the news, the more efficient its spread. An ethical problem arises when one tells, as fact and with malintention, a damaging story based on flimsy, hearsay evidence. In smaller locales or tight-knit academic communities, malicious rumors can cause considerable, undeserved harm. Reversing untrue stories proves next to impossible. Despite Bada's suspicion that Bing may not have supported his grant proposal, the ethically principled response would be to express doubt about the veracity of the story and to refrain from retelling it. (See also 14-2.)

Discussion Questions

1. Does harmful gossip plague your institution?

2. When you hear a campus story you know is false or distorted, do you attempt to correct it?

3. Can gossip reflecting something negative about individual faculty, staff, or administrators be ultimately valuable for the academic community? In what ways? What might be a fictional example?

Case 14-2. Warring Colleagues

> Professors Cain and Abel do not get along. They intimidate and embarrass each other during faculty meetings and gossip behind each other's backs. Sometimes the stories are quite foul or intrude deeply into personal matters. Their running feud is taking a toll on the department's morale, and students complain that both are cantankerous.

Professionals are supposed to show respect (or at least display overt behavior that suggests tolerance) for each other. This does not mean that they must *like* each other. However, conspicuous nastiness for no purpose other than to degrade a colleague is, in our view, unethical as well as unprofessional. Unfortunately, there seems to be an informal consensus that this kind of situation, in more or less extreme forms, is not uncommon on college and university campuses.

Harms extend well beyond the grief the primary actors heap upon each other. Students are short-changed because considerable energy is being diverted away from them. It is difficult on the enemies' colleagues, especially if choosing sides leads to a splintering within the department. Department spirit can be dampened, souring all teachers and affecting all students.

Institutional or departmental leadership should have the courage to take action to defuse the effects of feuding colleagues on the department.

Colleagues can be especially helpful if they make it known that they do not want to participate, even by listening to griping and gossip. Stronger sanctions, such as issuing a restraining order of sorts might ultimately be necessary, and such steps should be taken if the situation becomes intolerable. We know of a department, for example, that put the warring colleagues' offices in different buildings and required both to submit their comments in writing to the chair during departmental meetings. Sending the parties to sessions with a skilled mediator might prove successful if less formal mechanisms fail. (See also 14-1.)

Discussion Questions

1. Does the resolution plan for a situation like this differ for tenured as opposed to non-tenured and contract faculty members? More specifically, should uncollegial behavior by untenured and contract instructors be considered formally in the annual review?

2. What if colleagues intentionally shun both Abel and Cain? Is such behavior unprofessional or merely an acceptable behavior shaping technique?

3. Should salary sanctions (or related ones, such as ineligibility to teach summer courses) be used as a means of trying to change Abel's and Cain's behaviors? Should academic institutions establish policies allowing for this possibility in cases of entrenched and damaging uncollegiality?

Case 14-3. Colleague Interference

> Professor Collegial knew that the son of a member of her department was going to enroll in her class. She did not know the student and was prepared to treat the young man in an objective manner. What she was not prepared for was her colleague's intrusion into the process. He frequently asked her how his son was doing, requested a review of his exams, and once expressed that a paper on which his son had done poorly was a flawed assignment.

Although the father's behavior clearly violates Collegial's academic and employment rights, no single solution resolves all issues in this case. Professor Collegial may consider the following:

1. Approach the father and discuss the common goal of the welfare of the student.

2. Firmly refer the father to his son, explaining that to discuss his son's performance violates his son's rights to confidentiality.

3. Seek consultation from a colleague and/or the department chair.

4. Transfer the son to another class.

5. Bring a formal complaint against the father. It must be noted that the redress decision would complicate the matter considerably if the father is more powerful than Professor Collegial (e.g., a member of the promotion committee).

Collegial could capitulate, protecting her status in the department. But, this is a pale last resort that does not properly address—and probably rewards—the father's unethical interference.

Discussion Questions

1. Suppose another colleague is also having problems with the son and asks Collegial to discuss the matter, knowing that Collegial is also having problems with the son. How much can we share about students with others?

2. In most institutions, any member of the academic community may attend thesis defenses. Suppose the son is a masters student who is ready to defend his thesis, and Collegial is the committee chair. The student's father shows up ready to participate in the meeting. What would you do if you were Collegial?

Case 14-4. Stuck Between a Colleague and a Student

> Professor Middlestuck's disappointed advisee, Larry Scorched, shows Middlestuck a term paper he wrote for Professor Blue. Blue assigned Larry's paper a C minus. Larry believes Blue was biased against Larry's arguments because Blue favors genetic determinism and Larry's paper argued for strong environmental influences. Middlestuck briefly reviews the paper and judges it to be very well done. Middlestuck believes that Larry was ill-treated.

Academic ethics admonish us to respect the autonomy of our colleagues as well as to facilitate our students' educational development. Thus, this case poses an ethical dilemma for Middlestuck because cogent arguments can be made for both involvement and noninvolvement in the dispute between Larry and Professor Blue.

Most instructors do not have access to all of the information concerning the requirements and grading standards of courses taught by colleagues. On that basis alone, if Middlestuck feels strongly about the apparent biased evaluation that his student received, it is unwise for him to jump in prematurely with opinions about the grade that Scorched received, because Middlestuck has heard only the student's perspective. Middlestuck may opt for sharing his assessment of the paper with Larry if Middlestuck has accurate information about the assignment. Moreover, Middlestuck can offer Larry some ideas or options for finding appropriate relief from what may be an unfair situation. For example, Middlestuck might review procedures for filing a grade appeal, offer suggestions for ways Larry can approach Blue to request a re-evaluation of the paper and, under limited circumstances, might offer to serve as a mediator between Blue and Larry. (See also 14-9.)

Discussion Questions

1. What if Middlestuck was a faculty member in different department? Does this alter the interventions that Middlestuck might consider?

2. Imagine that Middlestuck decides to speak with Professor Blue about the paper. What are some ways he might approach Blue in a way that will not upset Blue?

3. Larry decides to file a grade appeal and asks Middlestuck to speak on his behalf. What considerations should influence Middlestuck's decision to do so?

4. The pre-existing relationship between Middlestuck and Blue would be an important factor in determining how Middlestuck responds to any matter involving a conflict. How would the approach change if:

a. Blue is a tenured full professor and Middlestuck is untentured?
b. Middlestuck is tenured and Blue is untenured?
c. Blue is known to be resentful and hold grudges for long periods?
d. Blue is a kind, gentle, apologetic man who is known for being fair to students?
e. Blue seems to be burned out and uninvolved with departmental affairs?
f. Blue is disliked by most students and most colleagues?

Case 14-5. Recommending
Colleagues to Students

> Professor Insider privately recommends one of his
> colleagues over another to students because, as he tells
> them, "One is far and away the better teacher."

Let us assume that Insider is sincere in his opinion, thus creating a difficult
situation in which one loyalty is pitted against another. On the one hand,
instructors should normally show outward respect for colleagues, and
Insider's insinuation that one instructor is not up to par could be construed
as disrespectful. On the other hand, if the unrecommended instructor is
indeed an incompetent teacher, Insider is helping students avoid a
potentially detrimental educational experience.

Some might argue that the student grapevine is sufficient to warn
students about incompetent, hostile, disrespectful, uncaring, or disturbed
instructors. Yet a browse through almost any instructor's teaching
evaluations reveals that the instructor one student rates as "poor" is another
student's "excellent." The same phenomenon may operate among
colleagues. We do not know, for example, the bases of Insider's judgment
of his two colleagues' abilities.

At the bottom line is the question, should instructors be in the business
of advising students about which instructors to take or to avoid? Our
response is a *very highly qualified* "yes," though not in Insider's brash way.
Our more intimate knowledge of our colleagues may allow us to help a
particular student link up with an instructor who is especially well-suited
to that student's special needs. For example, an instructor known to give
extensive special tutoring sessions may be recommended to a student who
seems likely to require such a service. Or a student with an intense interest
in some specific area might be directed toward the course section of an
instructor who is actively engaging in scholarly work on that topic.

Another approach would be to briefly enumerate the positive qualities
of the instructors the student is considering. Even if the list of positive
attributes is much longer for one than for another, the student is left to
make the choice. When any recommendations are based on a careful
consideration of individual student needs and are given in the form of a
suggestion (as opposed to Insider's uncharitable wording), ethical
problems are usually avoided. (See also 3-4.)

Discussion Questions

1. What if the instructor has information that a recommended colleague is

considering taking an extended leave, taking another job, or retiring, thus leaving the student in the lurch? Is the instructor making the recommendations at liberty to divulge this possibility?

2. What if Insider has confidential information that a colleague is being monitored as part of a sanction for showing bias against students with disabilities? Is it ethical to steer a disabled student away from that colleague's course without explaining why?

3. What should an instructor do with respect to a colleague known to make, in private, sexist, racist, or homophobic remarks? Is it permissible to steer affected students away from this colleague's courses?

Case 14-6. The Anonymous Charge

> **Professor Recipient finds an anonymous letter in his campus mailbox informing him that a colleague is a "rat who humps and dumps students right and left."**

Students have expressed to us that they feel they cannot make any open or public criticisms of, or charges against, instructors because the revenge their educators are in a position to take could result in even more damage. This dilemma has likely served to protect many instructors who should have been scrutinized.

Anonymous charges, however, are insufficient to substantiate an allegation. Recipient could, therefore, simply ignore the letter. Or, he may wish to show it to the colleague while making it clear that his motivation is not to accuse but rather to inform the colleague of an event affecting him. Unless Recipient has other information, he should assure the colleague that he need not defend himself. If the colleague is behaving inappropriately with students, learning that he is in danger of being exposed might have some salutary impact, especially if other colleagues also received letters. (See also 20-9.)

Discussion Questions

1. Are there any circumstances when anonymous letters should be given credence? Does the specific message or accusation make a difference?

2. Whether the letter is credible or not, does Recipient have an obligation to show it to someone? If so, who?

3. What are the arguments against showing the letter to the accused?

Case 14-7. Knowledge of Poor
Judgment Off-Campus

> Mary Jane offhandedly remarked to one of her instructors that Professor Hit attended a party where lots of students were present and that marijuana was smoked. Mary Jane seemed delighted that Hit joined in on the rounds.

The student might have found Professor Hit's behavior entertaining, but engaging in illegal behavior with students constitutes extraordinarily poor judgment. Hit should be told that renditions of the event are circulating and, if they are true, he has put himself at serious risk in more than one way. Furthermore, the reputation of the department and the institution is in jeopardy should Hit's behavior be made public. If Professor Hit fails to recognize the problems his behavior could cause, the department chairperson should be informed so that formal action can be taken. Finally, rather than being a "relevant guy," Hit is actually a very poor role model for students. (See 11-5, 12-2, 12-3, and 12-4 for other cases about outside social activities with students.)

Discussion Questions

1. Is Hit's presence at the party a where drugs are being used a problem, even if he does not participate in the illegal behavior? What would you do in that situation?

2. What if the adult students are not doing drugs, but are drinking liquor or watching X-rated video tapes?   Both actions are legal.   How should a faculty member respond?

Case 14-8. It's Not in My Job Description

> When attendance is taken in faculty meetings, Professor Shut is never there. Shut serves on no committees or other university posts. According to Shut, he was hired to teach, not to do administrative work or to sponsor clubs. He views himself as a dedicated teacher who intends to focus his efforts exclusively on the job for which he was hired.

Although taking on a college or university teaching position requires that helping students learn as our priority, institutions of higher education affect students in ways far beyond the classroom. The teaching staff should have input and influence throughout all functions of the institution. Active involvement in departmental affairs, institution-wide committees, and student activities are the mechanisms through which such influences are realized. Professor Shut fails to recognize, for whatever reason, that much of the impact that instructors have on students occurs outside of the classroom.

Conditions of employment may or may not specify which duties, other than teaching, are required of instructors. Nevertheless, Shut has drawn his calling much too narrowly.

Discussion Questions

1. What intervention can or should be imposed on Professor Shut?

2. What if Professor Shut has excellent teaching evaluations and students seem to flock to him? Should he still be admonished for his lack of campus citizenship?

3. Is it unethical for an instructor to err too far in the other direction, that is, becoming overly involved in activities, committees, and outside functions to the detriment of teaching responsibilities?

4. What if Professor Shut also has a large externally funded research program that provides paid research opportunities for many students in the department. Does this now excuse him from contributing to campus affairs?

Case 14-9. When a Student Informs
Us of a Colleague's Problem

> **A teaching assistant confides to another instructor that something should be done about Professor Spearmint. According to the student, Spearmint slurs his way through disorganized lectures and, despite attempts to cover up, his breath smells of alcohol.**

When personal problems conflict with professional responsibilities, instructors have the obligation to take action that safeguards students' welfare. The instructor in this case has a second-hand yet seemingly credible report suggesting that Spearmint is conducting his classes under the influence of alcohol. Furthermore, this practice appears to interfere with what Spearmint offers to students. The colleague might opt for approaching Spearmint directly, if the relationship with Spearmint is such that open discussion would lead to constructive solutions (e.g., Spearmint acknowledges his behavior as problematic and agrees to seek treatment). However, Spearmint may deny the student's report, or the colleague may feel the relationship she has with Spearmint is not conducive to a discussion. Spearmint may become abusive or threatening. Should untoward reactions occur, especially careful consideration would be called for. The colleague may want to pass the information to the department chairperson who is in a position to evaluate the situation systematically and take appropriate action, such as observing Spearmint's classroom performance or removing him from the classroom.

Fortunately, many institutions have recognized the need for identifying and assisting dysfunctional educators. Formal mechanisms may already be in place for dealing with student or peer reports of possible impairment, and a call to the appropriate office describing the problem (not necessarily revealing identities at this point) is a place to start. Such services highlight the need for ensuring that the students' welfare is protected and that the dignity, privacy, and welfare of impaired faculty are also considered. (See also 14-4 and chapter 19.)

Discussion Questions

1. Impairment resulting from substance abuse often results in noticeable signs. Other forms of impairment also exist, yet can be more difficult to detect. Examples include major depression and certain physical problems such as Alzheimer's disease. What criteria should instructors use to decide when to intervene when a colleague's performance appears to be impaired?

2. Colleagues are usually reluctant to confront their colleagues. How would you proceed with professor Spearmint?

3. As colleagues in a unit with a reputation to protect, to what extent are we our brothers'/sisters' keepers?

4. Does your institution have a program to assist colleagues with alcohol abuse?

Case 14-10. More Biased Assumptions

The undergraduate advisees assigned to Professor Wheel, a highly regarded scholar in his field, are all physically disabled. Wheel is a paraplegic. He enjoys advising students. However, he resents the seeming assumption that he is an expert in physical disability and that he, alone, is best suited to work with physically disabled students (and perhaps, by inference, less suited to work with able-bodied students).

Members of the academic majority group (White, male, and able-bodied) may often assume that instructors who represent another group may both be expert in their group status and make the very best role models for students in the same group. To stereotype minority group faculty (or women faculty) in that way is, perhaps unwittingly, insensitive. Furthermore, all students are disadvantaged if assigned to advisors who may not be the best academic mentors for them.

In this case, able-bodied students are denied easy access to Wheel, and disabled students are denied access to advisors who might provide assistance more relevant to their particular academic and career interests. If advisees are not matched (e.g., by request, similar interests, need for expertise in career counseling), then a random distribution of advisee assignments is probably warranted unless a particular advisor requests a certain type of student, and that assignment appears to be in the students' best interests.

Discussion Questions

1. A few students from a particular minority group approach the department chair and request that they all be reassigned to a faculty member who is also a member of that group, arguing that only members of their group will be sensitive to their needs. How should the department chair handle such a request?

2. Are there appropriate circumstances that warrant matching students according to ethnic, religious, or sexual orientation?

3. What if an advisor is expert in graduate school advisement? Would it be appropriate to assign only the best and the brightest undergraduate students to this advisor?

Case 14-11. Negative Comments About Another Specialty

Professor Adamant, whose specialty is neuropsychology, counsels students away from taking courses in clinical and counseling psychology, claiming them to be "soft-bellied." He tells students that if they want to be "real"

> psychologists, they will take only courses oriented toward the "hard" sciences. The clinical faculty members get wind of this advice and protest. Adamant responds that he can support his conclusions and that he "owes it to the students to steer them in the right direction."

Although Adamant is correct that courses in the physical and biological sciences are valuable to students, he is wrong to imply that such courses have a monopoly on scientific and intellectual rigor or that related professionals are not "real" professionals. Furthermore, Adamant's tactic and demeanor show disrespect for his colleagues. He breeds low morale and dissension, and his rigidity ultimately does not serve his students' individual needs and goals. He has his own point of view, to which he is entitled, but he expresses it inappropriately.

Academic advisors should tailor their advice to each student's circumstances and work with students' inclinations rather than forcing their own beliefs on them. For example, Adamant could point out that many psychological disorders have physiological components, and so indicate the usefulness to a clinician of a strong background in biology and neuroscience. It would be acceptable to present—with the prelude that a personal opinion is being expressed and that other points of view exist—the strengths and weaknesses of various specialties within a field. This expression of opinion can be voiced in a professional and respectful way and without resorting to pejorative language.

Adamant might also want to consider whether he is the best person to advise students whose interests appear to be very different from his own. It would be prudent to refer such students to colleagues in the students' areas of interest. (See also 3-4.)

Discussion Questions

1. What if Adamant has reasonably objective evidence, such as the results of an external review, that his colleagues are deficient relative to the accepted standards for their field? What are his obligations to his colleagues and to students in such a situation?

2. How best can faculty members remain true to their convictions and advise students whose interests are directly in conflict?

Exploitation
of Students

Financial and scholarly productivity pressures on faculty members are not uncommon. Unfortunately, such sources of tension can lead to engaging in activities that are ethically questionable. This chapter presents examples of how instructors can misuse students, often when they rationalize their actions in the course of fulfilling their own needs.

Case 15-1. Taking Over a Student's Idea

> Richie Bright submitted an outstanding research proposal as his senior honors project. After Richie graduated, Professor Loot conducted the study that Richie had designed, making very few modifications. When a colleague who had consulted with Richie mentioned the similarities, Loot explained that he had supervised the student from the beginning, so the idea was partially his. Furthermore, Richie had continued his studies in a field unrelated to this project. Finally, Loot noted that Richie did not have the skills to conduct the research or to write a publishable manuscript without considerable assistance.

This is not a case of outright plagiarism because Professor Loot was involved from the beginning and conducted the work that brought an idea to fruition. However, Loot still profited from the original effort of another without giving credit. This matter could probably have been easily resolved had Loot consulted Richie upon deciding that he wanted to implement Richie's design. Richie should have been offered direct involvement in the conduct of the research. In this case, it appears that Richie would have declined the invitation because his educational goals had since shifted. It is likely that some agreement about credit for Richie's original contribution could have been reached, such as a footnote in any published version.

That Richie did not possess the competencies to continue on his own is an irrelevant defense in and of itself because Richie might have resumed study of the same subject in graduate school, caught the interest of another faculty member, and run the study as his masters or doctoral thesis. Adapting from a senior project for such purposes is not unusual.

Students at any level can inspire us in ways that direct our own scholarly work. When that contribution is deemed to have had sufficient influence, instructors must assess objectively the question of the students' rights to involvement and credit. When in doubt, consultation with colleagues or the ethics code of the discipline may assist in resolving the matter. (See also 18-6.)

Discussion Questions

1. What criteria should be used to determine what kind of credit (e.g., authorship vs. footnote acknowledgment) students should receive for a publication to which they contributed an idea?

2. What if the replicated project is in the arts? How can one claim plagiarism of a painting, sculpture, musical theme, or theatrical idea if there is no exact duplication? What standards apply? For example, what if a photography instructor were to intentionally recreate a student's landscape photograph using the same location?

Case 15-2. Inappropriate
Handling of Disappointments

> The dean reneged on a promise to provide Professor Stubborn with a computer and upgraded laboratory space. Stubborn then refused to turn in the students' term grades to the registrar until the promise was made good.

Faculty members can have legitimate grievances against the institution's administration that cause frustration and anger. However, holding students' grades or any other "hostage" as a pressure point is inappropriate and unprofessional. (See also 6-8 and 9-2.)

Discussion Questions

1. What if, rather than holding students' grades hostage, Stubborn tells his students what happened and encourages them to write to the dean and the college president protesting the dean's treatment of Stubborn?

2. Would it be more acceptable if Stubborn takes his fight to the campus newspaper?

3. Is there ever a situation that justifies deliberately holding up grade submissions after the deadline?

Case 15-3. Outside Tutoring for a Fee

> **Professor Coacher offers private tutoring in accounting for a fee to students in his department, including students currently enrolled in his accounting courses.**

Profiting financially from current students is highly suspect. We are already paid to teach students what they need to know about what we are teaching them. Professor Coacher is vulnerable to a host of objections and charges, especially if the tutored students do better than the untutored students (which perhaps they should if he is any good at it). A conflict-of-interest situation occurs when money is exchanged, even assuming that the service is offered off-campus and after hours. If the tutored clients are not now current students, they may become Coacher's students later, raising the possibility of the expectation of special considerations.

It is certainly appropriate to help faltering students find qualified tutors. Instructors may also offer free and open review or tutoring sessions made available to all students. This activity would be considered a valuable service rather than a suspect business practice. (See also 15-4 and 15-5.)

Discussion Questions

1. Would it make a difference if Coacher were a part-time contract or adjunct faculty member?

2. Suppose Coacher has a colleague at another local institution who is also interested in tutoring for a fee. They agree to refer students to one another. Are there any ethical issues here?

3. Under what circumstances can Coacher ethically supplement his income by tutoring individuals for a fee?

Case 15-4. Using One's Own
Work as Required Reading

> Professor Author has written a textbook in his field and uses it as required reading in his class. One of his colleagues believes that Author's primary interest is the size of his royalty check.

An instructor may not adopt his own book simply as a means of making money. The use of one's published work as required reading need not, however, constitute a conflict of interest provided that certain conditions are met. These might include an evaluation of the text by colleagues or external reviewers, adherence to any institutional policy that provides criteria against which the text can be judged or conditions under which one may use work from which they benefit personally, and, most important, the *sincere* belief that the book is the best choice for the level and content of the course and that it will be used actively in the course. Failure to comply with some reasonable standards does constitute exploitation of students.

Making copies of the instructor's own work readily available in the reserve section of the library is also recommended practice when instructors assign their own textbooks. Some instructor–authors return royalties directly to students, others donate a portion of the earnings to a charity or purchase equipment for student use. These practices help obviate any criticism alleging conflict of interest.

Is an author obligated to return or refuse royalties? No, no more than he would be obligated to return royalties to another instructor's students if that instructor adopted the author's text.

Finally, institutions often have formal policies in place to deal with situations of possible conflicts of interest. Instructors should be informed about such policies well in advance because the approval process can be lengthy. (See also 15-3, 15-5.)

Discussion Questions

1. Does the price of the instructor–author's published work matter? Is there a difference, say, between a book that sells for $90 as compared to a small paperback that sells for $5.95?

2. Does it make a difference if the instructor's book is assigned as a "supplementary text" and not very actively referred to in the classroom or used for exam purposes?

3. Assume that the book is not part of the required or supplemental reading for the class. Is it then proper for an instructor to hold up his or her book in class and tell students that copies are available in the bookstore? That is, can the classroom be used as a forum to advertise one's product?

Case 15-5. Royalties From "Homemade" Reading Collections

> **Professor Collection puts together a group of readings and takes them to a print franchise near campus to "publish." Professor Collection adds a 15% royalty fee to the cost and requires the students in her large class to purchase copies. (Assume here that all permissions have been negotiated appropriately.)**

The selection of appropriate educational materials for a course is part of the job for which instructors get paid. If the packet is no more than a collation of the work of others and Professor Collection merely wants compensation for her trouble in gathering it, collecting royalties is unethical because it exploits the educational relationship the instructor has with students. If, however, she included *substantial* original commentaries on the articles, she could make a case for compensation for her original work. However, ethical issues still exist because she is requiring her students to purchase a scholarly product that will bring her personal gain without the peer review sought by most textbook publishers. (See also 15-4 for a related issue.)

Institutions may have policies regarding the creation and sales of such materials. Instructors should become familiar with such policies and adhere to them.

Discussion Questions

1. Is a price "mark up" appropriate if all proceeds are used for the class's benefit (e.g., paying for field trip expenses or consumable supplies)?

2. What if Professor Collection did not require that students purchase her product and did not test the students on any of the content, but recommended purchase by any student who was interested in more information? Are all ethical problems defused?

Case 15-6. Letting Go Is Hard to Do

> **Brigitt is a gifted senior who has been collaborating on scholarly projects with Professor Stuck for almost 2**

years. She has excellent grades and achieved very high Graduate Record Examination scores. When Brigitt brings up the subject of graduate school, Stuck attempts to convince her that she should continue to work with him for another year as a post-baccalaureate student. That way, he explains, she could get more relevant experience, allowing him to write a particularly strong reference letter for her.

This situation strongly suggests exploitation. Although we may mourn the departure of excellent students who continue their educations elsewhere—especially those with whom a good team relationship developed—this form of loss in inherent in the nature of the positions educators hold. It appears that Stuck is more concerned about his own needs than those of his student. He appears to have developed a dependency on Brigitt. If this is true, Stuck is acting unethically and unprofessionally by attempting to retard the continuation of his student's education.

Sometimes, we might note, an extra year as a post-BA student may be to a student's benefit. However, this advantage usually occurs because the student has some deficit (e.g., insufficient course work or experience) that will hamper chances for acceptance into an advanced program or employment. The extra year or two could bolster that student's record. Brigitt, however, is *not* one of those students.

Discussion Questions

1. What if it is Brigitt wants to stay for an extra year and continue to work with Stuck? Does Stuck have an obligation to strongly encourage Brigitt to get on with her education elsewhere?

2. Are there any circumstances that would justify a bright student like Brigitt staying on for an extra year (not leading to a degree or graduate level credit) to work with Stuck? What is a scenario that would make this extended alliance possible?

3. How can instructors deal with the inevitable loss of prized students in a way that protects instructors from separation pain and lowered morale?

Case 15-7. Selling Complimentary Books

Professor Pinmoney collects the complimentary books that publishers send to him and sells them to a used book vendor.

Publishers are usually responsive to faculty requests for examination copies of books and often send unsolicited books to instructors, hoping for a course adoption. This enormously expensive promotion and advertising process cannot easily be replaced, primarily because responsible instructors require an opportunity to review an educational product carefully before requiring students to learn its contents. The cost of complimentary textbooks is, of course, passed along to student purchasers.

Complimentary books do become the receiver's personal property. Therefore, it cannot be considered unethical to sell free books, especially those that arrive unsolicited. However, a moral alternative would be to return unwanted books to the publishers' field representatives or give them away to students, the departmental library, or worthy educational agencies.

The practice of requesting books from publishers for the sole purpose of selling them to used-book vendors is a tacky and unethical way of earning a few dollars at the expense of the publishers and, ultimately, of student consumers. Furthermore, a colleague who labored to create the work is deprived of hard-earned compensation.

Discussion Questions

1. How do you respond to the used book buyers who roam the hallways with little carts and hard cash?

2. If you solicit a book, carefully consider it, but do not ultimately adopt it, is there a moral obligation to return it to the publisher or dispose of it in some other way besides selling it to used book vendors?

3. Are there ethical differences between students selling their used books to the campus bookstore and instructors selling unwanted, complimentary books to used book vendors?

Case 15-8. Biased Evidence of Teaching Effectiveness

Professor Average is seeking tenure. She consistently receives mediocre student evaluations. The required evaluation form is brief, and Average believe it does not assess her teaching effectiveness. She asks several of her current and past students to write letters attesting to her teaching ability. She plans to add these to her personnel file.

We sympathize with this instructor's belief that mediocre evaluations from students do not necessarily reflect her effectiveness as a teacher. We are, however, concerned about her strategy. A tactic less likely to raise ethical problems would be to solicit letters of support from colleagues rather than from students. Or, if Professor Average does request letters from students, they should all be past students or students she is unlikely to teach again. Under no condition should any of them be currently enrolled in her courses.

It is very important that each of the students Average approaches be in a position to decline such a request or to write freely about the instructor without fear of retribution. A concern is that Average wants several letters (not just one or two) and that most or all of the students she is likely to approach are those whom she knew had liked her and valued her course. Can we really assume that none of these individuals would feel coerced by her request? It would not be unusual for some students to later want a letter of recommendation for graduate school or a job from this same instructor, and turning her down or writing candidly would jeopardize the reciprocity.

Another issue in this case is how these letters are presented to the tenure committee and what weight they are given. In principle, having carefully solicited letters of support from past students is no different from a job applicant soliciting letters of recommendation from current and former colleagues. The fact that such testimonials are selected by the candidate is standard procedure. For the case in question, the letters should be accurately identified as solicited by the candidate, who should probably ask these students to address their letters to the department chair so that the original copies will appear in her permanent department file. The tenure committee could decide what weight to assign to them.

Some tenure committees solicit their own set of letters about a candidate from individuals with appropriate knowledge of the candidate's professional contributions. If this process is available, Average could enhance the impact of student letters if she gave the committee names of students (10 or more, perhaps) who had agreed to speak on her behalf and leave it to the committee to solicit letters directly.

Discussion Questions

1. Is there a fundamental asymmetry in our relationships with students such that our future obligation to help them (e.g., with recommendations) will always overshadow any current request that they help us?

2. Would it be appropriate to invite all of this instructor's students to send letters about her teaching directly to the department chair after final course grades have been submitted?

3. Are teaching evaluations using a single, mandated form unethical?

Case 15-9. Textbook Adoption Choices

> Professor Addon must select a new textbook. She reviews various options and makes her final decision based on the wider array of complimentary, ancillary materials such as a computerized test bank, videotapes, overhead projector transparencies, web pages, and CD-ROMs.

As is true with so many of our case commentaries, the ultimate decision should rest with whether Addon's behavior in some way creates less adequate learning experience for her students. If the textbook chosen is weaker than other contenders, Addon's choice is inappropriate and self-serving. She has put personal convenience ahead of the quality of her students' education. However, if Addon chose a textbook that at least equals the competitors, the supplements may actually enhance her classroom presentations.

Publishers compete heavily for textbook adoptions, and the array of offered supplements is often dazzling. Instructors may need to pause to consider who is ultimately paying for these extras and remember that students are entitled to the best educational value for their money.

Finally, we would note that "teaching technologies" are increasingly encouraged at many institutions, despite the fact that their efficacy is still unclear. Some suggest that the traditional college-level classroom is the only remaining opportunity for people to experience an hour-long, in-depth lecture as opposed to sound bites and MTV-style glitz.

Discussion Questions

1. Some instructors openly admit that ancillaries, especially the more recent versions that provide many multimedia classroom activities, allow them to put in far less effort in their classes. Does this pose an ethical problem? Why or why not?

2. We know a professor who is an outstanding lecturer but who will retire rather than give into the pressures to teach using multimedia and other technological enhancements. Should instructors who do not feel comfortable with technology or who do not believe that it is the right way to teach students ever be forced to do so?

3. What value do you assign to the ancillary materials offered by textbook publishers?

Discrimination

Teaching is based on a special relationship, focused on student learning and educational development. Behaviors that interfere with this alliance, or that have the appearance of interfering, are ethically suspect and should be dealt with quickly before complications arise. The cases in this chapter illustrate how public comments or other behavior by an instructor that risks making others uncomfortable can impair the learning environment. Part of what is challenging here is that, by their nature, educational settings bring together people who differ markedly in background or perspective. Those with more influence should remember that the ethical risks are greater when some groups are in the minority, and that smaller groups may feel relatively powerless to inhibit unethical behavior.

Case 16-1. Out of Step

> Professor Anachronistic frequently appears to enjoy a sexist humor approach to making his point. For example, when a student asked him how long their responses to essay questions should be, he responds, "Your answers should be like the skirts you gals wear - long enough to cover the subject, but short enough to keep things interesting." To many students he seems harmless enough, but some women in the class feel that Anachronistic degrades them personally and jeopardizes them academically.

Professor Anachronistic needs to change with the times. Although he does not recognize it as such, his comments are likely to be experienced as derogatory by many contemporary students. He creates an uncomfortable learning environment for female students and is a poor role model for male students. His behavior may discourage many of the women from participating in class (e.g., asking questions or offering opinions) and may even undermine their perceptions of themselves as serious students. His behavior may also violate the institution's sexual harassment policy. Perhaps, as an intelligent man, he might respond to a vigorous consciousness-raising session with colleagues or students. Otherwise, the students will continue to have legitimate ethical (and possibly legal) complaints.

Closer inspection may reveal that Anachronistic has failed to promote the educational goals of women in his classes in ways that have caused substantial harm, such as writing "fluffy," off-target recommendation letters or failing to even consider nominating a woman for an award or special opportunity. (See also 1-3.)

Discussion Questions

1. Several of Professor Anachronistic's colleagues are aware of his attitudes, but have been unsuccessful in raising his consciousness. As a recourse, they steer their advisees away from his courses. Is this an appropriate response?

2. Professor Anachronistic argues that his free speech rights are violated when others attempt to curb his use of humor to teach students. What are his rights?

3. If the women students came to complain about Professor Anachronistic, what would you advise them to do?

Cases 16-2. Infatuated Students

Sam Puppy, a 19-year-old student, shows up at Professor Brown's office regularly, sometimes just to smile and say, "Hello," but more often to ask if there is anything he can do to help her. He sometimes brings little gifts, like a donut or a flower. Occasionally he waits outside her office and walks with her to her car. Lately, he has called her twice at home to ask her unimportant questions about the class. Professor Brown is not comfortable with the escalation of Puppy's attention.

Suzie Pepper, a 19-year-old student, stops by Professor White's office regularly, sometimes just to smile and say, "Hello," but more often to ask if there is anything she can do to help him, and sometimes bringing little gifts, like a donut or a flower.

> Occasionally she waits outside his office and walks with
> him to his car. Lately, she has called him twice at home
> to ask him unimportant questions about the class.
> Professor White is not comfortable with the escalation
> of Suzie's attention.

Both cases should have the same solution. That solution involves a combination of deliberately avoiding any encouragement of the student's advances and direct comment to the student about what is acceptable in a teacher–student relationship and what is not. Although both Puppy and Pepper may experience wounded feelings, this result is to be preferred over a continuing, unacceptable, and unwelcome situation. We also suggest that instructors might address only those behaviors that make them feel uncomfortable rather than recounting all of the unwelcome, attentive behaviors that Puppy and Pepper have shown. This can be accomplished by stressing the behavior rather than the unacceptablity of the person.

Although our cultural conditioning may lead us to see Puppy's behavior as innocent immaturity and Pepper's as seductive (even the author who named our case players later had to admit that a bias was unintentionally showing), both young people should be treated with sensitivity. College-level instructors are ready objects of respect and affection, and young people often do not have all of their emotional needs sorted out. We argue that it is difficult to tell whether students who pay us inordinate attention have a sexual attraction or are, rather, seeking a substitute parent, mentor, or source of mature support.

Finally, we acknowledge that the foregoing cases are based on heterosexual attractions and that students who are attracted to the same-sex instructors are not uncommon. The boundaries must still be drawn with sensitivity, using the same techniques suggested earlier.

Discussion Questions

1. Although most situations, such as those described in this case, involve students who simply need guidance about the boundaries of instructor–student relationships, occasionally we encounter students whose attention signals serious emotional problems. What might be some of the warning signs that suggest that a student's interest is becoming an obsession or that the student is interpreting interactions with us in an irrational way?

2. How should an instructor respond if a student confesses love for her or him?

3. Have you had an experience with a student who was apparently or obviously sexually attracted to you? If so, how did you deal with such an advance?

Case 16-3. The "Chilly Climate"

> Occasionally, during departmental faculty meetings, the
> women in the department are the subjects of mild
> ribbing, such as suggesting that a female colleague
> carrying a paper sack must have been out shopping for
> clothes. Or, during a meeting to discuss building
> renovations, it was suggested that the women should
> be in charge of designing the faculty kitchen area. These
> constant comments irritate the women in the
> department. However, they are junior faculty and fear
> that they will appear petty or be subject to retaliation if
> they make any comment.

Although women have made great strides achieving equal opportunity, it
remains true that they are underrepresented in most academic units. Even
in departments that can demonstrate equity between female and male
faculty in salary, teaching load, availability of resources, and tenure, subtle
indicators of gender stereotyping, such as sexist jokes, are common.

Sandler and Hall (1986) have written extensively concerning the "chilly
climate" for women in academia and suggest that when women are subject
to a cool occupational environment their accomplishments are devalued,
their contributions ignored, and they experience feelings of professional
isolation and demoralization. In short, women report that they are treated
like second-class citizens. Moreover, because in most departments women
are few in number and are concentrated in the instructor and assistant professor
ranks, they may feel powerless to take on the majority. Thus, stereotyped
comments may continue virtually unchallenged.

Faculty members have an ethical responsibility to protect the dignity
of others, and when the professional dignity of junior faculty suffers, the
senior faculty has an ethical obligation to respond. Expecting only the
women or only the men to address these issues is both inappropriate and
unrealistic. Furthermore, when males alone defend their female colleagues,
an impression may be created that the women need to be taken care of by
their male colleagues. And, when only the women confront sexist remarks,
they become typecast as having no sense of humor.

In dealing with the chilly climate, private conversations with those
making the remarks are often sufficient to eliminate future offense. Many
instances of offensive humor are the result of unintentional insensitivity
rather than deliberate hostility, and pointing out how the remark was
perceived is often enough to sensitize the offender(s). Some public "jokes,"
however, are simply too insolent and require immediate reaction. The

department chair should comment directly on the remarks and thereby set the tone for the rest of the faculty.

When attempts to sensitize the offenders through personal interactions are unsuccessful, a department may wish to consider organizing a workshop on gender stereotyping for its faculty. Often such programs are available through the assistance of the Affirmative Action officer. (See also 16-4 and 16-5.)

Discussion Questions

1. What if the annoying comments described in this case only take place in informal settings, such as the coffee lounge or at department parties? Is this still a problem?

2. Suppose the humor, rather than being sexist, is a subtle form of gay-bashing. Federal laws do not cover discrimination on the basis of sexual orientation. What recourse do faculty members who find this humor offensive have?

3. At what point does humor (which often, in our culture, involves some measure of cynicism, hostility, or ridicule) become overly repressed? For example, do jokes about a new drug to enhance male performance run the risk of insulting, unbeknownst to anyone, an impotent colleague? How sensitive do we need to be?

Case 16-4. Stereotyped Departmental Expectations

Traditionally the department has had a beginning-of-the-year reception for its faculty, a pre-winter-holiday reception for students and faculty, and an end-of-the year party for graduating seniors. In addition, small receptions for guest speakers follow their presentations. The women staff and faculty recognize that the planning and refreshment preparation fall on their shoulders, not by their choice but by custom. The women also realize that if they did not make the effort, the functions would be dismal. They find that prospect embarrassing.

The burden of planning and implementing departmental events should be shared equitably or run by a committee of members who are most interested in these events. Traditions die hard, even for women themselves, and the women should give the entire department a clear account of their desire to share the tasks. All department members can then decide if they want to discontinue the events or figure out how the responsibilities can be divided among more people. (See also 16-3.)

Discussion Questions

1. Issues of inclusion often arise in regard to departmental social events. For example, suppose a department always schedules its social events on Friday nights. Alcohol is always served. What groups might feel excluded, burdened, or uncomfortable with this arrangement? Should these issues be considered in planning social gatherings?

2. Suppose that faculty members rarely show up for department social activities involving students. Should faculty members be required to attend a certain percentage of such events?

Case 16-5. Offending Colleagues' Sensibilities

Professor Plainlook wrote a letter to the affirmative action office alleging harassment by four female colleagues. In it he describes their unending conversations in the faculty lounge about the prowess and superior physical shape of the football team members. He contends that these frequent discussions create an unfriendly and humiliating workplace environment.

At what point does harassment change from a hostile condition, making it difficult for employees to do their jobs, to a matter of personal oversensitivity, perhaps accompanied by collegial insensitivity and lack of empathy for others in the workplace environment? When is intervention necessary to limit behavior, and when is behavior within the legitimate purview of everyday human discourse?

Plainlook may be oversensitive, but the women are bothering him. It is up to him to take action. He might say, in a playful tone, something like, "Don't you have something else to talk about that the rest of us regular guys can relate to?" Sometimes a nonaggressive comment is sufficient to alert others that they may be unwittingly offensive or hurting someone else's feelings. But, the fact remains that the women are having a private conversation which is neither derisive of Plainlook nor sufficient to meet the criteria of harassing behavior. Plainlook may have to simply accept what is going on (without having to like it or join in) or choose not to be in the lounge.

It is likely that all of us occasionally endure annoying, subtle, and perhaps unintentional forms of mild uncollegiality. A colleague proudly notes that his wife has remained a size 10 after 30 years of marriage (Patai, 1995) without taking into account the fact that one of the woman to whom he is addressing is considerably overweight. Another colleague gleefully announces the acceptance of her article by a prestigious journal to a colleague whose paper has been rejected after six attempts to locate a publisher. A colleague gives a dismissive eye-roll to another's suggestion in a faculty meeting. The list is endless and ranges from ugly attacks or thinly disguised scholarly debates, to an offhanded comment that would be offensive only to a particular recipient. One of the prices of maintaining a scholarly community that thrives on open debate and criticism may be the suffering, with a stiff upper lip, of the personal style and foibles of others. (See also 16-3.)

Discussion Questions

1. What if genders in the foregoing case were reversed? That is, a female colleague overheard a group of men at the next table commenting on the splendid bodies of the female cheerleaders? Does this bring up a different set of feelings? Why?

2. At what point is a reaction to a comment a matter of personal oversensitivity, perhaps accompanied by lack of empathy for others in the workplace environment? Is it often just a matter of how comments are worded rather than the content *per se*? Consider the following:

a. A colleague tells a "short people joke" to a group that includes a 5'1" woman. (Is your response different if the joke is about a 5'1" man?)

b. An instructor trips and falls in the stairway, and a colleague says, "Your butt is going to swell up like the Hindenberg!"

c. In a faculty meeting, a colleague responds to your suggestion as "shortsighted and uninformed."

d. A colleague says to another, "Why don't you get a new briefcase? That one makes you look like a bag lady."

Manipulative Students
and Instructors

The teaching–learning situation quite frequently lends itself to opportunities to manipulate others. Students can find ways to influence the instructor's decision-making processes. Instructor's can "use" students for self-promoting purposes. This chapter considers examples of such behavior.

Case 17-1. Helping an Irresponsible Student

> Joe Irresponsible doesn't come to class for a month, which has put him hopelessly behind. Joe is now asking for a letter from the instructor to help him maximize the amount of his tuition refund upon his withdrawsal from the course.

Many schools have relatively clear policies about the conditions for dropping a course, and these should be well publicized to students and adhered to by instructors. When the decision is left to the instructor, or the instructor has an opportunity to influence the outcome, many might refuse to make any special effort on behalf of a student like Joe, perhaps just to teach him a lesson. An instructor might even point out parallel situations to Joe. For example, there would certainly be no refund if he signed up and paid for the Graduate Record Exam (GRE) but then failed to show. Or, if he chronically missed work, his pay would likely be docked and he could lose his job.

Nothing is inherently wrong with a strict stance as long as it is applied consistently and evenly. That is, an instructor who has helped more likable students get the most out of wasted opportunities should not refuse to help a student like Joe simply out of spite for failing to come to class. However, if Joe had earlier bouts of irresponsibility and ignored the feedback, most of us would agree that he deserves no extra help now.

As an argument for considering leniency, we know of a case where an instructor gave a second chance at a thesis defense to a student who fell asleep during her first orals. She was later diagnosed with a brain tumor. This example shows how, in rare instances, a strict judgment (e.g., the somnolent student is failed) might turn out to be inappropriate in light of later developments. Such examples are evidence for why we might at least consider giving second or even third chances to students, especially when the problems they present would be unexpected based on our prior experience with them.

An instructor who decides that Joe deserves a break needs to base a decision about writing a helpful letter (or making a phone call on his behalf) on whatever exculpatory facts are available. If Joe offers no other explanation than simply failing to act responsibly, it would be inappropriate for a letter to make any excuses. If there are mitigating circumstances (e.g., Joe has a medical or psychiatric disorder that disrupts his daily functioning), the instructor could weigh these circumstances and perhaps require, as a condition of getting his letter, that Joe listen to some advice about making sure next time to explain his special circumstances in advance. (See 8-1, 9-2, and 17-3.)

Discussion Questions

1. Sometimes a student who is failing the course asks for a simple "Withdrawal" instead of a "Withdrawal/Failing" to avoid hurting his academic record. If it is early in the term and the student theoretically could have passed the course had he performed well later in the term, would an instructor be justified in giving a "W" even when the student's overall grade at that moment is not a passing one? Why or why not?

2. What is your understand of the Incomplete (I) grade? If Joe has asked for an I, saying he would take the class again next semester, would you have agreed to that even though he was failing?

3. Does your school have a policy regarding I grades, and under what circumstances they are permissible?

Case 17-2. Skipping the Final Exam

> **Stan Settlesforless, an excellent student, tells Professor Sternum that he does not intend to take the Human Anatomy 462 final exam. Stan reasons that even if he**

earned a zero on on the final exam, his average would still be a B. Stan adds that he is happy to help out his friends in the class, none of whom are doing as well as he. Sternum is in a bind, knowing that Stan's zero will lower the class average upon which the grading scale will be based. He is also upset with Stan's stated intent.

Just as instructors have the right to set standards for performance in their courses, students have the right to choose how they will perform in a class. Unless Sternum has explicitly stated that all students are required to sit for the final exam, or there is an institutional requirement that all students take final exams, Stan is within his rights to choose to take his zero and settle for a B in the course.

Many instructors may have encountered a related problem at the end of the semester after setting a course policy that allows students to drop the lowest exam grade. Usually the instructor never intends for a student to skip the final exam, especially if the exam includes item that are comprehensive across the entire term. We recommend that instructors create a policy that requires all students to take the final exam.

Sternum had no such policy, however, and now must contend with Stan, who has an ulterior motive. Stan wants to do his friends a favor by adjusting the class average downward. Sternum may be able to deal with this problem by not including Stan's cumulative score in the calculation of the class average or by using the average of Stan's prior scores as an estimate of his score for the final when calculating the grade for others. Sternum would also be doing Stan a favor by pointing out the impression Stan is creating by choosing to perform at a level lower than his capability.

Discussion Questions

1. An absolute grading scale can avoid the problem encountered by Professor Sternum. What are the benefits and liabilities of this practice?

2. The practice of allowing students to drop their lowest grade is common. What are the benefits and liabilities of this practice? Who is harmed?

3. Stan's zero makes him an outlier in the final exam score distribution and, for a small class, would significantly lower the class average. Should students who perform *extremely* poorly in a class be eliminated from the calculations of final grades when the grade assignment is based on a class curve?

4. What about the opposite situation when one or two students in a class, perhaps like Stan, perform at such a superior level that the grades for the rest of the students are significantly lowered. Is it acceptable and fair to alter previously stated procedures?

5. How would you have responded to Stan?

Case 17-3. Too Many Chances?

Professor Softouch allows an irresponsible student considerable latitude for making up assignments. Softouch wonders if students like this deserve such charity from their instructors, or might actually be disserved by it.

Students derive many of their expectations about how they should cope with direction and supervision from their college-level instructors. If we reinforce the message that time extensions past the deadline are the norm, then many students will assume that all performance expectations will be similarly flexible. At the very least, our laxness gives them ammunition to use when criticizing other instructors who are strict about deadlines.

On the other hand, some students (e.g., students who had lenient teachers in high school) who are early in their academic careers often do not know how to manage their time effectively. If Softouch considers being flexible in a given instance, she might be able to draw a receptive student into a serious talk about the importance of working steadily on all assignments and completing them on time.

In our view, enforcing a hard and fast policy on deadlines is defensible as long as it is consistent and was announced well in advance, both orally and in writing. Some policies might take into account how much time the student has to complete the assignment (e.g., showing more flexibility with a short-term assignment than one students work on for the entire term). Many instructors effectively put the responsibility and consequences for missed deadlines back on the student by allowing lateness or repeat chances, but attaching nontrivial penalties to such exceptions (e.g., half a letter grade for a limited deviation, a whole letter grade or more for a significant departure). This arrangement allows the instructor to give extensions and second chances while not penalizing students who complete their work on time. (See also 5-6 and 5-7.)

Discussion Questions

1. Are the problems described in this case more likely to arise when the instructors for a given course or department vary widely in their policies regarding lateness or makeups? If so, should more uniform policies within departments be recommended as a way of minimizing student confusion? Why or why not?

2. How do you handle students who miss deadlines, claiming dire circumstances such as the death of a parent or serious illness? How do you draw the line between acceptable and unacceptable excuses?

Case 17-4. The Unexpected Quid Pro Quo

> A student volunteers to make an extra class presentation on a relevant topic about which she has special expertise. The instructor agrees, even though he could easily have given a similar presentation himself. The student works many hours to prepare the presentation. Afterwards she asks if the instructor will substitute her presentation for the required course term paper, which is due very soon but which she has not had time to work on because of the effort she put into the presentation.

Nontraditional students or others in one's class may have extensive experiences or backgrounds that are directly relevant to certain course topics. Such students can enrich a course. Such students are often proud of the special knowledge they have and are eager to share it.

Throwing herself into this opportunity to be professor for a day, the student apparently overspent the time put into her preparations and realizes too late that a serious toll has been taken on her schedule. Understandably, then, she feels it is appropriate to ask the instructor for a commensurate favor in return to even things out. A conniving student might even entrap the instructor in such a dilemma, volunteering up front to do something which she knows she can pull off safely and efficiently and prefers doing in lieu of the standard assignment. Either way, the instructor is over a barrel. Denying the student's request for a quid pro quo would give her some basis (however uncertain) for appealing her final grade. But, granting her request would be unfair to everyone, including the student in question who loses the benefit she would have gained from learning something new.

Students are very sensitive to what they see as an uneven playing field, and too often special offers will come with expectations for reciprocity that, in fairness, cannot be honored. We recommend, while designing a course, requiring all students to perform tasks or produce products that are explicitly tailored to the goals and learning objectives of the course. The work of different students should be at least roughly equivalent in kind and quantity, allowing for the inevitable differences among students in motivation and thoroughness. If any substitutions are allowed, these must be equally available to all students and publicized well in advance. Instructors should depart from such arrangements rarely, if at all, and then only for reasons that are sensible and unlikely to create predicaments like the one presented here. Instead of agreeing to a special presentation from one student, for example, the instructor who comes to learn of a student's special knowledge about a topic might announce to the class as a whole that this topic will be the primary focus of an upcoming class session, and invite the expert student to participate.

Discussion Questions

1. What about a situation where a particular student knows a great deal more about a topic than does the instructor (e.g., current practices or regulatory issues associated with a particular applied setting)? How can this student's expertise be appropriately showcased?

2. What would you have done if the student in the case made the offer to you at the beginning of the term?

Case 17-5. Ingratiating Students

> Ingrid Ingratiator takes classes with Professor Stoic and Professor Ego. She compliments both of them effusively, and has told each that he is her all-time favorite instructor. Her behavior makes Stoic very uncomfortable, and he is not sure how to respond. Ego, on the other hand, enjoys the flattery so much that after class he often unwinds by conducting friendly office chats on any manner of topics (not all related to class) with Ingrid. These sessions may last an hour or more, and only rarely are other students present.

Ideally our relationships with students are cordial, warm, and collaborative, and, at all times, they must also be appropriate. Other cases in this book have covered situations in which a faculty member pushes or exceeds the appropriate boundaries or tenor of a relationship with a student. It can also be the student whose behavior threatens an objective and professional working relationship.

If ingratiating behavior makes an instructor uncomfortable, the student's chances for a successful course experience may be jeopardized. Also, repeated ingratiation by one student is often reacted to negatively by others in the class (e.g., feeling threatened by the imagined advantages the ingratiator is gaining).

In terms of responding to ingratiating students, it is usually possible to handle milder examples (e.g., "I hear your section of this course is tops") with a modest, businesslike response (e.g., "I try to do a good job"). If the behavior is constant and repetitive, or if the remarks are so extreme and passionate as to cause discomfort, some sensitive but explicit feedback should be given to the student in private. Such feedback can help the student understand that effusive praise demands some sort of response from the instructor, and yet either agreeing or not agreeing with it puts him or her in a no-win situation. The feedback should also stress the instructor's need to maintain comfortable, even-handed relationships with all students in the course.

Professor Ego needs to be careful about Ingrid's behavior becoming so reinforcing for him that it affects his objectivity toward her and their respective role boundaries. Lengthy meetings outside of class could be very helpful to Ingrid if their primary focus is on material from Ego's course or field. It is more difficult to see the educational benefit of their frequent, lengthy conversations when the focus strays completely away from these topics. Ego is running a risk that sooner or later he will tell Ingrid things she has no business knowing (e.g., about himself, his colleagues, or her fellow students), or that she will think it is all right to share inappropriate information with him. Ignoring interpersonal boundaries compromises their professional relationship, and compromised relationships have a way of turning messy later on. If Ingrid is simply playing a game with Ego, she is winning.

More generally, we would point out that a course should be structured so that there is no significant advantage to be gained by ingratiating behavior on a student's part. That is, final grades should always be based on objective results of student performance in the course, with little room for the instructor's subjective impressions (whether positive or negative) to play a significant role.

Discussion Questions

1. In a mentoring relationship, how far afield can the topics of conversations and the nature of activities range and still be consistent with appropriate role boundaries?

2. Where do you draw the line between appropriate compliments and suspicions that your backside is being kissed? What are the markers for each?

3. Can you tell whether the student is giving a sincere compliment or is simply attempting to be manipulative? When in doubt, is it best to assume that the student is being sincere?

4. How do you react to extreme forms of flattery from students?

Case 17-6. Playing to Student Evaluations

> Student ratings of their teachers are weighted heavily in the department evaluation process. Professor Stumper studies the required course evaluation instrument and designs his class around "playing to it." He goes out of his way to get to know each student by name, to include intriguing little tidbits to spice up his lectures, to tell jokes, to invite students to his office to chat, to hold special tutoring sessions, to smile every time he runs into one of his students, and to never engage in any action that could alienate any of them. Stumper has done students favors that go well beyond what is expected of educators. Stumper admits to himself that he has to bite his tongue often.

Is Stumper a good teacher, despite his motivation of self-interest, or is he merely a caricature of a good teacher? Certainly, a number of Stumper's practices, such as trying to make his lectures more interesting and holding tutoring sessions, are pedagogically sound and to be encouraged. Also, to some extent, impression management with students can increase instructors' credibility and affect student learning positively. However, deliberate manipulation of students, such as providing unmerited praise for the sake of increasing ratings, is unethical because it is dishonest.

Ethical issues arise if course content is superficial or aiming primarily for a laugh or titillation. If Stumper's expectations of the students require so little effort that they neither demand much studying nor discriminte among weak, average, and better students, Stumper is not doing his job.

If Stumper simply ignores inappropriate behavior to avoid alienating students (e.g., overlooking evidence of cheating, not holding students to appropriate class-management standards such as showing up at a specific time for a make-up exam, or allowing chatting students to disrupt those around them), ethical issues are also present.

Stumper is also so focused on his goal of receiving high ratings that he places himself in possible jeopardy. The whole act could fall like a house of cards. If his classes are not challenging, or if his avoidance of proper discipline offends others, those who demand a high quality education may give Stumper poor ratings.

Ideally instructors take care with their teaching preparation and extend themselves to students for reasons that are strongly related to a commitment to the discipline, integrity, and their calling to teach. The danger (and irony) in *over*-using student evaluations in the personnel decision process is that *anything* that elevates good ratings is interpreted as constituting good teaching. For example, an unchallenging course in which every student receives a high grade may result in high evaluations but little learning. (See also 6-3.)

Discussion Questions

1. Are faculty members almost forced to adopt Stumper's primary motivation just to retain or advance on the job?

2. Do you think that students' teaching evaluations are ethical and valid measures of your ability as a teacher? Why or why not?

3. Do you think that it is ethical to place a very heavy weight on students' teaching evaluations when it comes to personnel decisions? Why or why not?

18

Supervising, Advising, and Collaboration With Students

The use, overuse, and misuse of students as teaching assistants has received widespread attention, in part due to the publicity surrounding the unionization of graduate assistants on university campuses. The last decade has also witnessed the development of extensive training programs designed to support the professional development of graduate students. These programs have helped alleviate the problem of inappropriate reliance on graduate assistants and have focused on preparing them for increasing levels of responsibility commensurate with their progress.

The multiple roles of student, employee, and junior colleague can strain the boundaries between appropriate and improper involvement of students in various professional capacities. In this chapter we present cases that help to distinguish healthy, productive, collaborative mentoring relationships between students (both graduate and undergraduate) and faculty from those that are lax in supervision, manipulative, and exploitative.

We would note that we use the term Student Assistant (SA) generically in this chapter. Titles intended to be covered include Teaching Assistant, Graduate Assistant, and Research Assistant.

Case 18-1. Student Assistant Responsibilities

> Professor Ledger's SA, Looksee Tell, divulges to his peers how they are doing compared to other students and imparts information about other identified students. For example, he told his girlfriend that Booby Dim got 7 points out of 20 on the last assignment.

All work by SAs should be carefully monitored. Students vary widely in their maturity and soundness of judgment, and it should not be assumed that SAs fully understand the trust that has been placed in them and the confidentiality responsibilities that attend their position. Instructors should carefully outline ethical as well as the task expectations to all supervisees at the onset of employment. As direct supervisors, instructors may even be liable should violations be reported. SAs like Looksee may be more common than we realize, and it is unlikely that we would easily detect such behavior ourselves.

As a general safeguard against violations of confidentiality, major responsibilities for grading students who are the SAs' peers in the same department should be avoided as much as possible. Such assignments create dual-role relationships among students that invite conflicts. (See chapter 20 for confidentiality issues.)

Discussion Questions

1. What if Looksee told his friends how bright a certain student is? Is that less ethically problematical?

2. What ethical mandates would you give to your SA at the onset of employment?

3. Are faculty members who, simply out of curiosity, compare notes with each other regarding the exam performance or classroom deportment of specific students engaging in ethically questionable behavior?

Case 18-2. Student Assistant Access to Test Banks

> Adam Assist, a senior majoring in speech com-
> munication, is the SA assigned to an introductory course
> in public speaking. Professor Orator has asked Adam
> to help with test construction and has given Adam the
> test bank for the required textbook. Adam's job is to
> select questions from the item bank for the next exam.

Is it appropriate for Adam to have access to the test bank? Assuming that Adam's selection as a SA was based on a reasonable screening process, there is no reason to believe that he cannot be trusted with the test item bank for Orator's course. There is always the possibility that any SA could misuse test information (e.g., selling tests to students, photocopying items), but it is difficult to predict which student might exploit the situation.

Most SAs who have responsibility for creating test items need close supervision. We strongly recommend a formal orientation session for SAs that includes guidelines for how to create good test items, a discussion of the potential limitations of test bank questions, and a review of test validity issues. Many students do not seem to realize that test items must coincide with course goals and learning objectives. One colleague told us that when questioned about how she selected items from the test bank, the SA indicated that she simply picked odd or even items. If a SA is given responsibility for test construction, it is the instructor's responsibility to carefully review the work and make necessary changes before the exam is finalized. SAs also need clear guidelines for maintaining test security.

Undergraduate SAs frequently find themselves in an awkward dual-role situation. They may be taking classes with some of the same students in the class they are assisting. Occasionally their peers may pressure them for insider information about exams and other course assignments. Reviewing the boundaries of the SA role and giving SAs suggestions for dealing with potential dual-role conflicts at the start of the semester is a recommended way to prevent problems later on.

Discussion Questions

1. What are the ethical issues when someone other than the course instructor constructs an exam?

2. Should there be criteria for the amount of experience or skill level that a SA should have before being given responsibility for test construction?

3. Should undergraduate SAs ever be included in test item construction?

Case 18-3. Heavy Use of Student Assistants

Professor Maxima uses SAs to the fullest possible extent to perform his undergraduate teaching responsibilities. For example, SAs create all the exams, grade all written work, and teach the class every week or two when Maxima is out of town or is busy with other work. SAs are also responsible for virtually all of the contact with students outside of class, including email communitions. Maxima defends this arrangement by saying that her students get a good overall "package" (i.e., two or

more instructors for the price of one), that her classes
cover the curriculum with adequate breadth and depth,
and that it is helpful to the SAs to be given such
extensive teaching experience.

Under some circumstances, Maxima's program may be adaptive, though
not ideal. Research professors at high profile universities are far more
likely to make considerable use of SAs in their undergraduate classes than
are their colleagues at smaller institutions. At the very least, however,
students in the class should understand and accept the arrangement from
the beginning, preferably through disclosure when they apply to schools
making heavy use of SAs in undergraduate classes.

What comes across in the Maxima scenario, however, is the profile of
an instructor who does not like to teach. The students appear to be receiving
less experienced and far less expensive instruction than they (and parents
or taxpayers) believed would be available to them. The students appear
to have virtually no direct access to their instructor and are at the mercy of
their advanced peers for both their educations and academic evaluations.
Maxima's tactics possibly violate university policies but, unless someone
complains, the predicament is unlikely to be detected.

If less experienced SAs are unsupervised, poorly monitored, or
teaching beyond their level of competence, students are not receiving a
minimally acceptable education. Furthermore, the instructor in charge is
neglecting a primary responsibility.

Discussion Questions

1. What if the instructor is an outstanding scholar who uses the time freed up
by SAs to produce scholarly achievements that bring great recognition to the
department and university?

2. What about Maxima's argument that the SAs are receiving invaluable
training? Does she have a good point here? Why or why not?

Case 18-4. Student Research Assistants

As a result of severe cutbacks in funding, Professor
Adapt offers students independent study credit to assist
him with his research. He gives the students a footnote
credit (and occasionally authorship credit if the students'
contributions were extensive) on his professional
meeting presentations and publications. The students

> do not complain because they get class credit and can claim research experience on graduate school and job applications. A colleague, however, believes that Professor Adapt is exploiting his students.

Considerable financial support for scholarly activity has become more difficult to attract in recent years. The requirement to produce scholarly work for the purposes of promotion and tenure, however, has remained constant in most comprehensive and research universities. Nonetheless, many educators welcome opportunities to conduct research or engage in other scholarly or creative activities because they enjoy them and take pride in making contributions to their disciplines.

It does not appear that Professor Adapt is exploiting students. As long as they are learning how to do research (a necessary condition for extending academic credit), are carefully supervised, and are receiving credit in proportion to their contributions, a partnership has been created that is advantageous to both the students and the instructor.

Ethical issues arise if the instructor is taking credit for work done by students, is not properly attributing credit to students for their contribution, is sloppy in supervision and therefore generating possibly invalid data, or assigns only tasks that involve considerable difficult or tedious efforts that result in minimal learning.

Discussion Questions

1. Should courses in which students act solely as research assistants and make no intellectual contribution to the project be graded, or should students be required to take the course on a pass–fail or credit–no credit basis? That is, should a student be awarded an A for collecting data or locating resources in the library? If not, what should a student have to do to receive a grade rather than a "pass" or "credit" entry on the transcript?

2. Sometimes students' work is sloppy or irresponsible. For example, a student who was initially excited about a research opportunity gets behind in her more structured courses and neglects her research tasks. What can be done in advance to minimize failed research alliances with students?

3. Professor Adapt typically takes on several SAs to help with his research. All of these students sign up for the same course, but Adapt assigns tasks to them based on their levels of experience. Students with minimal experience do clerical tasks, those with more experience collect the data, and those with the most experience analyze the data. What difficulties might Adapt encounter with equity in the course? How can equity issues be defused?

Case 18-5. Classroom
Students as Data Collectors

> Professor Convenient asks his undergraduate business
> students to collect questionnaire data from their friends,
> score them, and encode them in the computer as a way
> of gaining, as he put it, "valuable experience in the nuts
> and bolts of survey research." He then uses the data
> that the students collect as the basis for his scholarly
> publications. Colleagues who know of his methodology
> wonder whether this technique is good science and if
> students, who are never cited, are being exploited.

Professor Convenient has made several ethical errors. The haphazard data
collection by the students does not conform to scientific standards.
Researchers are ethically obliged to select methods to ensure the validity
of their data. His data gathering technique also models sloppy science.

A second ethical issue concerns the failure of Professor Convenient to
provide appropriate supervision and instruction to the students
throughout their participation in the project. He has also given them the
message that dual-role relationships are appropriate (i.e., collecting
questionnaire responses from friends). Another error concerns the
apparent failure to adhere to ethical guidelines concerning the treatment
of human research participants. The case description suggests that proper
informed consent may not have been obtained by the student data
collectors. Convenient also has no way of knowing whether some students
actually collected data. Compounding these problems is the fact that this
instructor may have exploited the student researchers because it is not
clear whether the students learned anything of value from this "nuts and
bolts" experience.

What if Convenient had extended authorship or footnote credits to
the students? Would that have addressed any of the concerns? We believe
that giving publication credit addresses only the exploitation
concern, and minimally so. It neither eliminates the dual-role issue nor
the unscientific methods employed for data collection.

Discussion Questions

1. What if the data the students collected were not published but used solely
for classroom demonstrations of data analysis and interpretation? Have the ethical
problems disappeared?

2. What would one have to do ethically to have students in a course collect data for publication? Is this even possible?

3. Let us say that Professor Convenient collects the data from his own students, using class time, that he later uses in a publication. Are there ethical problems? If so, can they be minimized?

Case 18-6. Authorship Order
on Publications With Students

> A student complains that Professor Initiator has denied him first authorship on a paper that is to be published in a prestigious refereed journal. The paper is based on a series of experiments that the student conducted as a part of his senior research project under Initiator's supervision. When questioned as to why the student received the junior authorship position, Initiator provides a two-pronged defense. First, he describes how he provided the student with the main hypotheses and basic designs for the experiments. Furthermore, he contends that the student is not a good writer and contributed little to the published manuscript.

Professor Initiator has two ethical obligations in this case. The first obligation is to assign authorship accurately on the basis of relative contributions to the research effort. The second is to provide instruction to his student during all phases of the research project. An undergraduate is typically not yet able to create a design that would be acceptable to a reputable scholarly journal. Few have yet attained the writing skills necessary to produce an acceptable draft. Moreover, most students are uninformed about what constitutes a substantive contribution to a research project and may overestimate their contributions. The extensive time commitments required to collect and tabulate data, for example, may seem to a student like the most critical contributions to a research project whereas those same tasks are viewed as functionary by research scholars.

All of these circumstances point to the need for the supervisor to create clear verbal or written contracts, *in advance*, with students regarding authorship expectations so that they are not misled or disappointed. It appears that Initiator did not adequately discuss his own intentions with his student at the beginning of this process. Instructors may initially assume, usually correctly, that a scholarly project conducted in collaboration with an undergraduate student is unlikely to be published.

But, sometimes promising work does emerge. So, it is better to have an agreement with every student just in case the work has potential.

It is probably acceptable for Initiator to take first authorship in this case, provided that the student was not the primary contributor to the design and the other major creative elements of the work. It would have been unethical for Initiator to deny coauthorship to the student because this student's participation appears to have included substantial contributions. Although Initiator was active in the interpretation of the findings, his work would have been much more difficult without the data and analyses provided by the student.

The second ethical issue is the research supervisor's pedagogical responsibility to the student. When a supervisor simply "takes student data and runs," the behavior is exploitative and is not fulfilling an ethical responsibility to the student. The contract is relevant here, too. By negotiating with the student regarding authorship, the supervisor is giving the student a model for working with collaborators. Regarding the student's poor writing skills, Initiator also had an obligation to incorporate the student into the writing process, because that is how students learn how to prepare manuscripts and how to improve skills. If the student, however, declines the opportunity to participate, Initiator is justified in proceeding independently with the project. (See also 15-1.)

Discussion Questions

1. What if the student was someone that Initiator hired with grant funds to collect, record, and analyze data using standard techniques as specified by Initiator? How does that change a response to the student's complaint?

2. We recommend reaching early understandings with students about the possible future use of student project data. But, what if circumstances change markedly during the course of the project? For example, what if the student performs far better than expected? Or what if the student competently collects the data, but then drops out of school? How can allowance for contingencies be built into the initial agreement?

Case 18-7. Excessive Mentoring

> Professor Pushy spends considerable time, by his own choice, counseling and encouraging the best students in the department. He recommends graduate programs and career directions. No one doubts the sincerity of Pushy's motivation to help students make good life

> decisions, but students have complained that he becomes very irritable if his advice is challenged or if he thinks a student is aiming too low in life. Sometimes he insists that students apply to certain graduate programs he recommends and scolds them if they do not comply. He threatens not to write recommendations to graduate schools or potential employers if he does not think they are commensurate with a student's potential.

Just as students may see us as parental figures, these feelings can be reciprocated and the result can be inappropriate. Because our responsibility is to help students maximize the educational benefit of their relationship with us, we may be disappointed when students we believe to have considerable potential decide to go in another direction or down a less-challenging path. Certainly no one can fault instructors for giving extra time to help students with graduate school and career advice. However, such advice should be presented as our own views and never as commands. We should also encourage students to seek advice from several sources.

If strong feelings emerge when advising a student, or an instructor finds him or herself using coercive tactics (e.g., holding a letter hostage unless certain decisions are made), it is time for a boundary check. We can express our opinions and give advice when it is sought, but we are not our students' keepers. They must ultimately find their own way.

We should note that perfectly legitimate reasons exist for writing stronger or weaker letters for the same student depending on the institution, program, or position to which the student applies. For example, one might feel very comfortable voicing strong support for a student's application to a master's program but not to a PhD program. (See also 15-6, 18-3, and 18-8.)

Discussion Questions

1. What about the opposite situation? How strongly should an instructor intrude when students of modest ability aspire to graduate programs or jobs that seem extremely unrealistic?

2. How assertive can an instructor be in urging a promising student to attend graduate school when the student's goal is finding a job?

Case 18-8. Misuse of Graduate Assistants

> Professor Overload has a demanding teaching schedule
> and an active research lab. His research assistants and
> teaching assistants typically devote close to 40 hours a
> week to the tasks Overload assigns, but their
> assistantship contracts stipulate a 20-hour commitment.
> Some of the students are concerned because their
> workload in the laboratory requires them to place a
> lower priority on course work. However, they are
> reluctant to complain because Overload rewards their
> contributions with authorships on publications and very
> favorable letters of recommendation.

This case raises several questions. Is Professor Overload knowingly
overburdening his assistants, or is he unintentionally underestimating the
amount of time it takes students to complete the work he assigns? Are
students required to do extra work, or is the extra work optional? Is
Overload using letters of reference or publication credit as a means of
manipulating his students to do extra work?

In most settings, graduate research and teaching assistants are
considered to be professional apprentices as opposed to employees who
earn an hourly wage. Because of this tradition, few instructors require
that students maintain a strict, hour-for-hour accounting of their time.
Many students seeking expanded opportunities for publishing and
teaching devote more time than is expected of them working in their
supervisors' laboratories and classes. The workload for some assistants
may ebb and flow as the demands of research or the classroom change
from week to week. For these reasons, we need to reserve judgment until
more information about Overload's practices is available.

This situation is resolved easily if Overload intends to make a good
faith attempt to stick to the stipulations of the assistantship contract.
Overload may simply be unaware that the tasks he assigns are resulting
in a heavier workload than some students can comfortably handle within
the 20-hour limit. Or he may not have made it clear to his assistants that
extra work is an option rather than an obligation. In this case, the concerned
students need to discuss the situation with Overload.

Perhaps, however, Overload believes that students' top priority should
be what they do with him and that he is justified in assigning significant
amounts of work beyond what their contract stipulates. Faculty
supervisors who share Overload's belief may rationalize a *quid pro quo*

system in which only those teaching and research assistants who log the most hours are rewarded with good letters of reference and authorship on publications. However, clear boundaries between assistantship duties and extra work need to be established at the outset. Graduate assistants may be offered the opportunity for extra challenges, and some may actively seek it out, but faculty supervisors need to remain aware of policies governing assistant positions.

Discussion Questions

1. To what extent could competition among graduate students play a role in this case? Do instructors inadvertently encourage students to become the "favorite apprentice"?

2. In some settings in which the apprentice model is endorsed, faculty members believe that any time spent working with and for one's research mentor is more valuable than any other activity, including other faculty members' courses. Are there ethical problems associated with this perspective?

3. What are (were) your experiences as a graduate student assistant with regards to hours actually spent working and expectations your supervisors had of you?

Case 18-9. Promoting Uncertain Futures

> In her senior-level seminar, Professor Inspire tries to persuade her students to apply to graduate school in her discipline. During one of the classroom discussions, Skip Tickle says "Isn't it true that there aren't very many jobs available in this field right now? Why should I get advanced training if I won't be able to be employed?"

Tickle's question raises the constant dilemma faced by many college level educators. A belief that study in a particular discipline or specialty is worthwhile has to be weighed against the reality that graduates may have considerable difficulty finding positions that will allow them to enter a career based on their educational training. Professor Inspire can encourage students to pursue her field of study, but she should also provide accurate appraisals, as best she can, of what may happen for students in the marketplace. This is one area where the Internet may prove to be a profitable exercise, allowing the students and the instructor to acquire current and projected employment potential. The level of need for various types of professionals tends to cycle, due to numerous factors, and it is helpful if instructors keep up with the latest projections. National publications, such as *The Chronicle of Higher Education,* or local campus resources, such as an career services offices, are other resources to consult.

For many disciplines it is also fair to indicate to students that only those who have a thorough background at the undergraduate level, an excellent record of success, and strong scores on standardized tests have a realistic chance of being accepted for advanced study. Inspire's honest love of her discipline and her enthusiasm provides a model, reflecting the standard they will need to attain to be successful in that field.

Discussion Questions

1. Do instructors have an obligation to report how well graduates from the home institution do compared to graduates from other schools?

2. Should instructors actively discourage students from majoring in their fields if the current employment outlook is grim? Why or why not?

Case 18-10. Counseling Students on Nonacademic Matters

> A teary student asks Professor Directive for advice about her unwanted pregnancy. Directive asks the young woman a couple of questions about her life goals and suggests that an abortion might be her best option.

Students frequently seek advice for personal problems from teachers who seem amicable, but does Directive's recommendation cross the line? We believe that the limits for advice should normally relate to the standard role of advisor, instructor, research supervisor, or mentor as opposed to advice that is in the domain of counselors or therapists. A possible criterion for deciding whether to offer advice might be to consider the decisions your own family would make. That is, if it seems inappropriate to you that a member of your family would take direction from a college instructor on the decision, then it is probably inappropriate for you to give such direction to someone else.

In this case, we conclude that Professor Directive greatly exceeded the role of an advisor. The student's difficult decision is best assisted by someone who has a close personal relationship with her or by an appropriate professional. Directive might have, instead, referred the student to the counseling center or an off-campus professional or agency.

At the very least, he can express sympathetic concern for the student's welfare, but gently express that he is not in a position to influence the decision or give advice. (See also 2-8.)

Discussion Questions

1. Does the fact that the student specifically asked for a recommendation make a difference?

2. Is it acceptable to offer several options without offering an opinion?

3. What are examples of student problems that should be responded to with considerable caution?

4. What experiences have you had with students who ask for advice on very personal matters, and how did you handle them?

Case 18-11. Sponsoring Controversial Student Projects

> Sid Squish approaches his art professor with his proposal for the annual construction display. To symbolize the "aggressive, uncaring, path of the corporate monopoly and its impact on citizen consumers," Sid plans to display a spinning truck tire with roadkill gathered up from a nearby wooded highway in its wake. Sid asks his professor to sign the sponsorship form.

Drawing the line between creativity or breakthrough ideas that should be encouraged and inappropriate projects is among the most difficult ethical conflicts that educators face. Whether the student proposal is about a sensitive topic, takes an extremely controversial tact, is likely to offend, or simply seems goofy, educators can be put in the position of deciding whether to encourage or squelch a student's enthusiasm.

Sid's instructor is in a difficult position. On the one hand, he can appreciate Sid's creative idea, eagerness, and plan of implementation. On the other hand, this event attracts many who will be unlikely to get past the sight of rotting, disemboweled squirrels, possums, and a cat. School children often attend this event, and the impact on some of them could be traumatic.

Educators may need to perfect a delicate role when the possibility for extremely negative fallout arises from legitimizing, as an agent of the institution, a student project. This role would involve the ability to communicate to the student that the project needs to be altered or even scrapped without dampening the student's enthusiasm and creative energy. It is far less difficult than educators may realize to stunt a student's development by summarily dismissing a proposal. On the other hand, instructors must also remain mindful that breakthroughs in any discipline often come from new approaches that may have seemed worthless, obtuse, or inappropriate at the time. Furthermore, colleges and universities are the soil from which many scholarly and creative advances germinate. Restrictive censorship goes against the purpose of higher education.

When students' propose to go outside the realm of traditional scholarly or creative study, we believe that their educators have an ethical responsibility to weigh the issues very carefully before making a decision about supporting or derailing their projects. Fear of retribution by the institution or unwanted publicity should not be the primary decision-making criteria. And yet, an educator cannot be faulted for wanting to avoid penalties or retain a position that might be jeopardized. When all is said and done, the final decision may involve a deeply personal and moral struggle.

Discussion Questions

1. What would you do if Sid Squish came to you for sponsorship of his exhibit?

2. This case was suggested from a story appearing in *The Chronicle of Higher Education* (1998). An art instructor created an exhibit involving hundreds of live goldfish (symbolizing Jesus Christ) in cups covered with plexiglass. As the fish suffocated and rotted, the word "sin" on the bottom of each cup was obscured by the murky water, representing the death of Jesus for our sins. Pressure applied by animal rights groups shut the exhibit down. What would you have done had this artist been seeking your endorsement?

3. Would you ever be willing to risk your position or reputation for the sake of your own or your students' academic or creative expression? If so, what might be some of the variables in play?

VI

Responsibilities to Students and Colleagues

Instructor Competency

During the past decade, colleges and universities have begun to focus more on assessment of learning outcomes among their graduates. Campus discussions of issues related to accountability in higher education have gone as far as to question the usefulness of our tradition of granting tenure to faculty. A key concern among some critics of the tenure system is the extent to which this system allows institutions to side-step concerns about instructor competence in the classroom.

In this chapter we offer scenarios about instructors whose competence can be called into question as a result of a number of causes. These include failing to remain current, psychological or physical impairment, apathy, working outside of one's area of expertise, lack of objectivity, and theoretical bias. Practical suggestions are offered to instructors and their departments for meeting their instructional obligations to students when resources are strained, when unexpected circumstances arise, and when individual faculty members are resistant to improvement or rehabilitation.

Case 19-1. Updating Lecture Notes

> **Students in Professor Oldstuff's sociology class complain that no work published after 1985 is presented or required as reading. They want to learn newer material, especially because they need to prepare for the Graduate Record Exam and graduate school.**

Competent teaching includes updating courses to reflect the current state of the field. Oldstuff's obligation to keep his course current does not restrict his lectures *only* to newer material. If he believes that nothing important has occurred since 1985, he could weigh his lectures toward the older material and provide examples contrasting past brilliance with current mediocrity, always striving to maintain accuracy and objectivity. Such a compare-and-contrast approach would also give Oldstuff's students examples of critical thinking that they can apply to their other courses.

Although older scholarship should not be discarded, critical information in many fields has flourished in recent decades. It is incumbent on instructors to familiarize themselves regularly with current material and to incorporate this knowledge into their teaching.

What is the minimum interval at which lectures and other course materials should be updated? The answer depends on the course because some fields advance more quickly than others, and the content of lower-level courses is probably more stable than that of upper-level and graduate courses. A rule of thumb might be to update lectures at least as frequently as substantive, as opposed to cosmetic, changes are made in the textbooks of major fields.

Discussion Questions

1. Not all older scholarship is outdated. Indeed, veteran scholars are both frustrated and amused when "new" findings simply replicate the findings of earlier work that has since been buried or not yet transferred to retrievable databases. How does one differentiate between work still worth teaching and outdated material?

2. Is the decision about Oldstuff's teaching pattern at all related to how close he is to retirement? Should he be forced to "keep up," even if he intends to step down after 1 or 2 more years? Why or why not?

Case 19-2. Oversticking to One's Guns

> Professor Watson has been teaching psychology for more than 30 years. He is recognized nationally as an authority in behaviorism and has an excellent teaching record. He finds the contemporary and active area of cognitive psychology to be a "return to our mentalistic beginnings" and "a step backwards." In the classroom, Watson extols the validity of behaviorism and frequently warns against the "onslaught of this new fad."

Does Professor Watson have an obligation to learn and objectively present a topic or more recent approach? Generally speaking, academic freedom accords instructors considerable discretion in how they structure their courses. This is an example, however, of an inappropriate fixation on one aspect of a field.

Cognitive psychology is much more than a "new fad." Whether Watson likes it or not, psychology students need to know about cognitive psychology. Disparaging or withholding information might be harmful to students having legitimate interests in it. Academic freedom allows Watson to criticize an approach after he has understood it and at least summarized it objectively for his students. In other words, he should know his antagonist and then distinguish his individual opinion from those of other authorities and conclusions that are supported by empirical evidence. Using a textbook that adequately presents the topic reduces the degree to which Watson is obligated to explain it fully himself.

Watson's behavior is a more extreme case of a common bias that occurs in lesser degrees. In a survey of college and university instructors, Tabachnick et al. (1991) found that more than three fourths of their national college level educator sample reported that they sometimes taught in a nonobjective or incomplete manner. Although instructors cannot be expected to present every relevant viewpoint or fact, we advocate careful preparation and instruction that is accurate, current, reasonably complete, and scholarly. Instructors are also expected to maintain their expertise (e.g., stay abreast of the latest information), minimize the effects of personal biases on their work, and model for students a scholar's respect for legitimate competing views. (See also 3-5 and 3-6 for cases involving purposefully biased lectures.)

Discussion Questions

1. How does one decide when something is "current" versus "historical"? Does this decision affect how the instructor prepares a class presentation?

2. Passionate teaching is rewarding to students, and Watson is passionate. Because he is only one of many instructors to whom the students will be exposed, is it all right to let him do things his own way and assume that students will pick up what else they need elsewhere? Does it matter whether the course is required or an elective?

3. Some argue that the ability to objectively evaluate various perspectives in one's discipline is not only desirable, but a preferred qualification for teaching and research. After all, many dissertation committee members expect doctoral candidates to be able to critique their work from alternative perspectives. Should colleges and universities take this ability into consideration when hiring faculty?

4. Should the inability to present a balanced view be characterized as "poor teaching" in promotion, tenure, and merit reviews?

Case 19-3. Physical Illness

> Professor Frail misses meeting with his statistics class almost half the time. He has not been well, and everyone is worried about him. His graduate-school-bound students, however, also worry about themselves and whether they are getting the background required to analyze data and compete at the next level. The department's budget is already overburdened, which precludes the possibility of hiring a substitute instructor or graduate assistant.

As sympathetic as we may feel toward a colleague with a physical illness, our obligation to students must also be fulfilled. The institution must provide adequate teaching coverage to ensure that students receive reasonably complete instruction. Although students in a statistics course require frequent and active guidance, the general principle holds for almost any course. Possible exceptions might be a course that involves mostly independent study allowing for flexible supervision, or a course for which it is relatively easy to provide meaningful, alternative learning experiences on short notice. Statistics, involving principles methodically building on each other, is not on such course.

If an administrative budget is truly exhausted, colleagues should be willing to pitch in and teach the course or supervise qualified graduate students. Personal problems that interfere with the ability to give adequate service to students require whatever action is necessary to protect the students' educational welfare. When an illness (physical or mental) renders the instructor incapable of providing adequate services, the instructor is ethically obligated to request a medical leave of absence.

Discussion Questions

1. When feasible, might an instructor who is often ill be able to tape some lectures and play them on sick days?, Or might the instructor post the lectures on a web page? Aside from any logistical matters, are there ethical concerns as well?

2. Does the appropriate response differ depending on whether the course is required in the major or an elective?

3. Would it be an acceptable solution for an advanced graduate assistant—assuming that he has access to a GA who knows the subject matter—be on constant call to fill in on the days that Frail is ill?

Case 19-4. Unprepared to Teach

> The washing machine broke, an upset friend needed to talk, and the cat threw up on the carpet. So much for the evening that Professor Adlib was planning to spend developing tomorrow morning's classroom presentation. She wonders if she should just stay home.

Instructors are only human and will be poorly prepared for work on occasion. A national survey (Tabachnick et al., 1991) revealed that most of a large sample of instructors have been unprepared to teach on occasion. However, simply calling off class is probably unwarranted in most cases. Instructors, like their students, are capable of pulling "all nighters" if they have to, and this may well result in an acceptable preparation.

Several options may be available to Adlib, including switching to an already prepared lecture that is coming up on the schedule or offering an alternative, pedagogically sound experience such as breaking into discussion groups or showing a relevant film. Because unplanned intrusions occur often enough, the best tactic is prevention: *Develop classroom presentations well ahead of time!* Finally, if the instructor is going to try to deliver a lecture or demonstration anyway (assuming that this material is not totally unfamiliar to the instructor and that she has previous teaching experience in the content area), the best she can do under the circumstances might be adequate.

Delivering a truly inferior lecture as a result of unmastered or poorly understood material is unethical because it violates the standard of competence and responsibility to students. The students may unfairly blame themselves for not "getting it." We also believe that if an instructor realizes that the presentation on a given day was inferior, she owes the students a brief explanation and, perhaps, an apology. (See also 19-5 and 19-7.)

Discussion Questions

1. How much of an explanation for a less-than-stellar performance is appropriate? For example, if Adlib's best efforts under the circumstances prove mediocre at best, she might say, "I apologize for not being as well prepared today as I had planned. Something unexpected came up yesterday which cut my preparation time a little too short." Will this explanation, however, teach students that making excuses for poor performances is acceptable?

2. How have you handled unpreparedness? (We have all had such days!)

3. Do you feel more sympathy for Professor Frail (Case 19-3) than for Professor Adlib? Is the instructor who is plagued with a physical problem held as less responsible than one presumed to have more choices and options?

Case 19-5. Emotionally Distraught Instructors

> Professor Sad had a terrible fight with his girlfriend. His underage son from a previous marriage was just arrested for driving under the influence of alcohol. When the alarm goes off the next morning, Professor Sad is so agitated that he calls in sick to cancel all of his classes.

An infrequent cancellation is probably preferable to teaching classes that may be totally useless or even counterproductive. We have learned of examples of upset instructors reacting in ways that caused additional distress. One instructor who had just discovered that his wife was having an affair unleashed unmerciful anger at a secretary for not having finished a letter and then stomped into his classroom declaring that today's students are stupid. These are difficult actions to later repair, and the instructor would have spared everyone had he stayed home to settle down.

As with physical illness (19-3), missing a class that cannot be appropriately taught because of emotional agitation is not considered unethical. However, should the distressed state prove to be other than very temporary, instructors are ethically responsible to seek the help they need and, if they cannot maintain professional standards, to refrain from teaching altogether. Some campuses offer counseling programs for emotionally impaired employees.

Individual faculty members and departments are encouraged to develop alternatives for those who cannot come to work because of illness, physical or otherwise. A buddy system could be created and activated whereby someone would take over another's classes for the day. Or the faculty member could preselect a film to be shown on any sick day.

We should note that sometimes instructors feel much better if they go to work, and can put in a good day even though their personal lives are in turmoil. This decision is, of course, a very personal judgment call. But, if the educator role can "kick in" once he or she gets out of the house and onto campus, the recovery process may actually be facilitated. (See also 19-4.)

Discussion Questions

1. How can one reasonably know in advance whether it is possible to make it through the day? What might be some of the signs and symptoms suggesting that everyone is better off if an instructor does not come to campus?

2. What if a distraught state is likely to be relatively temporary but will cause incapacitation for a week or two? What steps should the instructor or a department take to ensure that the students' education is minimally disrupted?

Case 19-6. Drinking on Company Time

> Wine is served at Professor Emeritus's retirement luncheon. Professor Crony has been a close friend of Emeritus for years and joins in on several toasts. Professor Crony, a wee bit tipsy, walks directly from the faculty center to teach his afternoon class.

Unfortunately alcoholism is a sad reality, even in higher education. It is assumed that a pattern of abuse is not, however, what we see in this case. The sentimental reason for drinking enough wine at lunch to become "tipsy" is probably understandable and might be acceptable *if* Crony's work day had been completed (and it will be a while before he drives home). But the question remains as to whether even minor inebriation is acceptable given Crony's remaining professional duties before his workday ended.

Teaching in a classroom as well as conducting research trials, holding office hours, grading exams, reviewing a manuscript for a journal article, and so on, require a high level of mental clarity. To indulge in a personal pleasure that diminishes the responsibilities for competent teaching and related activities raises concerns about professional obligation. The damage to our role as models is also extensive should students notice (or smell) a difference. In short, Professor Crony's choice to consume alcohol at the reception was not appropriate.

Discussion Questions

1. Are there other, legal substances that can be abused? If an instructor ingests considerable caffeine, such that each class is a frantic event, is drinking too much coffee unethical?

2. Are chronic sleepiness or other side effects from prescription drugs ethical concerns?

3. Crony is, presumably, engaging in a one-time act that may carry some consequences but is unlikely to cause any permanent harm to anyone. Are we all allowed a small fall from grace when the consequences are temporary and minimal? Or must instructors be held accountable for every faulty decision they make?

Case 19-7. Disorganized Lecture Presentations

> **Professor Flustered is described by students as a disorganized person who shuffles notes around and does not deliver an organized, coherent lecture.**

Some instructors are more organized than others, and it is partly the variation in teaching styles that makes getting an education interesting. Furthermore, some of the world's most brilliant scholars have been described as mediocre lecturers.

If student evaluations consistently indicate, however, that lectures are not useful or understandable experiences for students, serious questions about teaching competence arise. The department's chair or a peer should visit Flustered's classes to ascertain whether the lectures are only slightly disjointed or just boring, or whether the content is presented in an incomprehensible way. If Flustered is to remain in the classroom, he should be responsive to peer judgments that his presentations are not understandable and work to remedy the problem.

Discussion Questions

1. What if Flustered believes he is well-organized? How should the department chair proceed?

2. Should scholars who lecture so far above their students' heads, and who are incapable of "dummying down" their material, not be allowed to teach undergraduates?

3. Is the true sign of an outstanding instructor the ability to communicate difficult material to those being taught, regardless of level?

Case 19-8. Burned Out

> **Once a vibrant and active member of the department, Professor Decline has steadily backed away from contributions to the college over the past couple of years.**

> He has become quiet, cuts students short when they come by, assigns students minimal work, and often expresses to colleagues how he "just doesn't care anymore."

Professor Decline appears to be burned-out. Colleagues should be concerned when one of their own undergoes such a major transformation. Although Decline may be experiencing trouble in his personal life, this possibility does not excuse the ineffectual learning opportunities he is offering to his students or the withdrawal of his commitment to the institution.

Because Decline does not appear to be rekindling his passion for teaching or handling his outside problems adequately on his own, someone should encourage him to seek appropriate intervention. This confrontation may require mustering up the courage to deliver "tough love," but it may be the only way to reach Decline.

Teaching is a high-risk profession for burnout because one gives, and then gives again to never ending waves of students. The fruits of our labor are out there somewhere, but we rarely have a chance to see how they ripened. Instructors need to find their own rewards and develop programs to revitalize their energies. Some find renewal in research or other scholarly or creative productivity, including self-directed continuing education. (See also 3-1 and 19-5.)

Discussion Questions

1. Is this a case of employment burnout or is this a case of an impaired faculty member? How can we tell the difference?

2. Have you had periods when you felt burned out? What did you do to revive yourself?

3. How is burnout different from laziness? What might be some markers that differentiate the two?

Case 19-9. Retreading to Teach New Subjects

> Professor Change did not receive graduate level training in psychopathology and abnormal psychology, but would very much like to teach the undergraduate course entitled "Behavior Disorders." She spends the summer

> **reading several relevant undergraduate textbooks as well as five other advanced books on the subject. She also meets for several hours with instructors who have taught the course for years. From these experiences, she develops an undergraduate course.**

Instructors have ethical obligations to provide only those services that are within their areas of expertise and to remain current within those areas. These principles imply that instructors should continue to develop expertise after completing their earlier formal training. In addition to reading books on a subject, plans to retrain might also include tutorial experiences or workshops from recognized experts. One intent of a paid leave is to allow faculty members to acquire expertise in a new area within their disciplines, and some instructors elect to retrain for teaching new courses. Departments that require faculty members to teach courses outside their areas of expertise should help them find sufficient means for retraining.

This case raises the issue of the level on which the course is offered. A summer's worth of reading may be sufficient for some introductory undergraduate classes or for survey courses in some specialties, especially those that overlap somewhat with one's own expertise. However, readings alone may be too meager for an advanced undergraduate course and are likely to be insufficient for courses at the graduate level, both of which require considerably more preparation and supervision or evaluation by someone who has been formally trained.

As stated in the scenario, Change wishes to teach a course in behavioral disorders. Graduate-level training in psychopathology normally includes direct experience with a range of persons who experience diagnosable behavior disorders. Professor Change should include opportunities for some observational or direct experience in an applied setting before she attempts to teach the behavior disorders course. Such additional considerations are also present in many other specialties.

This case also highlights a potential dilemma for small departments, many of which require faculty to teach courses outside their original areas of specialization. Departments like these may need to wrestle with this issue when hiring and curricular decisions are made. It may sometimes be preferable not to offer a specialty course until qualified faculty are hired to teach it or until current faculty have had an opportunity to adequately prepare.

Finally, we wish to acknowledge instructors' ability to teach themselves, and to encourage efforts among faculty to broaden their educational bases. These practices ultimately have positive effects on students.

Discussion Questions

1. What would it take for you to retrain to teach a course you have never taught in your discipline and believe that you would be proficient at it?

2. Should there be a formal review mechanism within the institution to certify that faculty members are qualified to teach courses on a topic for which they have no formal training?

Case 19-10. Course Section Variability

> Ten sections of an introductory survey course are offered by 10 different instructors from six different specialties in the field. The instructors range from graduate students to full professors. Assigned textbooks range from those designed to attract students' interest in the field to hard-nosed works for the serious student scholar. The number of exams and grading standards vary in the sections. The student grapevine is rich with fodder as to who is the hardest and easiest grader, who is the least and most fun, who is the best and worst teacher, and so on.

This case describes a common situation in larger undergraduate programs, especially when a survey course is part of the institution's core curriculum. Ideally all introductory students are exposed to a high-quality educational experiences because for many students this course will be the only one they will ever take in a given discipline. Although great variability in grading, textbooks, and types and numbers of exams is not an optimal condition, it is a reality at colleges and universities with a high enrollments.

Departments have the option of dealing with variability formally or informally. Formal options include standardizing the course to some degree, such as selecting one text or using a single exam format. A less formal option is to schedule discussions among the introductory course instructors regarding course goals and content.

Despite options for dealing with variability among sections, it is unrealistic to think that standardizing elements of a course will eliminate differences among sections. It would not be in the students' best interest to force faculty into a format that undermines the benefits of each instructor's presentation style or ignores academic freedom. An important component of a student's education is learning to adapt to different demands and different evaluation methods. Given these considerations, this case, as described, does not show clear ethical problems.

Ethical issues do arise, however, when variability is so wide that students from some sections receive less than the minimum content expected from an introductory course. This deficiency can place students at a disadvantage in subsequent upper-level courses because they are inadequately prepared. For others, wide variability results in a skewed view of the discipline. It is unethical to offer sections that are clearly inferior, and departments have an obligation to ensure that students have access to adequate learning experiences. (See also 19-12.)

Discussion Questions

1. Is there an ethical justification for mandating that the same textbooks, exams, and class syllabi be used in multiple sections of a given course?

2. Should first-year students who are planing to major in the department enroll in the same introductory section so they will all have a similar background for later courses?

Case 19-11. Offering the Big Class, Regardless

Mammoth State University's history course entitled "The Civil War" draws huge enrollments. Next semester, however, one of the two instructors who routinely teaches the course is on leave and the other had been promised that she would teach only one section. Professor New, an assistant professor with a specialty in the history of Southeast Asia and a limited background in American history, is told that he must teach a section of Civil War.

Colleges and universities should not be run at the expense of the very people upon whom the academy is built. An instructor without competence in a particular area should not be forced through administrative fiat to teach it. Unfortunately, Professor New may feel powerless to protest. Senior members in the department should monitor such circumstances and try to intervene when junior members are exploited. Sometimes a new instructor will volunteer for a popular, albeit unfamiliar course (see 19-9), yet his or her colleagues are still obliged to ensure that the instructor is adequately prepared.

A department in this bind should try to renegotiate with the instructor to whom a promise was made or hire a part-time person who has adequate preparation in the subject. If this becomes a chronic problem, the department should hire a qualified instructor or give another person sufficient time to re-specialize. If options like these are unavailable, the best response would be to not offer the additional section.

Discussion Questions

1. Would the issue be different if Professor New was an experienced instructor instead of someone who is just starting out in his career?

2. What if the instructor who had been promised only one section is now pressured to teach the extra one as well? She agrees, but in return will give only half the usual number of writing assignments. Does this create an ethical issue?

3. Have you ever felt pressured to offer a course that you did not feel prepared to teach? How did you deal with it?

Case 19-12. Gaps in Survey Course Coverage

> **Professor Selective teaches Introduction to Psychology. He usually neglects, however, to cover sections concerning perception, physiological psychology, and research methods because he is weak in these areas. He also fears that when students ask questions, he will be perceived as inadequate because it is unlikely that he will know the answers.**

No one who teaches a survey course is likely to be equally comfortable with every subtopic. Nonetheless, we have an obligation to cover the necessary basic material. Simply deleting important material from a survey course neglects professional duty and may harm students who continue with the major under false pretenses and are inadequately prepared. In this particular example, omitting research methods especially distorts the students' image of an entire discipline.

Selective should work to improve his background in his weaker areas. He can probably find some aspect of each topic sufficiently interesting to compose a good class session. Studying the unmastered material in several textbooks, which enables him to view the subject from slightly different perspectives, is also helpful. He might also confer with colleagues to learn and discuss newer material, or to swap guest lectures. Such arrangements can be reciprocal and can enrich collegial relationships. If Selective cannot master the material at the relatively low level required for introductory students, he should not be teaching the course.

Selective must also learn to feel more comfortable admitting to students that some areas are outside of his realm of expertise. Any effort to conceal this information—especially if Selective simply makes up answers—only harms students and gives the false impression that instructors know everything. In our experience, revealing limitations does not cause students to lose respect for their educators. Students can understand and accept the quick and simple explanation that disciplines are so vast (and most are constantly changing) that no one scholar can know it all. (See also 19-10.)

Discussion Questions

1. What if Selective considers the material problematic because his students consistently find it too difficult and seem to learn very little? Would that justify giving it short shrift?

2. How does one decide what constitutes the "necessary basic material" in a survey class? Do we simply let the content of the textbook make those decisions for us?

3. How do we optimize the trade-off in survey courses between covering many topics in brief vs. fewer topics in more depth?

Case 19-13. Remembering Students' Names

> Although there are only nine students in her advanced seminar class, Professor Noengram learns none of their names. Students complain to another professor that they feel invisible and that Noengram could not possibly care about them.

Learning students' names is not usually thought of as an ethical requirement for instructors. Large classes preclude that possibility for all but those few who have extraordinary memory faculties. However, at some point along the census continuum, instructors should know all or most students by name. A very small seminar is certainly a situation in which students should receive personalized recognition.

Noengram's aloof attitude creates an inferior, perhaps even hostile, learning environment and presents a poor role model to the students. One might legitimately question how much energy Noengram puts into her teaching role in general if she is so uninterested in her meager number of students as individuals.

Discussion Questions

1. Should Noengram's colleagues inform her of the students' complaint? Does this jeopardize the few students' status in Noengram's classes? What helpful role might a colleague play?

2. What solutions are available for personalizing larger lecture sections?

3. Do you learn the names of most of your students? What are the conditions that have allowed you to know most students' names? What conditions make learning student names difficult or impossible?

4. Do you have any good tricks to share that help you recall students' names?

20

Confidentiality
Issues

College and university faculty members are privy to sensitive information about others. Our sources of insider information come from our official duties, as in the cases of students' grades and in-class behavior, or from unofficial channels, as when students and colleagues tell us about themselves or each other. Knowledge of sensitive information naturally raises the issue of confidentiality. When, if ever, is it appropriate to disclose such information to third parties? To whom is it appropriate to make such disclosures? To whom do we owe our primary loyalty? The cases presented in this chapter provide starting points for a discussion of these thorny ethical questions, some of which have legal implications.

Case 20-1. Lectures Based
on Stories Students Tell Us

> During a lecture on victimization, Professor Grimm recounted a detailed story of a young woman who had been raped by her husband's brother. One of the students recognized the story as being that of her best friend. She told her friend about Grimm's presentation. The victim had been in Professor Grimm's class the previous semester and had detailed her plight to him during an office-hour conversation. The victim was devastated upon learning of Grimm's public recounting of her story, but she never spoke to him about it.

It must always be remembered that removing an identifying name does not necessarily protect confidentiality and privacy rights. Instructors must also realize that what is relayed during office hours is presumed by the student to be private, even though we do not typically issue a "limits of confidentiality" statement as is ethically required by mental health professionals. Professor Grimm was wrong to tell the story in class without substantially altering the details. Educators strive to ensure no harm. This caution might help an instructor remember to pause and reconsider before telling a thinly disguised story.

This case also reveals another possible harm about which instructors must remain alert. Professor Grimm never learns from his poor judgment because the student, feeling vulnerable or embarrassed, never confronts him. Trust in her educators has likely been eroded, but Grimm has no clue as to his role in this process. (See also 20-2.)

Discussion Questions

1. Are we ever justified in repeating sensitive stories told to us by students, even when an attempt has been made to fully disguise the identity of the major players?

2. If the student had confronted Grimm, what would be Grimm's most appropriate response?

Case 20-2. Gossip After Hours

> At the weekly TGIF session, the department faculty enjoys telling stories about what students did during the week. These stories often reflect actions or comments viewed as stupid or weird, and the students are often identified by name.

Students are known to gossip about instructors by name, and it is not always flattering. So, it may be tempting to see this turnabout as fair-play. However, educators have a responsibility to protect their students from harm and disgrace. In an informal setting, telling unflattering stories that identify the students by name or other means can influence the way other instructors see these students.

Deleting the identification may alter the situation. Instructors are like everyone else with a job. Blowing off steam in the presence of sympathetic others can help release work-related stress and frustration. However, if the story sessions have a ritualistic or obsessive quality (e.g., the weekly event is a contest to see who can tell the most outrageous student story), the appropriateness and constructiveness of this social tourney must be questioned, even if identities are protected.

There will be times when naming students during a discussion is acceptable or cannot be avoided. An instructor who is having trouble dealing with a student may seek counsel from a colleague known to be wise in such matters or who has previously taught that student. This may be especially necessary for inexperienced instructors. But if such consultations take place they should occur in a professional setting (e.g., university office rather than the local pub), and the student's welfare should be the primary purpose for holding the discussion. (See also 14-4.)

Discussion Questions

1. If stories that identify students by name were to reflect good performance or excellence, does this change the ethics of the situation?

2. If the student's behavior is in the public forum (e.g., the student newspaper), does this change the legitimacy of discussing it during a social hour?

3. What and to whom do you communicate when a student does something that is extremely funny, stupid, or insulting?

Case 20-3, A & B. Sharing Information
Between Student Assistants and Instructors

Toby Tutor is the student assistant in Professor Plato's upper-division Philosophy class. Toby meets with students during office hours and clarifies course material, offers study suggestions, and gives guidance for completing course assignments. Moe Manipulator, a student in the class, has taken Plato's courses before. In previous courses Moe missed class frequently, routinely made excuses for missed assignments, and was caught cheating twice. Lately, Moe has been asking Toby for considerable extra help and Moe's attendance in class has again dropped off. Plato wonders if he should tell Toby about Moe's mode of operating.

Connie Confide is a student in Professor Miro's Art History class. She is also an acquaintance of Miro's teaching assistant, Laura Listensalot. Lately, Connie has been telling Laura of her troubles in school, at home, and with her boyfriend. Connie is having trouble

> maintaining her grades and tells Laura that she is going to miss the next Art History exam because the stress in her life is becoming too much for her. Laura wonders how much of Connie's story she should share with Professor Miro. She feels an obligation to protect Connie's privacy, but feels an equally strong obligation to apprise Miro of Connie's situation. When Laura suggested to Connie that she speak with Professor Miro, Connie refused and reminded Laura that their conversations are confidential.

What are the ultimate boundaries of confidentiality in these situations? To what extent should teaching assistants be expected to share confidential information about students with the instructor of the course and vice-versa? Do issues of informed consent apply here?

These two cases raise the issue of how much confidential information about students should pass between the instructor and the SA. We believe that the instructor and the SA are obligated to inform one another when this information meets three criteria:

1. provides genuine help to the student,
2. is necessary for the effectiveness of the SA's contribution to the class, and
3. maintains the academic integrity of the course.

A good rule of thumb is to provide information on a "need-to-know" basis. Gossiping about students would clearly be unprofessional and off limits. SAs should not be expected to be tattle-tails, either. For example Toby could be warned in general terms about Moe's prior history of irresponsibility without revealing unnecessary details, thus precluding Moe's manipulation of Toby. Likewise, Laura should inform Miro of Connie's need to miss the next exam due to "personal problems," but she need not describe the details of Connie's distress. An added benefit of encouraging instructors and SAs to share basic information about students is that the SA gains experience in learning how to deal with difficult teaching situations.

These two cases highlight the need for instructors to give SAs clear guidelines for interacting with students and regular opportunities to discuss any issues that arise. Professors Plato and Miro need to explain the difference between appropriate and inappropriate help, provide assistance with renegotiating prior relationships (like that of Connie and

Laura), clarify professional role boundaries, and define the situations in which a student should be referred to the instructor or a counselor for further help. Regularly scheduled supervision meetings are always good practice.

Instructors have some control over how the SA is viewed by students in the course. Formally introducing a SA on the first day of class and describing the SA's responsibilities can help students understand the professional role of the SA and foster interactions that remain within the boundaries of a student–instructor relationship. This announcement should inform students that the instructor and SA communicate regularly and share information about students' progress in the course.

Nevertheless, instances such as those described in this case are likely to occur. Even if the SA is introduced as a junior colleague, it is fairly common for students to feel more comfortable approaching the SA rather than the professor when questions and concerns arise. Therefore, it is not surprising that Moe meets frequently with Toby or that Connie seeks out Laura. Unfortunately, a corollary of this is that students may also think it will be easier to manipulate the SA, and this perception should also be discussed with SAs at the onset of the course.

Discussion Questions

1. Do SAs have an ethical duty to inform someone about a student in jeopardy? If you were Laura, what would you do after talking to Connie?

2. How much information should Professor Plato give Toby about Moe's history?

3. Are there different standards for how much a SA should share with the instructor as compared to how much an instructor should share with a student? If so, what are they and why?

Case 20-4. Knowledge of a Student's Illegal Act

> A student, while attempting to explain why he has been doing poorly in class, confesses that he is feeling guilty because he took part in an unarmed robbery of a gas station last week, and an attendant was punched in the face by his companion.

Instructors are generally obligated to keep students' confidences when there is a presumption of privacy. However, this situation is more complicated. To whom does the instructor owe loyalty? The instructor can suggest that the student turn himself in, but what if the student refuses or indicates that he will do so, but does not follow through?

If the student were directly responsible for the battery of the service station attendant, or if the victim was very badly injured or killed, the decision might actually be easier to make. Increasing numbers of legal statutes governing the disclosure of information shared in confidence include a duty to warn or inform appropriate others if the person is viewed as dangerous to others (or to him- or herself). In these difficult situations, with complex legal ramifications, we strongly encourage instructors to consult the institution's legal counsel before deciding how to proceed.

Discussion Questions

1. Should the instructor reveal this student's identity to the institution's legal counsel?

2. How does an instructor distinguish a major offense that should be reported from a minor one that can be ignored?

Case 20-5. Instructors' Private Lives

> While chatting comfortably with Professor Vintner, Gary Grapevine, a student of Vintner, mentions that everyone is saying that Professor Chablis is a lesbian. Vintner is a friend of Chablis's and knows that Chablis is, in fact, a lesbian. But, she is not open about it and wishes to keep her private life private.

The primary ethical issue confronting the instructor in this case is not the accuracy of Grapevine's information, but the fact that the student has introduced a topic of conversation that crosses over two boundaries. The first boundary violation is of Chablis's privacy. The second boundary violation is across the point that separates a professional relationship from a more intimate social relationship.

In responding to this situation, Vintner has several choices. One choice is to simply ignore the remark, thereby sending the indirect message that such topics are off limits, although the student could interpret the nonresponse in any of a number of other ways. Commenting in a way that tries to avoid the situation (e.g., "I don't know," "You would have to ask Professor Chablis about that") also gives ambiguous feedback that can be interpreted as a "yes." Lying to the student, ("No, Professor Chablis is straight") is an untruth and also sends the message that the question was appropriate because it was answered.

We believe that Vintner should neither confirm or deny any private information. Even if Vintner has Chablis's permission to comment (which is unlikely given the information in the scenario), discussions between students and faculty that center on nonacademic or nonstudent development issues (aside from innocuous chit chat) set the stage for dual-role relationships and are, in the main, not in anyone's best interests. The preferable option for Vintner is to shift the conversation away from the question itself and directly confront Grapevine about the inappropriateness of discussions about the private lives of faculty members.

Discussion Questions

1. Does Vintner have any other ethical responsibilities in this situation? For example, should she discuss with Grapevine the ethics of rumor transmission?

2. Should Vintner tell Chablis about the session with Gary Grapevine? Why or why not?

3. Does it matter if the student's question is about private happy matters, such as inquiring about a colleague's engagement to be married, a wanted pregnancy, a promotion, or some other pleasant situation?

Case 20-6. Dispersing Papers

> At the end of the term, the graded personal journals for Professor Pickemup's writing class are left in a box sitting on the floor of the department office for students to retrieve.

Although Pickemup may be using a convenient mechanism for students to fetch their papers, it raises questions about students' right to privacy. This scenario is troublesome because personal journals may contain sensitive information that snoopers could easily access. Even for more traditional term projects, it is still best to avoid this method of returning papers if at all possible. Or, at the very least, grades and evaluative comments should appear inside a folder rather than on the outside page.

Centralized pick-up boxes also carry a risk of unauthorized removal, which further reduces the attractiveness of this dispersal method. It would be better to have the office staff (if they have the time) disperse the papers and ask for proper identification if a student is not already known to them.

Concerned students should be able to receive their papers some other way.   Students could be allowed to provide self-addressed/stamped envelopes, and the instructor could return papers or journals by mail. Instructors who are willing to mail papers should announce it in advance because students may not think of it themselves. (See also 7-2.)

Discussion Questions

1. Are there comparable problems when handing back papers or exams in class? For example, passing exams "across the row" may reveal grades or comments to some who should not see them.

2. How much effect does the size of the class have on the technique used for returning assignments? What are effective ways that minimize privacy invasion when returning assignments in a very large lecture class?

Case 20-7. Publicizing Others' Private Information

> **Professor Outing is openly gay. His work in the classroom and in the laboratory is beyond reproach, and he has favorable recommendations for both tenure and promotion.   Recently, however, he has started identifying other colleagues who are gay but have not revealed this in any public manner.**

Sometimes information can slip out, such as dropping the news that a colleague is dissatisfied with the administration and is looking for another position. However, this is not the case here. Outing's behavior is an unethical invasion of privacy and violates the level of confidentiality expected among colleagues. Exposing publicly such private information about others shows inadequate respect for their dignity and welfare and would very likely do lasting damage to his collegial relationships. If his long-term interest is the promotion of human dignity, Outing was a more successful role model before he commenced this selfish and impatient behavior which, in the end, may alienate people and actually set back Outing's cause.

The incident described in this case would be rare and serves primarily as an example of a more general concern about revealing information about colleagues that may serve the needs of the revelator, but does not consider the rights to privacy of those being exposed. The underlying issue can be generalized to spreading any kind of information about colleagues' characteristics or behavior that is private, does not raise legal questions, and has no bearing on current competence or professionalism. Other examples could include a previous history of alcoholism or drug abuse or mental illness, most incidents of poor judgment occurring in one's youth, and opinions about sensitive matters that a colleague may share in a private venue. (See also 14-1 and 14-2.)

Discussion Questions

1. Suppose Outing is an energetic member of an activist animal rights organization and posts an inflammatory poster on his door that lists members of the academic community who have been seen wearing fur coats. Assume that the list is accurate. Do ethical concerns apply?

2. What are more common types of information that colleagues may be privy to about their peers that could cause considerable harm should that information be widely cast across campus?

Case 20-8. Unintended Effects of Cooperative Programs

> In an attempt to improve retention of first-year students at Keepem University, a program that pairs several classes together has been developed. The instructors for these classes plan overlapping activities designed to enhance the learning experiences of the student. The goals are to create a bonding among the students and that more of them will decide to stay in school.
>
> The instructors get together a number of times during the semester and discuss the progress of the program. These discussions involve reflections on the work of individual students. After one such meeting, Freddie Findsout's history instructor mentions to Freddie that she knows he is doing poorly in his English class. Freddie is upset that his English instructor has revealed his performance to another of his instructors.

Here is an example of a true gray area regarding the welfare of students. The 1973 Buckley Amendment ensures the privacy of one's records, and Freddie's privacy has been invaded when his grade in one class is revealed to another instructor. Moreover, as research has shown, the expectation (based in this case on the conversation about Freddie's English performance) may influence subsequent performance evaluations by other instructors.

Although Keepem University should be praised for trying to encourage students to complete their educations, such programs must be monitored for possible ethical dilemmas. In this case, training the instructors before the term starts should include a warning regarding the sharing of information about students, indicating what is appropriate and what may unfairly be of detriment. Students should also be made aware of the sharing policy provisions beforehand, allowing them to make an informed decision when selecting a college or a special program within the institutions. It may well be that Freddie's performance in both classes can be enhanced if the teachers who share their information look for ways to coordinate their efforts to help Freddie. But, it must be kept in mind that, by doing so, they could also work against Freddie's best interests. (See 20-3.)

Discussion Questions

1. Are there times when discussing an identified student's performance with colleagues will most likely help that student? What circumstances might justify "bending" considerations of privacy when attempting to help a student?

2. Some students might be willing to forsake the privacy restrictions if there was the promise that the program would help their overall performance in college. With the pairing of classes such as this, should the instructors develop a limited confidentiality waiver for students to consider signing?

Case 20-9. Unwanted Knowledge

> Because it is placed in an unaddressed envelope, Professor Inmiddle opens and reads a short note he finds in his mail box, written to a married colleague by an undergraduate student. The student confesses everlasting love, and the content suggests that an affair may already be in progress.

In this case, Inmiddle has unwittingly fallen into a situation in which he has information that may have implications for a student's welfare. However, he has little information about the veracity or the specifics of the situation. How and whether Inmiddle chooses to react depends on many factors. How explicit is the evidence? (e.g., "Could we meet again at the same time and place tonight?," as compared to "Could we meet sometime soon?") Did the note leave room for interpretation? Could the student be idealizing the relationship with her teacher? Could the letter be a hoax? If Inmiddle chooses minimal or no intervention, a student may be harmed. If he acts on the basis of incomplete information, his colleague could be unfairly harmed.

Assuming the note contained explicit detail that left little room for doubt, many would argue that this case depends on whether the identified faculty member is currently evaluating the student or may evaluate the student in the future. Others would argue that the current status of the professional relationship does not matter because once the power differential between an instructor and student has been established, it is always present. But, regardless of one's position on whether it is ever permissible for an instructor to date a student, Inmiddle may not be able to determine if the student is being harmed by this relationship.

If the content of the note leaves ample room for multiple interpretations, as seems to be the case here, Inmiddle might approach the recipient and cautiously attempt some informal inquiry. Such a solution might be necessary if Inmiddle's institution has no guidelines for reporting cases of suspected sexual harassment. Even the most productive response, however, may be altered by variables such as the relationship between Inmiddle and his colleague, the relative ranks of the two, and whether they have a close or distant relationship. Inmiddle should consult a trusted advisor before proceeding. (See also 14-6 and 14-7.)

Discussion Questions

1. If Inmiddle decides to report his knowledge to the appropriate university official, is he obligated to let the instructor and student know of his intentions? What are the pros and cons of making either choice?

2. Suppose Inmiddle learns of this affair during a meeting with the student. The student believes she is the victim of sexual harassment, but wants Inmiddle to keep their conversation confidential. Some professional organizations (e.g., the American Psychological Association) have ethics codes that prohibit violation of confidentiality in most circumstances regardless of local institutional policy. What options does Inmiddle have for dealing with this apparent conflict of interest?

3. What would you have done if the note was delivered to your mailbox?

Political and Public Statements

How do we negotiate the boundaries of our influence over students when the focal topic is socially or politically charged? Media saturation makes controversial issues and conflicting interpretations impossible to avoid on a college or university campus. Educators are often admonished, however, to remain objective and to avoid taking advantage of our opportunity to unduly persuade our students in matters unrelated to pedagogy. Defining the line between fostering civility and the right to free speech has been sorely tested in the academy, but not fully resolved.

The cases in this chapter examine the possible impact of one's political or religious views on everyday interactions with students, both in and out of the classroom. Examples include race, abortion, free speech, and hot-button campus issues. The significance of our influential role requires sensitivity to what students think about us and how they incorporate our beliefs and values into their own.

Case 21-1. Politics in the Classroom

> **Professor Partisan is very active in politics and her political party. She observes that many of her students, however, hold political ideals very different from hers. She uses her classroom pulpit to interject her views into the discussions at hand by, for example, telling accounts of the negative impact that results when other ideologies have prevailed. In addition, during political campaigns she wears buttons while teaching class and puts posters favoring her candidates in the classroom where she teaches. Outside of the classroom, she tries to persuade students to vote as she will. Students begin to grumble that Partisan's political views cloud her presentation of relevant course material.**

Being active in political affairs outside of one's responsibilities as a faculty member is both acceptable and an inalienable right. On the other hand, partisan politicking in the classroom or otherwise while on the job is inappropriate, and may violate school policy.

To a limited degree Partisan's enthusiasm for proselytizing among students is understandable. The facts are that students do differ from us in many ways, and many are uninformed. Part of our calling may be to help them change certain attitudes, at least regarding their understanding of the subject matter we are teaching. However, instructors should avoid steering students towards their personal agendas, and Partisan's use of her authority to attempt to convert students to her political values goes way out of bounds.

That said, do instructors have any latitude in giving straightforward and honest answers to questions concerning their personal beliefs? It can be difficult to eschew political values and implications entirely when helping students understand certain subjects. With some courses or topics it is all but impossible to avoid politically sensitive issues or questions. So, what criteria should be used to cope with this unsettled situation? Our view is to accept that political values are inevitably implicated in at least some of what we tell students, and it is better to acknowledge this fact whenever it seems appropriate than to believe (or at least claim) that we always remain impartial. We should also acknowledge, whenever appropriate, the legitimacy of holding views other than our own. Furthermore, our actions as instructors should never involve coercion (e.g., grading essays based entirely on the their adherence to the instructor's political views). However, it is not always clear how persuasive various actions (e.g., wearing a button) are for some students. Our built-in authority over students gives our actions the potential to be more coercive than we realize.

Instructors should include enough information and context to allow students to distinguish a instructor's personal, partisan ideology from "regular" course content. Students should also understand that they are free to accept or reject the former as a qualitatively different kind of information from that making up the substantive area of knowledge they are studying. In the end we are most successful when we help provide the groundwork for students to make their own informed judgments and choices. (See also 21-5 and 21-6.)

Discussion Questions

1. What if the instructor's agenda is simply to increase students' political

participation in a nonpartisan way? Examples might include encouraging students to vote and providing information about how to register, or encouraging their involvement in campaigns that have widespread, nonpartisan support (e.g., campaigns to neuter pets, cease smoking, or drug abuse). Would apathetic students or those wanting to remain entirely outside the system have any legitimate complaint regarding undue coercion?

2. What if Partisan never openly spoke of her political stance on issues, but wore buttons or ribbons almost every day that identified her political alignments, including those that are openly controversial? Is that more acceptable than how she was portrayed in the vignette? Why or why not?

3. Is it unethical for an organized group of faculty to underwrite and sign their names to an ad in the student newspaper endorsing a sensitive position that has divided support at best (e.g., a petition against the U.S. stand on military tribunals)? How about the local newspaper?

4. Is it ethical to hold students accountable on exams for material that was identified as personal opinion?

Case 21-2. Religion in the Classroom

A student, Peter Pious, frequently cites Biblical passages and other religious texts to support (or refute) positions taken by himself, the instructor, and fellow students. He also makes liberal use of such sources on essay exams. When the instructor offers Peter feedback that this kind of evidence is not germane to the course, Peter protests that his spirituality is so central to how he experiences everything that he cannot simply turn it off and be expected to think, integrate material, and make original contributions to the class. Peter further notes that the course syllabus invites students to "think for themselves" and "share personal views" on the material.

In spite of the instructor's continued admonitions, Peter persists. Other students are complaining that his behavior is making them uncomfortable and wasting class time. The instructor decides to inform Peter that from now on he will be recorded as absent from any class when his contributions to discussions are explicitly religious, and that any exam answers that include religious arguments will receive no credit.

How do we deal with students who insist on approaching our course strictly on their own terms? How do we grade and explain our grades to students whose religious or other deeply held values lead them to very different conclusions from those reached by the instructor or a discipline? Peter cannot be faulted for his deep commitment to a set of personal beliefs. His primary responsibility as a student, however, is to meet the expectations of the course. It is helpful if the course syllabus and early explanations are clear about what is considered relevant. In addition, students' grades should be based on objective indicators of performance.

On essay exams, students should be allowed some latitude, albeit with the risk they will be judged to have come up short if they omit substantive ideas or data simply because they clash with their personal beliefs. If Peter learns to couch his views in more secular terms, his ideas may serve to invigorate class discussions by the insights they offer while avoiding overtones that could distract or repel others.

We do not, however, agree with this instructor's handling of Peter's stubbornness. For purposes of classroom management, the instructor may need to arrive at a special understanding with Peter about what is appropriate for his in-class contributions. However, evaluations of Peter's academic performance (attendance and exam scores) are a different matter. When Peter is present he should not be marked absent, no matter the nature of his "contributions." Similarly, his exam responses must be graded fairly on the basis of how well they addressed the questions, with appropriate credit given for whatever relevant material Peter includes.

As noted with respect to several other cases, imparting new values is a big—if often unstated—part of what we do as college-level instructors. Part of our mission may be to show sensitivity when we help students learn to recognize the difference between their beliefs and empirical data, historical research, or other perspectives and interpretations. In this way we help them expand their critical thinking abilities without denigrating their personal values. As difficult a task as that may be, that mission is impossible to achieve if we, ourselves, cannot serve as models for our students. (See also 2-10.)

Discussion Questions

1. What if Peter does not directly espouse his strong religious views until the very end of the course, such as on the final exam or the term project? Is the instructor justified in failing him for the exam (and perhaps the course)? Or, could an Incomplete (with arrangements to be made later) be justified in such an unexpected case?

2. What if the perspective to which a student like Peter is strongly committed happens to correspond closely the instructor's personal views? Can instructors recognize the possible bias and still remain objective when it comes to grading such students?

3. Most campus policies allow for a student to be removed if consistent behavior substantially disrupts the learning process. Does Peter meet this criterion?

4. Is it a mistake for an instructor to encourage in the syllabus speaking out and thinking for oneself? (After all, Peter ultimately used these statements to his own advantage and caused problems for everyone else.)

5. What would you do if Peter Pious was your student?

Case 21-3. Hot Topics in the Classroom

> **Professor Oneside discusses abortion in his Social Issues class as a decision that should be left up to the woman. He takes an empirical approach to this controversy, using a number of data-based research studies to support his point of view. Several students protest that he does not give equal time to the arguments on the other side and is, therefore, misusing his power to shape student attitudes.**

Presenting highly controversial issues in class, even when the issue is a legitimate aspect of the course topic, can be tricky for several reasons. The instructor may have well-formed opinions about these issues that are different from those held by many students. Instructors can also hold a substantial influence over students, and part of an instructor's job involves helping students learn to appreciate the relevance of empirical evidence and alternative scholarly interpretations in understanding complex issues. However, when personally held core values are also at stake, the place of empirical data is more complex.

Rather than arguing only one side of an important controversy, as in the present case, an instructor should outline all the important sides (including any relevant data) and let the students participate fully in a critical discussion of the issue. Oneside may voice his opinion that his side of the abortion debate has more empirical support, and he should document this assertion on the basis of scientifically and professionally derived information. For a course like this, it may be appropriate to mention in the syllabus (and reiterate in class) that the instructor has well-formed opinions on some of the issues to be presented. He might add and that students may disagree strongly with the instructor without risk of ridicule or censure, and that they are encouraged to discuss issues with him outside class. If Oneside cannot offer students who disagree with him a genuine, nonpunitive forum, then ethical problems exist. (See also 21-8.)

Discussion Questions

1. What if the students seeking equal time belong to extremist hate groups? Is an instructor obligated to attempt to present their ideology and purpose in a constructive manner by attempting to enumerate their "good" points?

2. How critical is it for an instructor to present minority viewpoints on issues when the majority view is widely endorsed among experts in the instructor's field and also has widespread public support?

Case 21-4. Campus Political Organizations

> Professor Staunch is an avid opponent of capital punishment. He has organized a group of students on campus with similar beliefs. He leads the group at meetings and has organized trips to large rallies. Staunch often makes a point of telling all of his students who come to see him before or after class, or during office hours, about upcoming events. Students who do not share his beliefs feel threatened if they express their true feelings. Some complain that they feel pressured to express support for statements that do not reflect their belief in capital punishment.

Although there is usually no problem with organizing or leading an appropriately registered campus group (even a controversial one), power differences between students and faculty and the risk of misusing the trust and influence we enjoy require scrupulous sensitivity to the distinction between personal and professional activity. Thus, once instructors are involved in a controversial cause they should go out of their way to separate this involvement from their role in the classroom. If questions directly relevant to the focal issue come up in class, for example, the instructor should either decline to comment in that context or scrupulously acknowledge all other sides of the issue.

Discussion Questions

1. What if Staunch never mentions capital punishment in his classes, but students who are active in support of the death penalty must take his class? These students are personally known to Staunch because they openly face off from time to time. What precautions should Staunch take to maintain his objectivity when evaluating these students?

2. What if the issue is somewhat less polarizing (e.g., welfare reform), and Staunch considers it directly relevant to his course (e.g., a social work course lecture on the history of welfare policy)? Would his recruitment of students in an activist activity be ethically justified?

3. What if an issue is widely popular, such as the sharp rise in patriotism after September 11, 2001? Is it ethically acceptable to encourage patriotic activity during class time? If so, in what ways?

Case 21-5. Controversial Speakers

> **In announcing the visit of a Ku Klux Klan Grand Wizard to campus, Professor Screech encourages the students to show up and "boo the man down."**

In our view, Screech's encouragement to deny the Ku Klux Klan (KKK) or any other group its right to free speech is unethical, whether delivered in the classroom or elsewhere. Most instructors want students to think for themselves. Whether a presentation is benign or grotesque, it is inappropriate to tell students whom they should or should not hear unless the speaker's presentation is directly related to the course.

We are not suggesting that Screech must ignore the occasion of an official KKK visit, because encouraging students to attend such an event is appropriate, or even desirable, as a device to further their educational experience. Screech may also express his own laudatory or condemnatory opinions about the group or its message as long as these personal views are identified as such. Spending too much time in a class unrelated to the topic, however, would be inappropriate. Finally, Screech could promote competing ideas by participating in a peaceful protest (noncoercively and outside class) or by arranging for an opposing speaker to come to campus.

Postsecondary institutions are uniquely suited to the exercise of free speech, and there is nothing like an odious guest speaker to remind us of this fact. Furthermore, ethical principles obligate instructors to respect others' rights to hold attitudes or opinions differing from their own. Instructors should be visible models of this principle rather than misusing the influence they have over students.

Discussion Questions

1. Should limits on free speech exist on a college or university campus?

2. Should extremely controversial speakers ever be invited to campus in the first place?

3. Given his obligation to serve as a role model for students, is it ethically questionable for Screech to participate in disruptive confrontations or civil disobedience, even as a private citizen at an off-campus location?

4. It is a common and accepted practice for instructors to require students to attend campus-wide events when the topic is directly related to the course. Are there types of on-campus events or speakers that would be *unethical* to require of *every* student in the class? For example, should an orthodox Jewish student enrolled in a religion class be required to go to an evangelical Christian church service and marked down if she refuses?

Case 21-6. Political Display in the Office

> Professor Political has slogans and posters on his outside office door and inside office walls that leave no doubt about how he feels on various contemporary issues. Topics include animal rights, nuclear power, capital punishment, women's rights, and various partisan political personalities. Political does not mention any of his causes in class, nor does he talk to students about his beliefs unless he is asked.

Although under most conditions Political's behavior would be protected under a First Amendment right to free speech, several points are worth consideration. First, because institutional (college or university) property is involved, Political would be wise to investigate whether policy statements exist relevant to his poster passion. In state-supported schools, legal risks may be incurred. There may also be some meaningful distinction between Political's personal office area and the space he shares with others (e.g., the hallway, classrooms, or lobby area).

Legal or policy issues aside, there are subtle ethical risks in trumpeting beliefs on the walls and doors of our offices. A major concern is the possibility that students and others will confuse Political's personal views with his professional opinions as a faculty member. We want students to take serriously what we say, and yet we also expect them to distinguish the information conveyed in our teaching from those that express only our personal beliefs. However, when in doubt, it is our responsibility to clarify the boundaries dividing our professional roles or positions and our private views. Displaying partisan statements reflecting one's personal beliefs on school property makes these beliefs public, and students, parents, and other visitors will readily view an instructor's office and decor as official trappings of his or her position as a faculty member and, perhaps, representative of a professional discipline.

Given the substantial differences in power and authority between faculty and students, adverse effects can occur even when views (political or otherwise) are clearly understood to be the instructor's own. For example, a tasteless display (e.g., a blood-drenched pictorial poster for a slasher movie) could be offensive or intimidating enough as to prevent a student from being comfortable in the instructor's office, or even from seeking assistance in the first place. Also of concern would be less blatant material which might have a *differentially* negative effect on certain others (e.g., partisan materials concerning far left or far right political orientations). Considering the complexity here, the more traditional among us would be likely to opt for official neutrality on partisan political issues. (See also 21-1.)

Discussion Questions

1. Suppose Political has colleagues with views opposed to his who push the envelope with their own partisan displays. Does this give Political somewhat more latitude to respond in kind than he otherwise would have?

2. Several faculty members in many departments have a sign that says "SAFE" on their door to indicate that the instructor does not discriminate against lesbians and gay men and is open to discussing educational issues with gay and lesbian students. Might this be intimidating to those who hold antihomosexual views, or does this otherwise pose ethical problems? Should we care?

3. A Caucasian instructor's spouse is Asian, and a wedding photo of them is prominent among the instructor's personal office decorations. Another is in a committed gay relationship and displays a photograph of the two with their arms around each other. Should it matter to these instructors that their photos might offend a student who is uncomfortable about interracial marriage or a homosexual life style? What if a student was so upset that she refuses to come into the office? Is that just her problem?

4. What are the limits of personal photographs or other displays in our own offices? Should there be any?

5. A colleague we know who teaches human anatomy has human brains in jars in his office. He argues that this is the only safe place to keep them. Many students, however, will not enter his office. Because this colleague is limiting the contact students are having with him, is he unethical? Or, is the problem with the squeamish students?

Case 21-7. Self-Presentation Off Campus

> The Independent Star, a local newspaper, carries a flaming guest editorial lambasting the governor's state budget plan. The editorial is signed by Professor Hotpen, a political science instructor, and includes her title and affiliation. Some colleagues are upset because they do not agree with Hotpen's analysis. Others are upset because they do not wish to offend the governor lest he further cut the state-supported university's budget.

Any articulate and well-informed citizen, whether a college faculty member or not, performs a valuable public service by contributing to reasoned public debate. When imparting personal opinions in a public forum, however, faculty must attempt to assure that the public does not assume institutional sponsorship or endorsement of the position expressed. Hotpen could have avoided misinterpretation by omitting her university position after her name.

Often enough, however, what one does and where one does it is revealed anyway. Occupational status is easily obtained information that others often want to know in order to assess the credibility of the source. If faculty members wish to express opinions publicly, they should explicitly communicate to their audiences that the opinions are their own, that they are not acting as representatives of the college or university, and that their opinions do not necessarily correspond to those held by the university administration, other faculty members, and staff.

Discussion Questions

1. What if an editorial or other public comment is so extreme that it embarrasses almost everyone on campus. What appropriate responses are available to Hotpen's colleagues?

2. College and university faculty members are often called by media journalists or reporters to comment on various issues in the news. The inclusion of the caveats (i.e., "This is my own opinion that does not necessarily represent those held by other members of the college") is not under the instructor's control. In such cases, should instructors be especially cautious about what they say when it is clear that their affiliation will be identified? Would any institutional mandate to be cautious amount to curtailing free speech?

Case 21-8. The Bully Pulpit

> Professor Tickoff bursts into class one day waving the campus newspaper, obviously upset about something. When the class starts, Tickoff shouts out, "Did you see today's paper? Look at this? They're buying out the contract of a lousy coach and paying him a fortune! They pay off somebody who does an inferior job, but tell me they can't even afford a basic computer for this classroom. If they won't support me, why should I support them? What the..." Tickoff continues a tirade that lasts for most of the class period. Several members of the class are troubled because there is an exam scheduled very soon on difficult material that was supposed to be discussed that day.

We believe that a college education is more than just what goes on in the classroom. Students are usually unaware of the big picture of an institution's finances and agendas and could benefit from an open, frank, and fair discussion to put the situation into perspective. It might be all right if Tickoff wanted to very briefly discuss the buyout of the coach, pointing out the difficulties with financial policies as he sees them, thus helping the class to understand the overall picture of campus commitments. To shortchange his students by teaching very little during the class period, however, is an abrogation of Tickoff's responsibilities and unfair to the students.

Discussion Questions

1. What if the foregoing issue is reasonably relevant to the content of the course, such as one on educational administration or a physical education course on coaching? Does this change the acceptability of Tickoff spending considerable time on a specific event?

2. What if a critical event occurred that has nothing to do with the course, but everyone is talking about it. An example would be the days following the terrorist attacks on the World Trade Center and the Pentagon. Would it be all right to spend a full class period on that subject? Why and why not?

Responsibilities
to the Institution

This chapter looks at the sometimes hazy boundaries between acceptable and unacceptable use of campus resources. Most decisions as to what is acceptable and what is not are more difficult to make than they might seem at first blush. For example, most instructors take work home, and some do much of their grading and scholarly activities away from their busy offices to avoid disruptions. However, how many institutional supplies or equipment are too many to end up on the instructor's home desk? Questionable use of job-related resources and related work place integrity issues are the themes found in this chapter.

Case 22-1. Royalty Producing Work

> Professor Goodwords is writing a textbook. He asks the department secretary to proofread the manuscript, add changes and corrections to the file, and otherwise help with the development of the book during regular business hours.

No single and simple answer would cover the resolution of this situation in all circumstances. Generally, allocating resources to help produce royalty-producing work should not supersede routine departmental service. For example, if Professor Goodword's book is getting attention ahead of exam typing or assistance with a manuscript submitted to a non-compensated scholarly journal, there is an ethical problem because a personal enterprise is interfering with other normal campus activities.

The type of project probably makes a difference. Some works for which the instructor may receive some form of compensation also benefit the institution and the society. A textbook is not necessarily of that status, and far less likely to fit the criteria are nonscholarly works such as those in the "check-out-stand" genre.

Circumstances may arise in which no ethical complications exist. Some extended specialty scholarly projects are, by definition, royalty producing because they will be published as books. However, the monetary rewards will likely be very small, and the original purpose was to produce a body of scholarly work as opposed to creating a best-seller. In addition, department staff sometimes seek extra work during the down-times (often between terms) to stave off boredom. In addition, some support staff members may enjoy this type of challenge. However, it must be ascertained that the staff is not being coerced or charmed into doing work they neither want nor have time to do. Finally, sometimes it may be appropriate to agree in advance that some portion of the royalties will be returned to the department.

Some colleges and universities have disclosure and conflict-of-interests policies regarding the support of individual's income-generating research and scholarship that utilizes institutional resources. Instructors using institutional resources for work for which they will be compensated from outside the institution should check these policies carefully. As institutions of higher education increasingly recognize that their faculties can be a source of income, it is especially necessary to be aware of—and fully understand—intellectual property policies.

Discussion Questions

1. Suppose that Goodwords is the department chairperson to whom the secretary reports directly. Given this power differential, can a department secretary ever comfortably say no? To what extent should differences in power limit the requests that are made of staff members?

2. Although this case focused on the use of a secretary's time, other types of institutional resources are often involved in book writing. These include office computers, duplication of resources, paper, and other supplies. The argument can even be made that the instructor's time could be dedicated to course improvement rather than writing. What are the determinants of the appropriate use of these other resources, especially the intangible ones such as time?

3. What if Goodwords writes a best-selling trade book that garners the institution considerable favorable publicity and attracts many students to enroll? Should authors with this kind of "star potential" receive extra support from their departments?

Case 22-2, A, B, & C. Using Institutional
Resources Off Campus

> An instructor is also a free-lance consultant to the personnel divisions of many local corporations. She frequently conducts workshops and provides consultation on specific problems for personnel managers. Her college owns several films and tapes that include content relevant to topics covered in these workshops. She frequently checks out these materials and equipment from the library and incorporates them into her workshops.
>
> An instructor teaches full-time at a university and also teaches a Wednesday evening course at a local community college. Several of the required readings for the course are unavailable in the community college library. The instructor checks out these materials from the library at his home institution and places them for the entire term in a reading room at the community college.
>
> An instructor accepts an invitation to give a lecture at the local Rotary Club. She checks out a video segment and equipment from the library for use in her presentation.

The issue underlying the first two of the three cases is the use of institutional resources for activities that result in private gain. Neither instructor appears to have sought permission for the intended use of the resources.

When consultation is not *pro bono*, as in the first scenario, and the instructor is earning money for applying her expertise to deliver a nonuniversity-related, private service to the private sector, we believe that an ethical problem exists. It would be more appropriate for her to rent the desired materials. She can declare these costs as business expenses for tax purposes.

The community college teacher may be able to obtain university permission for short-term loans of the needed materials, as long as the students at the lending institution are not disadvantaged by the absence of the borrowed materials. A more appropriate solution is to negotiate the purchase of the books with the community college.

The third case appears to be the kind of activity that colleagues and universities actively support. Unless the instructor is using her Rotary Club speaking engagement to drum up business for her private consulting firm or to make a presentation that runs counter to the mission of the university, using resources to inform and enlighten the community is an activity worthy of appropriate institutional support.

Colleges and universities usually have their own policies on such matters, and these should be consulted. One may find, for example, that certain kinds of workshops or other continuing education programs conducted for personal gain do bring credit to the university or have such strong, legitimate educational goals that the institution is willing to lend the supporting materials. A common example might be the instructor who requires a data projector for a presentation and who also receives an honorarium that helps with expenses associated a professional meeting (e.g., travel).

Discussion Questions

1. Should the fact that expensive equipment (e.g., data projectors and laptop computers) is beyond what the average faculty member could ever afford alter an acceptable reason to take resources off campus for an income generating opportunity? For example, say that the university has many data projectors and the community college has none, should the instructor in the second scenario be able to borrow the equipment every Wednesday evening?

2. Does your institution have borrowing policies in place? If so, what are they?

Case 22-3. Double-Dipping

> The department chair assigns a new instructor, Steve Slick, ABD, a favorable teaching schedule. It is verbally agreed that the purpose of this arrangement is to allow Steve blocks of free time during the work week to complete his dissertation. Instead, Slick is discovered to be teaching part-time at a small college in a neighboring community.

At the very least, Slick's behavior has seriously abused the good will and support of his colleagues and has jeopardized his favorable teaching schedule (if not his entire job) at his primary campus. This case should also give fair warning to department chairs and others who negotiate with new hires that any understanding about how soon a degree will be completed should be discussed, agreed upon, and formalized in writing. Even in the event that Slick somehow manages to complete his dissertation more or less within the time agreed upon, he would have to do considerable fence-mending with his colleagues at the primary institution. If, in the more likely scenario, Slick miscalculates and fails to meet the understood deadline for completing his degree, it is then up to the department to decide if he keeps his job. Breaking trust is difficult to repair. (See also 22-4.)

Discussion Questions

1. What if a more senior colleague (rather than a new hire) obtains a paid leave to pursue a research or professional development project but, in actuality, spends much of the time in unrelated activities?

2. What if Slick responds to the discovery that he was abusing a privilege with a convincing argument that his pay is so low that he could not meet his basic monthly expenses? Does that constitute an acceptable excuse?

Case 22-4. Moonlighting

> **Professor Moonlite carries a full-time teaching load at a university and works 25 hours a week in his private consulting business.**

Instructors often complain that their salaries are far from commensurate with those of other professionals possessing a similar degree of educational training. However, instructors have chosen to accept positions requiring teaching and advising students, departmental and university committee participation, and, often, scholarly research productivity. Although our in-class hours may amount to 12 or fewer, the time involved in performing all the other duties meets or often exceeds a 40-hour work week. Even when no outside work is performed, undergraduate students probably need more of our time and attention than we are able to give them.

A case can be made that some off-campus work activity may actually enhance teaching, especially hands-on experience or the application of the discipline in which one teaches. Many instructors write scholarly books and, although the time commitment is extensive, ethical questions about this activity are rarely raised. The question is, what and *how much* outside activity enhances or detracts from one's full-time job commitment?

Full-time faculty involved in nonrelated business ventures or avocational activities abound. Sometimes the time and energy commitment is minimal (e.g., following a passive investment) or is a hobby (e.g., the talented physicist whose paintings are saleable). Such avocations are also unlikely to pose any ethical concerns. Other faculty members, however, have businesses that take many hours each week. The most egregious example brought to our attention involved a tenured full professor who taught his "full" load from 7 to 9 a.m. and 7 to 10 p.m. on Tuesdays and Thursdays, and could be found at his boat sales and repair shop all day, every day, during the week. Clearly an outside activity can ultimately become one of fraud. Certainly there comes a point when fatigue, stress, diverted interest, and time expended erode the competence and commitment available to the institution and to ones' students. When an instructor zips through lecture preparation, tensely indulges office hours with one foot out the door, is absent from any departmental or university support activities, and scurries off to somewhere else after class, the institution, colleagues, and students have been failed. Ethics becomes very much an issue.

It is difficult to come up with a specific guideline (e.g., "10 hours a week is ethical, more is not") because people differ markedly in their energy levels and available discretionary time. A tireless worker without relationship obligations may well be able to handle a substantial number of hours of outside employment without jeopardizing the quality of teaching and other campus responsibilities. We believe that it is every instructor's moral responsibility to assess whether outside activities short-change the institution or impair the ability to perform duties competently and responsibly. (See also 22-3.)

Discussion Questions

1. Can you create a scenario involving an instructor who spends 20 hours a week working off-campus in which no ethical problem would likely arise?

2. Is what one actually does during off-campus hours the institution's business?

3. Imagine a young, unmarried instructor who moonlights only on Friday and Saturday nights for a total of 6 hours a week. His job is to strip at a local club. Does the job performed, irrespective of time, have ethical implications? What if the instructor was a young female stripper? Does that change your answer? (In an unpublished survey of attitudes toward instructor's moonlighting [Keith-Spiegel, Tabachnick, Klimek, & Welsh, J.] students rated stripping as a side job as unacceptable, especially so if the instructor was female.)

Case 22-5. Using Institutional Resources During Leisure Time

> Colleagues wonder whether Professor Solitaire's game playing and personal web-surfing during lunch and after hours violates any institutional policy about use of the institution's computer and Internet services.

When in doubt, ask. Assuming that there are no explicit rules against use of one's office computer and what one accesses on the Internet during off-hours, instructors are probably not violating any ethical standard. However, can lines be crossed? Instructors usually have a few hours during the day when they are neither teaching nor attending meetings. Therefore, what constitutes "off hours?"

It can be argued that some Internet sites would be improper and unseemly for faculty to access from campus. We suggest that, in the absence of any specific policy, leisure use of computers and computer services be used fairly sparingly. We would argue that computer activities, such as a few games of Solitaire during a break or looking up the disease your friend has recently contracted, should not raise any eyebrows.

Discussion Questions

1. Do you know if your institution has policies regarding personal use of the institution's computers and its services?

2. How might you differentiate between acceptable and unacceptable use of the institution's computer and computer services?

3. More specifically, what types of web sites would be unethical or inappropriate to access from campus?

Afterword: Prevention
and Peer Intervention

As stated in our introduction, we believe that very few instructors intentionally behave unethically. If this casebook has sensitized readers to some ethical dilemmas not previously considered, we will have accomplished our goal. Ethical problems that are foreseen can often be avoided. And, although it is not always possible to avoid ethical conflicts, sometimes merely placing oneself in certain circumstances creates a risk that significantly elevates the potential for unethical outcomes. This afterword provides some suggestions for avoiding ethical dilemmas and for assisting others who appear to have been involved in ethical lapses.

Prevention

Knowledge and awareness of potential ethical dilemmas in academic settings are important prevention tools. Remaining sensitive to students' vulnerabilities also protects us from harming students. Many students are not as mature as they look and are very sensitive to critical comments from those in authority or those they hold in high esteem. Instructors may not always pay sufficient attention to the power differential between themselves and students and the implications for creating a positive influence or crushing defeat.

Another prevention tool is knowledge of policies and expectations for faculty conduct at your employing institution. Although many are likely to be obvious, such as the admonition to never show up to class under the influence of alcohol or drugs, others may be more subtle or governed by local norms such as the steps to be taken in an instance of observed academic dishonesty.

Ethical problems can also develop when people attempt to rationalize their decisions. Academics are no exception to this interesting but ultimately self-defeating process. Common forms of rationalization

include, "If there's no rule against it, it's OK," "I'm just doing what was done to me first," "No one got hurt," "Nobody else needs to know," "I can
still be objective," and, "Everyone else does it." Whenever you find yourself using any of these rationalizations, it is wise to pause and ask yourself whether the process is masking ethically risky behavior.

Ethical dilemmas may also arise during the course of instituting innovative teaching techniques or tools, even when the instructor has the best of intentions. We are *not* suggesting that creative approaches to teaching should be avoided, but we do recommend that any potential consequence of a planned innovation be considered in advance. In an actual case, a high school teacher was concerned because young people often either steal condoms or do not use them at all because they are too embarrassed to buy them. In an ill-conceived attempt to alleviate a serious social problem, he gave students extra credit for purchasing condoms from a clerk of the opposite sex. He was promptly suspended. His motive was honorable enough, but his judgment was poor.

Instructors should anticipate ethical issues and then protect themselves from confrontations whenever possible. Protective techniques include putting specific conditions, policies, and information about any controversial issues in writing (e.g., in a course syllabus) and making oneself available for individual consultation with students who feel upset or disadvantaged by or uncomfortable with any aspect of your classes.

Mental health professionals who find themselves in the position of defending against charges of unethical behavior are often coping with heavy life stressors or are suffering from other emotional problems (Koocher & Keith-Spiegel, 1998). There is every reason to believe that this phenomenon applies to members of any other professions. Preoccupation with difficulties is fertile ground for poor judgment, insensitivity to the needs of others, neglect of fiduciary duty, insufficient attention to one's work, or acts of thoughtlessness that result in the affliction of harm or wrongs to others. Avoiding burnout and other emotional problems by taking good care of yourself and, if indicated, seeking professional assistance are wise ways to avoid unintentional acts of poor judgment.

Peer Monitoring and Intervention

Someone who directly observes an ethically problematic act is often the best person to attempt to mitigate it. Indeed, many of the "grayer" instances presented in this casebook may require collegial intervention lest the questionable practice or action persist unabated. Authors of books critical of the professorate often accuse college and university faculties of protecting each other, ignoring blatantly unethical actions, and supporting a conspiracy of mediocrity and fraud. Although one may refute these overgeneralized—and often overblown—charges, it is far better and ultimately more productive to take a strong, proactive role in facilitating internally generated solutions.

It is easy enough for us to strongly encourage direct and active involvement in situations involving the ethically questionable behavior of colleagues. Indeed, making the decision that an unethical act has occurred is the easier task. Mustering the courage to become actively involved in mitigating the matter is something else again. After all, the people involved are faced every day. We may have to live with them during the daytime hours for many years. Some are friends. Some are disliked. Some hold higher rank and, therefore, hold power that could be wielded in revenge. Even in academia, a person who attempts to intervene after perceiving an ethical problem may be viewed as arrogant and self-righteous, or even as a trouble-maker or a "snitch." Getting involved is a personal test of integrity and mettle.

The decision to intervene and the method of confrontation will depend, to some extent, on the nature one's extant relationship with the people involved and any power differentials. We offer some suggestions, adapted from Koocher and Keith-Spiegel (1998), for approaching colleagues who may be exhibiting unethical behavior.

1. Objectively determine what ethical principle, policy, or code of conduct has been violated. Consider why it is wrong, what harm may have accrued (or could accrue), and how the integrity or image of the department, school, or institution may have been (or could be) compromised. Ask what legitimate loyalties may be in conflict. This preconfrontation exercise will help to clarify any duty you may have as well as raise your self-confidence and commitment to your decision to be actively involved.

2. Attempt to assess the strength of the evidence that a violation has been committed. Is it mostly hearsay? How credible is the source of information? This process is important because it assists in making the decision to intervene and, if your involvement is warranted, helps to formulate the appropriate approach for a confrontation.

3. Be aware of your own motivations to engage in (or to avoid) a confrontation. In addition to any fears, angers, or other emotional reactions, do you perceive that the conduct, either as it stands or if it continues, could undermine the integrity of the teaching profession or harm one or more campus members? If you answer this question in the affirmative, then some form of action is required.

4. At this point, we recommend that you consult with a trusted and experienced colleague who has demonstrated a sensitivity to ethical issues, protecting any confidentialities that may be relevant. If you personally do not know such a person, representatives of professional organizations may provide assistance or recommend a colleague in your field who can be contacted.

5. Schedule a confrontation in advance, but not in a menacing way. (For example, do not say, "Something has come to my attention about you that causes me such grave concern that I must talk to you about it. What are you doing a week from Thursday?") Rather, indicate to the suspected offender that you would like to speak privately, and schedule a face-to-face meeting. An office setting would normally be more appropriate than a home or restaurant. Handling such matters over the phone or by email is not recommended.

6. When entering into a confrontation phase, remain calm and self-confident. The suspected offender may display considerable emotion. Expect that, but do not become caught up in it. Remain nonthreatening. Avoid a rigidly moralistic, holier-than-thou demeanor because most people find it offensive.

7. Set the tone for a constructive and educative session. Your role is not that of accuser, judge, jury, or penance-dispenser. Your role is that of a concerned colleague. The session will probably develop better if you see yourself as creating an alliance with the person, not in the sense of agreement with the problematic behavior, but as facing a problem together. You might use such phrases as, "I am confused about why you chose to do it this way," or "Something came to my attention that perplexed me, and I thought maybe we could discuss it ." This approach can be less threatening than a direct accusation and may elicit an explanation rather than defensiveness. Also remember that the basis of your concern could be faulty or distorted. Or, there could be an appropriate reason for the act that was perceived as unethical.

8. If confidences require protection (e.g., another person involved in the situation agreed to allow you to confront the colleague but insisted that his or her identity be protected), explain this circumstance and expect an uncomfortable reaction. No one relishes an unseen and unknown accuser. You should also inform the person on whose behalf you are acting that it is unlikely that any formal action could be taken unless he or she agrees to be identified.

9. Allow the suspected offender time to explain and defend in as much detail as required. The colleague may be flustered and repetitive. Be patient.

10. If the colleague becomes abusive or threatening, attempt to head toward a more constructive discussion. Although some people need a chance to vent feelings, they often settle down if the confronting person remains steady and refrains from becoming abusive and threatening in return. If a negative reaction continues, it might be appropriate to say something calming like, "I see you are very upset right now, and I regret that we cannot explore this matter together in a way that would be satisfactory to both of us. I would like you to think about what I have presented to you, and if you would reconsider talking about it, please call me within a week." If a return call is not forthcoming, other forms of action should be considered.

11. If the suspected offender is a friend or acquaintance with whom no previous problematic interactions have occurred, the teammate role described in Point 7 is easier to implement. You can express how you want to be the one to deal with the matter because you care about the person and his or her professional standing. The danger, of course, is that you may feel that you are risking an established, positive relationship. If the confrontation has a satisfactory outcome, however, you may well have done a favor by protecting your friend from embarrassment or from more public forms of censure. Discomfort, to the extent that it ensues, is likely to be temporary.

12. If the suspected offender is someone you dislike, handling the situation will be, by definition, more difficult. If the information is known to others or can be shared appropriately, consider asking someone who has a better relationship with the person to intercede. If that course of action is not possible (e.g., when confidentiality issues preclude sharing the matter with anyone else), and objective introspection leads to the conclusion that the misconduct requires intervention on its own merits regardless of who committed it, then one must consider informing the individual's supervisor or some other form of proactive intervention.

13. If the suspected offender is of higher rank or holds a position of power over you, you may be able to get the support of someone not affected by the person's position. We encourage the establishment of a mentor system in every department so that contract and junior faculty members have a senior colleague with whom they can speak freely about issues such as these.

Finally, we fully understand that confronting a colleague about an ethical concern is in the same league with calling in a student suspected of cheating. It is distasteful and takes a certain brand of courage to act. We discourage two safer-feeling but less effective alternatives: gossip and sending anonymous notes. Neither can guarantee a solution to the problem, and both have a high potential of making things worse. We also recognize that not all ethical dilemmas are amenable to informal resolution. Sometimes one will have no choice but to report a problem to one's spervisor or other institutional office. If entire departments become embroiled in matters with ethical ramifications, formal intervention, perhaps involving a skilled mediator, is indicated.

In closing, we can say with confidence that several types of the dilemmas we have illustrated will arise and directly affect you in the course of your teaching. We hope that we have imparted ideas for recognizing and resolving what will surely come your way.

References

American Psychological Association. (1992). Ethical principles of psychologists and code of conduct. *American Psychologist, 46*, 1597-1611.

Anderson, M. (1992). *Impostors in the temple.* New York: Simon & Shuster.

Caron, M. D., Whitbourne, S. K., & Halgin, R. P. (1992). Fraudulent excuse making among college students. *Teaching of Psychology, 19*, 90-93.

Chronicle of Higher Education (1998, May 15). Short subjects: Art student's fish killings angers animal lovers. A10.

Dyer, W. G. (1995). *Team building* (3rd ed.). Reading MA: Addison-Wesley.

Hill, G. W., Palladino, J. J., & Eison, J. A., (1993). Blood, sweat, and trivia: Faculty ratings of extra credit opportunities. *Teaching of Psychology, 20*, 209-213.

Johnson, D. K. (1996). Cheating: Limits of individual integrity. *Journal of Moral Education, 25*, 159-171.

Keith-Spiegel, P., Tabachnick, B. G., & Allen, M. (1993). Students' perceptions of the ethicality of professors' actions. *Ethics and Behavior, 3*, 149-162.

Keith-Spiegel, P., & Wiederman, M. W. (2000). *The complete guide to graduate school admission* (2nd ed.). Mahway, NJ: Lawrence Erlbaum Associates.

Keith-Spiegel, P., Whitley, B. E., Perkins, D. V., Balogh, D. W., & Wittig, A. W. (2001). Ethical dilemmas confronting graduate teaching assistants. In L. R. Prieto & S. A. Meyers, *The teaching assistant training handbook.* Stillwater, OK: New Forms Press.

Keith-Spiegel, P., Wittig, A. F., Perkins, D. V., Balogh, D. W., & Whitley, B. E. (1993). *The ethics of teaching: A casebook.* Muncie IN: Ball State University Office of Academic Research and Sponsored Projects.

Koocher, G. P., & Keith-Spiegel, P. (1998). *Ethics in psychology: Professional standards and cases.* New York: Oxford University Press.

Norcross, J. C., Horrocks, & Stevenson, J. F. (1989). Of barfights and gadflies: Attitudes and practices concerning extra credit in college courses. *Teaching of Psychology, 16*, 199-203.

Patai, D. (1995, October 27). What price utopia? *The Chronicle of Higher Education*, A56.

Prieto, L. R. (1995). Supervising graduate teaching assistants: An adaptation of the integrated developmental model. *Journal of Graduate Teaching Assistant Development, 2*, 93-105.

Rodabaugh, R. C. (1996). Institutional commitment to fairness in college teaching. In L. Fisch (Ed.), *Ethical dimensions of college and university teaching* (pp. 37-45). San Francisco: Jossey-Bass.

Sandler, B. R., & Hall, R. M. (1986). *The campus climate revisited: Chilly for women faculty, administrators, and graduate students.* Washington, DC: Association of American Colleges, Project on the Status and Education of Women.

Schneider, A. (1998, March 27). Insubordination and intimidation signal the end of decorum in many classrooms. *The Chronicle of Higher Education*, A3.

Swartzlander, S., Pace, D., & Stamler, B. L. (1993, February 17). The ethics of requiring students to write about their personal lives. *Chronicle of Higher Education*, B1-2.

Sykes, C. J. (1988). *Profscam: Professors and the demise of higher education.* NJ: Regnery Gateway, Inc.

Tabachnick, B. G., Keith-Spiegel, P., & Pope, K. S. (1991). The ethics of teaching: Beliefs and behaviors of psychologists as educators. *American Psychologist, 46*, 506-515.

Trout, P. A. (1998, July 24). Incivility in the classroom breeds "education lite." *The Chronicle of Higher Education*, A40.

Whitley, B. E., Jr., & Keith-Spiegel, P. (2001). *Academic dishonesty: An educator's guide.* Mahwah, NJ: Lawrence Erlbaum Associates.

Wilson, R. (1997, November 14). A professor's personal teaching style wins him praise and costs him his job. *The Chronicle of Higher Education,* A12.

Additional Readings

Blevins-Knabe, B. (1992). The ethics of dual relationships in higher education. *Ethics and Behavior, 2,* 151-163.

Braxton, J. M., & Bayer, A. E. (1999). *Faculty misconduct in collegiate teaching.* Baltimore, MD: Johns Hopkins University Press.

Cahn, S. (Ed.). (1990). *Morality, responsibility, and the university.* Philadelphia, Temple University Press.

Fisch, Linc. (Ed.). (1996). *Ethical dimensions of college and university teaching.* San Francisco: Jossey-Bass.

Getman, J. (1992). *In the company of scholars.* Austin: University of Texas Press.

Hogan, P. M., & Kimmel, A. J. (1992). Ethical teaching of psychology: One department's attempts at self-regulation. *Teaching of Psychology, 19,* 205-210.

Hook, S., Kurtz, P., & Todorovich, M. (Eds.). (1997). *The ethics of teaching and scientific research.* Buffalo, NY: Prometheus Books.

Johnston, P. (1988). *Intellectuals.* New York, Harper & Row.

Long, E., Jr. (1992). *Higher education as a moral enterprise.* Washington, DC: Georgetown University Press.

May, W. (Ed.). (1990). *Ethics and higher education.* New York: Macmillan.

Payne, S., & Charnov, B. (Eds.). (1987). *Ethical dilemmas for academic professionals.* Springfield, IL: Thomas Books.

Prieto, L. R., & Meyers, S. A. (2001). *The teaching assistant training handbook.* Stillwater, OK: New Forms Press.

Strike, K. A., & Moss, P. M., (1996). *Ethics and college student life.* Needham Heights, MA: Allyn & Bacon.

Sullivan, L. E., & Ogloff, J. R. (1998). Appropriate supervisor-graduate student relationships. *Ethics & Behavior, 8,* 229-248.

Whicker, M. L., & Kronefeld, J. J. (1994). *Dealing with ethical dilemmas on campus.* Thousand Oaks, CA: Sage.

Subject Index